"Sessions' book is a wonder, f wonderful teacher. It dips down for being who we most truly at̲, ̲ ̲ ̲ ̲ ̲ up no formulas, no one-trick ponies. Sessions ranges in readings from ancient philosophy to modern politics, and uses them to tell of his life, and of yours. The authenticity we seek, he concludes, is not either/or. It is both/and. It is both love and courage, hope and faith, autonomy and connection, male and female, right and left, small town values and big city awareness. Spend a day with this marvelous philosopher of work and life. You owe it your authentic self."

> —Deirdre McCloskey, University of Illinois at Chicago, and author of *Bourgeois Dignity: Why Economics Can't Explain the Modern World*

"I have known and admired the work and ideas of Bob Sessions for several decades, and this book is no exception. Like Bob himself, it is wise, intelligent, compassionate and, to put it simply—real. Well-researched and well-written, *Becoming Real* effectively challenges sacred cows across the political spectrum, including some of mine. At a time when much of academic philosophy seems an ivory tower competition of the opaque and semantic, *Becoming Real* examines real issues in a clear and practical manner. It is part of the new road map we need to create a livable future. I have only one bone to pick with the author. In this book, he says he is not "cool," but in fact, he definitely is—in the best sense of the word—and so is this book. It deserves to be a best-seller"

> —John de Graaf, co-author, *Affluenza* and *What's The Economy For, Anyway?*

"Most of America's big problems in life and our failure to address them as leaders and citizens are traceable to a lack of personal authenticity, integrity and moral character. These traits are admittedly hard won in life. Forging an identity that is authentic and genuine, one that lines up our words with our deeds, is the challenge of a lifetime for all of us. *Becoming Real* is a solid companion on that journey, in part because it draws upon the wisdom of the ages and its sages to guide us through the serious distractions, excesses and disintegration so prevalent with Modernity and its massively false beliefs in unlimited material progress and endlessly rising material affluence, which brings not happiness but woe. It is also a book whose real authority comes from the authenticity of its author, who himself spent time wandering through a dark woods before finding some light, and has been circling around that universal experience and sharing humanity's learnings about identity with his students ever since."

—Rev. Benjamin Webb, author, *Fugitive Faith*

"Robert Sessions has put his finger on one of the chief problems of the modern age, an affliction out of our consciousness but affecting every day of our lives. He shows that at the root of our efforts to fit in, be cool, pad our worth with material stuff, and try on new belief systems as if they were clothes is the lack of an authentic core. We aren't comfortable in our own skin, because our authenticity has been coopted by marketers, mediators, and technology. He makes an eloquent case that this planet would be a lot more livable if we could just get real."

—Joe Robinson, author, *Don't Miss Your Life*
and *Work to Live*

BECOMING REAL

AUTHENTICITY IN AN AGE OF DISTRACTIONS

ROBERT SESSIONS

ICE CUBE PRESS
NORTH LIBERTY, IOWA

Becoming Real—
Authenticity In An Age of Distractions

ISBN 9781888160574   1 3 5 7 9 8 6 4 2

Library of Congress Control Number: 2011924025

Ice Cube Press, LLC
205 N. Front St.
North Liberty, Ia 52317
www.icecubepress.com

The paper used in this publication meets the minimum requirements of the American National Standard for Information Sciences—Permanence of Paper for Printed Library Materials, ANSI Z39.48-1992

Credit: Jane Kenyon, "Happiness" from Collected Works. Copyright © 2005 by the Estate of Jane Kenyon. Reprinted with the permission of The Permission Company, Inc. on behalf of Graywolf Press, Minneapolis, Minnesota, www.graywolfpress.org
Credits/Permissions on-file with publisher.

This book is dedicated to my beloved children. My hope is that by reading what I have written you will learn something meaningful about yourselves, me, and the world you are inheriting.

&

"If you are what you should be, you will set the world on fire."
—St. Catherine of Siena

CONTENTS

FOREWORD

I believe we have created a culture in which it is very difficult to develop an authentic self. Inauthenticity is a kind of psychological or spiritual hunger, a deep yearning for an integrated and coherent identity that is tied into reality. If having a coherent and solid sense of identity depends on integrity, on integrating the aspects that form the self, then the endless distractions of our lives are not merely inconveniences but profoundly affect who we are...or cannot become. For many people, our endless comforts and conveniences, toys and games, and near-frenzied busyness are more effective than Odysseus's sirens in taking our eyes and minds from any serious quest to become a person of character and gravity. We live in a world of "whatever," of bling and endless messages, and of work without end. For many people the deep hunger I have named is not even noticed, so ubiquitous and cacophonous are the distractions.

I have come to realize that I have been pursuing authenticity for much of my adult life. When I was a college student in the mid-1960s, my life was thrown into turmoil by the Vietnam War and the Civil Rights Movement. The small-town world in which I had grown up did not prepare me for the seismic changes that happened around and in me, and like many in my baby-boom generation it took decades for me to find my way. The world changed in that watershed decade, in ways that drove wedges between parents and children and society and its youth, and internally many of our moral compasses were spinning wildly. I had a difficult time not only believing in the America of my childhood but in the person I was, for like anyone at 18 I embodied the truths and values and stories with which I had grown up. As the decade spun on, further aspects of the American Dream of my childhood were challenged as women sought equality, some of the environmental implications of that dream were revealed, and the incompatibility of Christianity and the unbridled materialism of post-World War II America became apparent. Adrift, I sought to make sense of our collective lives in the aftermath of these great upheavals and realizations and in the process I tried to make sense of my individual life. Looking back I realize I sought, like many of my peers, resolution in strategies learned in childhood, which for me was individualistic and quintessentially American—back to the land to lead a simple life. Intellectually I was drawn even more dramatically than I had been in college to the literature, art, and philosophy of people who pulled away from society to seek solace in simple living and small, rural communities. Eventually the life I built to escape the great winds of change came crashing down as I lost my job, marriage, and farm one sad summer when I was in my late 30s.

Although I did not realize it at the time, my first attempt to make sense of my life and the 1960s was to write my PhD dissertation about autonomy. This concept embodies much of what I had learned and become, and pursuing its ideal had much to do with my journey to a small farm in northeast Iowa where I tried homesteading. What I discovered, in a very personal and dramatic way, is that the quest for autonomy and independence led me to misunderstand most of what

I had experienced, and my hungry pursuit of more autonomy was in significant ways responsible for my failure to forge an identity. For what I was searching for and desperately needed was an identity that I could believe in and from which I could act with integrity. I wanted to become authentic, to feel that my life made sense and that I was real. Instead, the diagnosis and direction the idea of autonomy gave me created a great gaping hole in my being, for it pulled me away from the nurturing sources my floundering self needed.

The quest for authenticity that obsessed me and many of my generation continues to plague people today. At the end of the first decade of a new century, we again live in a time of great transformation. As the engines of technological change combine with, and often help cause, dramatic ecological degradation, and as globalization creates unprecedented economic, political, and cultural realignments, it is not surprising to find people everywhere increasingly uncertain and confused. I see it in my community college students and in reports about young people across the land. This generation is not experiencing the draft or protests in the streets as I did in my youth, but nevertheless the upheavals of this era are causing an identity crisis in a new generation of youth as well as in many of their elders, a feeling that the sources once available to form a firm sense of self are unstable or evaporating. What is striking is how many distractions lure people away from any serious quest to become real. 'Attraction' means to bring together, to join what was separate, while the root meaning of 'distraction' is to pull apart or to separate. These new seismic forces leave people hungry for meaning, for a coherent sense of what it is to be human amidst the shock waves of change that overwhelm many. And again, I believe that the proper name for this hunger is a desire to become real, to be authentic.

Often the root of a problem can be there from the start and can arise from the same sources that also bring benefits. The rise of modernism from the ashes of the medieval world brought glorious inventions that generated social and political riches we take for granted. Liberal democracies, with their political, economic, and personal freedoms and rights, modern science and technology, and new ways of organizing work and society not only freed people from severely limited lives or even bondage, they often set people adrift in unfamiliar territories. As writers such as Dostoevsky, Kafka, Nietzsche, and Sartre powerfully lamented, the underbelly of the freedom to invent one's self is a deep anxiety that has led many people to shirk or escape this overwhelming responsibility. Thus out of the swirling chemistry that spawned the modern human we have also seen the birth of collectivist states, alienated labor, obsessive consumerism, and unthinking fundamentalisms. If we have learned nothing else, we should realize that telling people to go forth and create themselves is, as Mary Shelley warns us in *Frankenstein*, to make monstrous failures nearly inevitable.

While grave and large dangers such as violent fundamentalisms or racial hatred hover in the background of contemporary societies, I believe we can learn more about this soulful hunger for reality that plagues people by looking at more benign versions of social anomie and the resulting desire to be more authentic. More people today seek to form an identity, for instance, through work or technology or joining a group rather than by aligning with a neo-Nazi group or terrorist cell. While such strategies are less damaging than their more horrific cousins and can also more adequately satisfy the desire to be real, many people find themselves yearning for something more. We see evidence of this in the proliferation of self-help gurus, programs, and materials, and also witness it in the abilities of advertisers to convince us to buy endless arrays of things by appealing to our incessant desires for valued selves that are recognized as real. It shows up in our political lives where identity politics has become the norm as we seek leaders who, above all else, are genuine. We seek, nostalgically, for heroes to enshrine in our halls of fame, or collector's items to grace our homes and museums, hoping to be in touch with something authentic. A nearly endless list of such strategies has led philosopher and journalist Andrew Potter[1] to argue that the pursuit of authenticity has become our modern religion. He believes that this pursuit is highly corrosive of our personal and social lives and that we would be noticeably better off giving it up.

Thus we must proceed cautiously. Naming what ails us is crucial. Whether in medicine, auto mechanics, ecological or economic crises, our ability to respond adequately begins with proper diagnosis. But naming can deceive us into believing we understand when all we have is a label, and often what we believe to be true about a properly named reality is mistaken. If we try to fix our ailment based on inadequate understanding we can make things worse. We must be careful and patient. In contrast to Potter, I believe that if we are committed to follow where the trail leads and be open to past mistakes, we can find our ways to more genuine lives. *do people know this?*

To diagnose what ails us as a deep desire for authenticity is to point in a direction where we might begin to look for clues about what has brought about our illness and for possible cures. When searching for authenticity you first notice what prevents its development: our quest for authenticity is occluded by several centuries of misunderstanding as well as by a multitude of distractions. From the beginning of liberal societies in the sixteenth century poets and philosophers have noticed

---

1 *The Authenticity Hoax: How We Get Lost Finding Ourselves.* I will discuss Potter's excellent book at some length as he presents a powerful critique of the idea of authenticity. While I agree with much of what he says, I differ from him in my belief that, properly defined and understood, authenticity can be a very useful concept.

that forging an authentic self is difficult for modern people in ways that it was not for those who preceded us, and by the late nineteenth and early twentieth centuries, exposing inauthenticity had become a cottage industry. However, most of the diagnoses tended to be based on the belief that what ailed people was a lack of independence from cultural and social influences, with the result that the recommended cures tended to exacerbate the estrangement from legitimate sources of authentic selves rather than help to lessen it.

If this book is to help solve rather than add to the problems it addresses, it must provide an alternative understanding of authenticity and an alternative strategy for becoming authentic, one that taps into a strong vein in our culture similar to the idea of autonomy. Instead of seeking personal identity through independence from culture and society, I propose the building of strong communities of the right sort that include exposure especially of young people to a variety of narratives that can provide the building materials for strong selves rooted in reality. Instead of pursuing the frustrating Stoic ideal of self denial and moral purity, I propose that happiness, properly understood, is a much more fruitful avenue to authenticity because happiness requires being enmeshed in meaningful relationships and communities. Finally, I contend that it is easier for people who develop strong selves through rich community relationships to hear and respond to their own callings, to the deepest voices from within as well as without that call them to become more fully human.

Many people have had a hand in shaping this book, and to each I am humbly grateful. Melissa Connor set the process in motion by seeing, when I did not, that I wanted to write it. Steve Semken believed in me and my project from the beginning, and his careful midwifery has been critical to its birth. My friends and colleagues Scott Samuelson, Jim Throgmorton, David Depew, and Chris Vinsonhaler read parts or all of the manuscript and nudged me gently in ways that have improved the book substantially. I am especially grateful to Dan Kitzman who read and commented on the entire manuscript. Without his thoughtful insights and careful editing *Becoming Real* would have been a lesser book. I am also very grateful to Janet Freeman, who took considerable effort to read and comment on the manuscript, saving me from many errors. I thank Kirkwood Community College, my professional home for the past quarter century, for institutional and personal support for this and many previous projects that have fed me intellectually and professionally. My loving wife, Lori Erickson, has supported me with her extraordinary patience, good humor, gentle but probing insights and spiritual sustenance, and her substantial editing talents have helped make my writing clearer and more accessible to non-academics. Finally, echoing in the background are the ideas of my graduate advisor and friend, Frithjof Bergmann, whose wisdom is at the core of what I have written. In the end, however, I bear sole responsibility for the mistakes contained herein.

INTRODUCTION

The signs and symptoms are everywhere: contemporary humans, especially in America, are hungry. They are searching for something difficult to name or describe and thus doubly difficult to find. Many people join groups such as those that revolve around motorcycles or tailgating parties only to discover that these associations offer only thin gruel to feed this hunger. Others seek extreme, adrenaline-driven activities to fill the void they feel deep in their beings, only to realize that such thrills fall short of satisfying this deep desire. Still others flock to gated communities to live among people just like themselves only to learn that the comfort and convenience they find provides a lightness of being rather than the gravity they need. You can almost hear the refrain of those who desperately try to fill this void with recognition of their material success or being a cool trend-setter: *I have exercised my freedom to define myself and have succeeded in becoming unique and recognized, yet I still feel a deep yearning in my soul.* Perhaps the people who are most serious are those joining fundamentalist religious groups where they find the kind of strong medicine most other paths fail to deliver. The costs of membership in such groups is high, however, and the elixir they find may not truly satisfy their deepest desires.

What people desire, I believe, is authenticity: a deep sense of being real. I have come to believe that many people cannot attain this elusive quality of being because of the myriad distractions that keep them from a genuine quest and because they are looking for the wrong thing in the wrong ways and in the wrong places. In this book I hope at least to clarify what authenticity is and how our distractions keep us from it. I also hope to suggest some fruitful paths people might follow in their quests for a more authentic life.

Searching for Authenticity in America

I grew up in the South Dakota Kathleen Norris writes about in *Dakota*[1], near enough to the West (which officially begins on the other side of the Missouri River from where I lived) to have my life permeated with the strong strain of independence that marks the frontier attitude still alive in ranching country. Self reliance was taken for granted in my town, my school, and my family. From an early age I was expected to do substantial chores at home, and beginning after the seventh grade, I worked entire summers on farms or doing construction work, saving the money I would need to pay for my college education. My parents never paid a penny for my education and I was surprised to find college classmates whose parents were paying parts or all of their bills. Given this background it was not surprising that I would write my doctoral dissertation on autonomy, or that I would find the Existentialist take on authenticity attractive.

While I have never been entirely convinced by the "negative Existentialists" who viewed freedom as a burden from which we desire es-

---

1 *Dakota: A Spiritual Geography.*

cape, for many years I naturally found their "self-made man" perspective attractive. As I studied the social sciences and an array of social philosophers, and as I learned how to live in community with others, I began to realize the inadequacies of the individualist philosophy that permeated my growing-up years and place. The philosophy (or perhaps better, *story*, as that is how people learn and live it) that I inherited helped me get through some difficult times, although it was also responsible for many of my difficulties; but slowly I came to realize that with regard to authenticity this story not only is off base, but that it helps create many of the problems with authenticity that we face.

Consider the example of a highly successful retirement community in Florida. In his recent book, *Leisureville*,[2] Andrew Blechman describes life in The Villages, our country's largest gated retirement "utopia." Covenants in The Villages are fairly standard: no children, extensive rules that govern everything from paint colors to garbage collection, standard closing hours, and so on. The amenities are so extensive that residents need never pass through the gates to the outside. There are multiple golf courses and swimming pools, a multitude of shops and restaurants, and the social life is intense and never-ending. In fact, the social life is so active that such retirement communities have the dubious distinction of currently having the greatest increase of STDs in the country!

Blechman spent a month living among the residents (the longest outsiders are allowed to visit), trying to acquire an insider's feel for life in this idyllic setting. He was amazed at the near-frenzied social lives of those he met, and at first he was impressed by the ease of living in this carefully-planned "community." As he became more acquainted with his new friends, though, Blechman had a growing sense that something was missing. He came to see that the lack of medical

2 *Leisureville: Adventures in America's Retirement Utopias.*

facilities indicates a denial of the realities of the aging population in The Villages and is a symptom of something deeper amiss in this "gray utopia": no amount of fun and friendliness can completely mask the deep emptiness in the lives of its "citizens." But what could possibly be missing? Aren't these people living out a common and attractive version of The American Dream? Indeed they are. Most of them have worked hard to reach the point in their lives when they can quit working and worrying, where their lives are filled with fun and relaxation away from the cares and concerns that occupied them throughout their working years.

Residents of places such as The Villages seem to have avoided the mistakes of the people who populate Robert Putnam's world in his poignant study of increased isolation and alienation in America, *Bowling Alone.*[3] Putnam's extensive research indicates that a growing number of Americans feel lost because of the breakdown of traditional communities and associations, be they churches, bowling leagues, political organizations, clubs, or neighborhood associations. His solution for people who live in lonely crowds is to re-establish community ties such as those found in The Villages. Yet for many, such ties do not seem to bind in ways that satisfy all the cravings Putnam's subjects have. Those who are "bowling alone" are lonely, they feel as though they are aliens in their own lives not mainly, as in Marx's classic critique, because of their work, but because in their personal lives they do not have communities where they can receive the kinds of recognition and caring they need and desire. Residents of "leisureville" have community in spades yet, according to Blechman, they still lack something important.

---

3 *Bowling Alone: The Collapse and Revival of American Community.*

Consider a third example. In his second major book on manhood in America[4], social psychologist Michael Kimmel describes the intense communities of white males in America between sixteen and twenty-six years of age. Kimmel finds that this crucible in which middle class white males become men is troublesome in a myriad of ways. In this guy world he finds avoidance of adulthood rather than processes through which young men might become mature and capable adults. His analysis of the many activities so typical of "guyland"—the video games, sports, drinking, hooking up, and initiations—is that they are full of anger, violence, and even hatred. In these communities, especially those found on college campuses across the country, loyalty requires that members deny crimes and misdemeanors of all kinds protecting their "bros."

Residents of guyland, like those in The Villages, do not lack for friends or community activities. Furthermore, their activities have a kind of rawness to them that is lacking in most retirement village activities, which gives these guys a strong dose of reality that often seems to be lacking in The Villages. Kimmel describes some very unpleasant initiation rituals or other male bonding activities that would make hardened parole officers cringe. The key to understanding what is missing from their almost tribal existences, which may also reveal something important about the sense of loss or emptiness found in our other examples, is that like most newly-independent young people they are in the process of forming adult identities. These are the proverbial "Bohemian" years, to borrow a term from Kwame Appiah[5], when

---

4 *Guyland: The Perilous World Where Boys Become*. His earlier work is titled *Manhood in America*.

5 *Ethics of Identity*. Also see his essay, "Identity, Authenticity, Survival: Multicultural Societies and Social Reproduction" in Amy Gutman, ed, *Multiculturalism: Examining the Politics of Recognition*. This book begins with an extended essay by Charles Taylor followed by commentaries by Jurgen Habermas, Steven C. Rockefeller, Michael Walzer and Susan Wolf.

young people have always learned about and tried out new identities like shoppers trying on new clothes. Kimmel's guys are in transition from childhood to adulthood. They are searching, however inchoately, for stories that will help them make sense of manhood, of male adulthood, and his book chronicles many facets of what he considers to be troubled if not failed strategies in this perennial quest.

Most of the youths in guyland are suburban whites, products of remarkably privileged upbringings, who, according to Kimmel, are angry and frightened at the prospect of their "entitlements" being eroded—that the wealth and the comfort and convenience it has brought them at least will be difficult to match and possibly will be out of their reach in an economy gone bad and a diversified culture that no longer automatically privileges them. Thus many of their activities are laden with anger and violent language and images against the easiest scapegoats for their loss, women and gay men. Instead of the serious yet properly playful exploration of other identities that is legendary among college students and that might make their transformation into men successful and positive for them and society, Kimmel describes the unfortunate fallout from their desperate attempts to cling to outmoded identities. I believe Andrew Kimbrell[6] accurately pegs this failed strategy as one where masculinity is defined as whatever is not feminine and as women have come to share domains, power, roles, and characteristics with men, what is left for men that is uniquely their own has shrunk

---

6 *The Masculine Mystique: The Politics of Masculinity.* Kay S. Hymowitz, in *Manning Up: How the Rise of Feminism Has Turned Men Into Boys*, expresses similar concerns with the difficulties young men are having finding adult identities but she believes other factors contribute to this growing problem.

dramatically. No wonder these young males believe their entitlements have eroded![7]

More Extreme Attempts to Find Authenticity

Shift your imaginations to less privileged Americans who lived in and survived more difficult circumstances—veterans who experienced the rigors and horrors of combat. Everyone is familiar with "post traumatic stress syndrome," that lingering malaise that haunts those who have been in the thick of battle and who cannot shake the recurring imprinted nightmares. For many veterans of war, however, there is an equally strong "upside" to those incredibly powerful experiences. Just as the horrors of war are difficult to leave behind, so too is it difficult to forget that it was precisely in those adrenaline-driven, life-threatening moments when they were most alive. Many veterans find themselves organizing their life stories around those unforgettable moments when everything superfluous was stripped away and they had to find the courage and strength to measure up to the most strenuous of tests. Everything they experience after their defining moments pales by comparison, and the more comforts and conveniences life offers, the less satisfied they are. Many veterans report feeling a sense of loss and pine for the camaraderie and sense of being fully alive that marked those days of fear, anxiety, dread, and horror.

We can begin to fill in another piece of the puzzle by considering briefly a very strong response to the emptiness that drives people to seek

---

7 I would be amiss not to note parallels between the residents of guyland and some members of America's new Tea Party. Many of them, too, fear for their loss of place in society where white men, especially, are being replaced by women, foreigners and people of color, and often their rhetoric is filled with anger at a vague "other" whom ready demagogues such as Sarah Palin and Glenn Beck are quick to label progressives, Muslims, socialists, liberals, and so on. Clearly in the shifting sands of 21st century social change, scary shifts in security, power and status can rouse strong responses and often important social movements.

relief from the false promises of modernism—religious fundamentalism. Religious historians tell us that religious movements which promote a "return to fundamentals" are relatively recent, only dating back about 200 years—to the rise of modernism. Modernism is characterized by the birth of secular nations, humanism, and diverse, multicultural societies. With all the various benefits such as increased freedom and equality, greatly improved material well-being, technological and scientific progress, increased longevity, and decrease in toil, a concomitant feature is a decrease in dogma and certainty including an awareness that your way of living is but one among many viable forms of life. What fundamentalism offers is the lure of a return to a (mainly fictional) simpler time when people knew who to be and what to do and believe, and this promise is secured by holding up (a version of) a sacred text with (supposedly) straightforward eternal verities.

As populations become more diverse and trade more global, and as knowledge changes and grows more rapidly, fundamentalisms (including secular as well as religious versions) are more attractive to more people every day. In his recent book[8] Reza Aslan discusses how fundamentalism in his Muslim tradition has morphed from local to national to become international in its perspective. Aslan contends that in the process radical Islam has become a virulent refuge from uncertainty that insulates its adherents from any doubts about how their increasingly violent tactics affect other people *including* their fellow Muslims or countrymen. He believes that members of groups such as Al Qaida are following a simple-minded ideology of good vs. evil rather than living the deep and complex religion that is Islam, and he asserts that responses by nations or groups that simply reverse the polarity and attach labels to them, such as "the axis of evil," play into the hands of the radicals by supporting the arc of their metaphysical

---

8 *Beyond Fundamentalism: Confronting Religious Extremism in the Age of Globalization.*

story.[9] Whether or not we accept all of Aslan's rich and helpful analysis, what he can help us see are the extremes to which people will go to escape the uncertainties of living in the modern world. The desire for a clear identity, for a deep sense of reality, for living authentically, is powerful and can be dangerous.

One of Andrew Potter's central points is that in the quest for authenticity, much of what is valuable in modernism—open societies, scientific and technological advances, dramatically improved longevity and health, moral progress, and ease of living—gets jettisoned in favor of a retro-romantic (nostalgic) return to some illusory past. Thus, even though most contemporary strategies for achieving authenticity do not involve the wanton violence associated with extreme Islam or American religious zealots killing abortion workers, under the skin they have much in common. The stories that guide many who seek authenticity have similar patterns: they decry the emptiness of modern life and associate it with materialism and a lack of traditional values, they paint a picture of a lost civilization wherein people had clear values and noble identities, and they urge participants to throw off the yoke of modernism and return to the lost "Eden." A past and future utopia.

Many of the features of such narratives probably are inevitable. When we attempt to change anything about our lives, especially if they are major changes, we tend to demonize what we are trying to change and lionize our alternative. Furthermore, part of what makes modernism wonderful is the incessant drive to improve, to progress. The difficult necessity is to think in complex, objective, honest, and

---

9 In his very helpful analysis of happiness (*The Happiness Hypothesis: Finding Modern Truth in Ancient Wisdom*), which we will discuss at length in chapter five, Jonathan Haidt contends that humans have a strong tendency to set up good vs. evil dichotomies. He claims that this "naïve realism" is "the biggest obstacle to world peace and social harmony," and is based in the fact that "we are convinced of our own virtue, but quick to see bias, greed, and duplicity in others." (73)

realistic ways so that the proverbial baby is not thrown out with the bathwater. Probably the most important example of this difficulty looms for anyone today trying to figure out how to change, individually and collectively, to more sustainable ways of living. I am especially indebted to Andrew Potter for raising this issue for my attempt to articulate an understanding of the quest for authenticity that avoids the retro-romantic pitfalls of the versions of stories that have fundamentalists and many others under their spells.

When Authenticity Occurs…and Doesn't

We need not turn to such extreme examples to begin to see what seems to be missing from the lives of the denizens of Guyland, The Villages, Bowling Alone, or Islamic radicalism. Most people have had experiences where the soft trappings and numbing routines of life were absent. In June of 2008 many residents of eastern Iowa awoke to rising waters from epic floods that brought thousands of people from around the country and even from other countries to help raise sandbag dikes to try to prevent the worst damage and then to help clean up the monumental mess left in the wake of waters that would not be denied. As with war, no one would wish for the floods to return. Yet many who spent hours battling the raging rivers throughout the Mississippi watershed felt something that is typically missing from their normal lives. Engaging in the basic tasks of sandbagging or tearing out moldy drywall brought many people the same kind of direct and guileless physical and social experiences that combat veterans extol. They felt they were doing something solidly connected to reality. They felt real. They felt *authentic*.

It would be a mistake simply to identify authenticity with crisis experiences. If anything, people only get a taste of authenticity when struggling through challenging times, and we are looking for what might bring long-term relief to the boredom, alienation and sense of loss that permeates everyday existence for so many people today. However, we can begin to see why the strategies we typically follow in creating a good life often leave us feeling hollow, as if in easing our burdens and insecurities we are escaping from essential ingredients of full human existence. Doing electronic combat on an endless array of video games with endless levels of expertise will never come close to the full dimensions of one moment of real combat any more than viewing the endless variety of porn sites on the web (those who count claim there are over one million available!) can ever match one experience of actual love-making.

Turning in another direction, James Howard Kunstler[10] contends that suburbs were never the real "country" they pretend to be, with the result that suburbanites are neither country folks nor city dwellers. Instead, Kunstler says, suburban living is a kind of limbo in between the realities of urban and country life. In the same way, the goals of consumerism tend to be more symbolic than real. As we will discuss at length in chapter two, continually striving for more wealth tends to put us one step removed from the straightforward realities of making a living that have occupied people for millennia. Using a related marker, social scientists[11] studying happiness tell us that for more than half a century the ways Americans have been pursuing happiness runs counter to strategies that might actually help us achieve this elusive state. The endless pursuit of material goods (Bill McKibben calls this

---

10 See especially his video, *The End of Suburbia*, and also his book, *The Geography of Nowhere*.

11 Besides Haidt, see Bill McKibben, *Deep Economy: The Wealth of Communities and the Durable Future*; Richard Layard, *Happiness: Lessons from a New Science*; Matthieu Ricard, *Happiness: A Guide to Developing Life's Most Important Skill*; Martin Seligman, *Authentic Happiness: Using the New Positive Psychology to Realize Your Potential for Lasting Fulfillment*; Gretchen Ruben, *The Happiness Project*; Sonja Lynbomirsky, *The How of Happiness: A Scientific Approach to Getting the Life You Want*; and chapter five in this book.

the "endless more") that has occupied us since the end of the Second World War has not increased our happiness and for many it has lessened it. Happiness and authenticity are not the same thing, but they are intricately related, especially in that neither comes easily if we are too materialistic, as we will show in chapter five.

Kathleen Norris chronicles yet another way to comprehend the magnitude of our contemporary struggles with inauthenticity in her recent book, *Acedia and Me*.[12] Resurrecting a medieval Catholic concept, Norris shows how *acedia* afflicts many people today just as powerfully as it did monks attempting to live holy lives. She urges us to broaden the common translation of *acedia* as "sloth" to include phenomena such as *busyness* that usually are viewed as the opposite of sloth. For this "noonday demon," so familiar to monks, is characterized by a *lack of care*, and she believes that many people today experience and respond to care-lessness by being busy. (Or perhaps it is that busyness brings carelessness.) Norris does not discount the power and ubiquity of clinical depression, but she believes we are making a monumental mistake when we medicalize all bouts with lassitude[13], and she makes a convincing case that we need to see that the lack of care so common in our world is often a spiritual crisis rather than (or as well as) a biochemical one. In chapters one and two we will discuss in detail her important insights about how slothfulness *or* busyness are common experiences in relation to work and technology (especially the media), and how they are the face of inauthenticity as most people experience it. While some people are able to recognize the loss or alienation or emptiness that grows in our souls as we become evermore distant from reality, probably the more common symptom is the

---

12 *Acedia and Me: Marriage, Monks and a Writer's Life.*

13 For a related critique of our over-medicalization of depression see Allan Leventhal and Christophe Martell, *The Myth of Depression as Disease: Limitations and Alternatives to Drug Treatment.*

ubiquitous "whatever" in response to the challenges and obligations[14] the world brings us daily. As a defense mechanism against an overwhelming world this common avoidance of involvement (care) can get us through the day. Eventually, though, this form of disengagement is asphyxiating and we gasp for reality. Unfortunately, reality comes with a price tag many people have grown unwilling to pay. In this book I hope to show exactly what that price is, why it is sometimes worth paying and other times how to avoid having to pay.

From Authentic Things to Authentic People

In his book on authentic living, Richard Todd[15] catalogs the many ways Americans pursue authenticity: we seek authentic art and crafts, we desire authentic experiences and places, we seek political candidates and heroes who are authentic, and most of all we search for personal authenticity.[16] With each example Todd reveals more about this elusive quest. Sometimes finding authentic art or knowing whether or not a given work of art is authentic can be difficult, but pretty clearly what we want is art that is not fake, but is original or genuine. Authentic experiences and places are more difficult to pin down. Can you have an authentic experience in Disneyland? Is any place transformed by humans authentic? If so, why is any place more or less authentic than any other? Or, isn't our judgment that an old farmstead is authentic while one with new buildings and a manicured lawn is inauthentic simply based on our image of a real farm or our prejudice favoring the

---

14 Philosopher John Caputo, who argues that any kind of coherent ethic is impossible today, nevertheless recognizes that the fundamental motivation for morality is undeniable: "obligation happens." See his book, *Against Ethics: Contributions to a Poetics of Obligation With Constant Reference to Deconstruction.*

15 *The Thing Itself.*

16 Mythologist Wendy Doniger gave a talk in Iowa City, Iowa, in November, 2010, about women and jewelry wherein she discussed the close connections between authentic art (jewelry) and the desire women have to be authentic.

old? Such questions abound, and often it seems that Todd is merely telling us about his peculiar tastes, but the buildup to his final section on authentic selves reveals several important things. First, the hunger and sense of loss among Americans that motivates my own book has been noticed by other observers such as Todd and Potter. Todd also believes this deep existential yearning has to do with the loss or lack of authenticity. Todd's analysis can also help us see that people seek personal authenticity through things, places, and experiences. I believe this is a key insight that suggests that we intuitively believe (know?) that selves are constructed from the material and symbolic worlds provided by nature and culture.

Pursuing these insights, a central thesis of this book is that being authentic has to do as much with what occurs in the world around us as it does with what we experience subjectively, and it has to do with how the external and internal aspects of our selves fit together. Put differently, *authenticity is about whether or not we identify with our identities,* whether our subjective sense of whom we are fits with our social selves. Authentic selves take shape "in-between," as we will discuss at length in chapter four. Because I believe that who we are, and thus whether or not we are authentic, is greatly a function of the world around us, rather than beginning with a journey inward, as the classical theorists of authenticity have done, we will spend much of this book exploring how outward processes and events shape and affect us before exploring our inward experiences of authenticity or its absence.

My focus will differ from Todd's in many ways, as I bring a more philosophical than literary bent to my ruminations. I hope to make a strong and explicit case for what Todd only suggests—that personal authenticity is an accomplishment, a perpetual task always in process and made difficult by many of the sources of modernism, such as the media, work, and freedom, that make it possible in the first place. And when the difficult journey to authenticity has been traversed, there is no guarantee that the authentic self that emerges will be particularly attractive or even virtuous. What the journey does promise, though, is a life more like working in flood relief or fighting a war than one like the somnambulant hours propped in front of a screen seeking salve for the hidden wounds of boring work or a hollow social life. Humans desire to be genuine, to be in touch with reality and to be recognized for their real accomplishments and deepest being, and whether or not that happens depends a great deal on what kind of society we live in and what kinds of stories we live through. My view is that authenticity has as much to do with stories and communities as with individual efforts. Thus my offering is a *narrative* and *communitarian* account of human authenticity.

Why Authenticity?

At first I thought that continuing to write about the concept I pursued in my dissertation and early professional writing—freedom—but with a communitarian twist, would be the best way to convey my maturing perspective. Freedom, however, is a term that is so overworked that the only remaining uses of this term may be rhetorical. While the prey I stalk, like personal freedom, has everything to do with identity, the problems I have described are not necessarily caused by lack of freedom. Many theorists of freedom contend, in fact, that the multiplication of the kinds of distractions I will catalog add to our choices and thus to our freedom. While I do not accept the view that all choices benefit freedom, I do believe that too many of the wrong kinds of choices (distractions) can keep us from living authentically.

Thus I have chosen a close cousin of personal freedom, authenticity, to do the heavy lifting I hope to accomplish in this book.

Authenticity is a holdover from a long philosophical and cultural dialogue beginning at least with Rousseau and traversing a path through Hegel, Romanticism, the Existentialists, and the Bohemian 1960s. Recently the intellectual historian and philosopher Charles Taylor[17] has resurrected this discussion and has been followed by a number of incisive thinkers including Henry Bugbee, Kwame Anthony Appiah, Jurgen Habermas, Susan Wolf, Michael Walzer, Gordon Brittan, Jr, Charles Guignon, Charles Lindholm, Cory Anton, and Jacob Golomb.[18] Because of its historical pedigree the concept of authenticity has not been as overused[19] as the idea of freedom and thus has real potential as a relatively problem-free conceptual tool to help us think through a range of significant contemporary realities. I believe that several common misunderstandings about human identity (which is where authenticity resides) are causing many of the very real existential difficulties I discussed briefly in this Introduction. I hope that clarifying these misunderstandings will provide a kind of conceptual therapy which will help people lead more authentic (and I hope happier) lives.

An Overview of This Book

To that end I have organized this book in the following way. Inauthenticity is a kind of alienation, a distancing from the world that leaves people hungry for reality. There are many sources and contexts for this abstraction from reality and I will focus on three central ones—

? K

---

17 *Sources of the Self, Ethics of Authenticity,* and *A Secular Age.*

18 See footnote number one in chapter four for a full listing of these and other contemporary philosophers writing about authenticity.

19 As we have said, Potter contends that misunderstanding and misusing the concept of authenticity has done mischief similar to the many unfortunate uses of the idea of freedom.

work, technology, and nature—as a way of uncovering how we have conspired, however inadvertently, to create widespread inauthenticity. While many things can wrench us away from the lives we wish to live, to a great extent most people in America stray from developing and being themselves because of seemingly benign *distractions*. To paraphrase Hannah Arendt, what prevents the flowering of our authenticity is more banal than harsh, more mundane than dramatic, and in significant ways we simply are lured away from our true paths by very attractive and common distractions.

Work, whether paid or unpaid, is a fundamental context in which human identity is forged. We have built a jobs system in America that ignores or downplays the values of that formation and instead fosters mis-fits, people who fit neither their work nor their non-work lives. They become aliens in their own lives. This is complex and well-trodden territory, of course, but the connections between work and identity, and thus between work and authenticity, have not received adequate attention. I believe that work not only is a material necessity, but as monastic traditions from all parts of the world have shown, it is also a psychological and spiritual necessity. Thus it is nearly criminal when these most important functions of work are downplayed, ignored and even ravaged in favor of the bottom line gods of efficiency and profit. My argument in chapter one will be like the environmentalist argument that we must internalize all costs in our accounting if we are to begin to take seriously the tasks of sustainable living: in like manner we need to put these most fundamentally human aspects of work at the center of our reckoning as we construct work and leisure lest we run the risk of mis-shaping or even destroying the *human* nature that needs good work. From Plato through Freud some thinkers have contended that people need work to discover, develop, and express themselves, and just as religion can be used to twist and deform people because it is in touch with such fundaments of existence, work, likewise, can become a tool of great harm instead of a place where we find much-needed assistance on the road to becoming authentically human.

Chapter two takes on an equally expansive and pervasive reality, technology. Through the prism of several examples I will try to show how we are shaped and mis-shaped by many of the technologies that permeate and define our worlds in ever-increasing arrays. The media, including cybernetic devices, clearly are having such profound effects on people that many observers believe there is a fundamental and human-caused change underway in human nature itself. Technologies need not render us inauthentic, of course, but the valences and uses of many contemporary devices tend to exacerbate rather than reduce our difficulties in feeling and being connected to reality. Television and video games, e.g., tempt people to live vicarious lives where even "reality tv" is spectacle, one more form of entertainment used by people to escape from the unpleasant or even harsh realities of unfulfilling work and leisure. At the very least, time spent on screens is time not spent interacting and living with flesh and blood people and other natural beings. A major example in this chapter is how mediated lives can become devoted to surfaces, such as in the contemporary quest for "cool," with the result that the depth of character necessary for authentic being gets ignored and never develops to maturation. Finally, in this chapter we will begin to explore the complicated ways identities are formed in those rich interstices where individual and culture meet as a lead-in to the central philosophical chapter of the book (chapter four).

In chapter three I contend that as we have "successfully" overcome and distanced ourselves from the vicissitudes of nature, whether through our buildings, our transportation, our increasing time in our virtual lives (or through other "techniques" as Jacques Ellul[20] calls our technological strategies and objects), we separate ourselves, physically and psychically, from a major source of authenticity. Much of this chapter explores how and why being close to nature seems to be a crucial ingredient in human nature, and thus essential in forging a healthy identity capable of authentic being. I argue that, like it or not, we are natural beings who need contact with the stars, the elements, and other creatures in order to be whole and feel that we are truly in touch with reality. Many people have articulated this perspective, including a host of recent studies about the physical and mental health effects of time in nature as well as claims about the spiritual, educational, and social benefits, but to my knowledge none have connected it to a comprehensive theory of authenticity.

While there are quite a number of sub theories of authenticity, I have found four major views: 1) Essentialist views that argue or assume there is a deep core to human identity built into each person and that can be decked out in many ways but at root is invariant; 2) Existentialist (or Bohemian) perspectives that posit individual choice as the sole true determinant of identity; 3) Postmodern views that focus on the roles of society and culture in shaping identity; and 4) "in-between" views that see the self, and thus authenticity, as dialogical (to use Taylor's term). I believe the first three views are inadequate and that their manifestations have contributed substantially to many of the social maladies I catalogued earlier. In chapter four, I will sort out the views of various thinkers both historically and conceptually, and following Taylor and his disciples such as Guignon as well as skeptics such as Potter, I will try to show how these mis-conceptions have played out variously in damaged or wasted lives. In contrast to Potter, I will argue for a version of the middle path that takes its orientation from, but also differs from, contemporary philosophers such as Taylor, Appiah, and Bugbee who

---

20 *The Technological Society*

have inspired my view. I will also call upon ancient Chinese Daoism as well as Nietzsche and Heidegger to explore my alternative. Unlike many postmodern thinkers who build upon the Existentialists in this regard, I do not believe the self is merely a social construct basically imposed by society for various purposes. I also do not believe that the real me resides at some deeper and more essential level apart from our social interactions and roles. The theory I develop says that the self is real and consists mainly of lived stories (narratives) brought to the ongoing construction project that we are from within *and* without the individual. We are simultaneously social and individual, the locus of an ongoing dialogue that can result in identities that are genuine or fake, becoming or malformed, happy, or unhappy.

My perspective draws from literature and social science as well as from philosophy and religion. In chapter five I will try to show how theories and information from contemporary social scientific students of happiness, so-called "positive psychologists," can help us understand why so many of the strategies people today choose to achieve happiness and authenticity instead bring the opposite of what they seek. Not all authentic people are happy, of course, but it might well be that all happy people are authentic. For according to positive psychologists, happy people are those who find meaning in relationships, religion and other activities where they take the time to experience life thoroughly and passionately instead of through too-busy or too-materialistic lives that barely slow down enough to touch reality. The "flow" of absorption in the moment that these social scientists (and religious figures such as Ricard) believe holds the key to happiness is also a crucial dimension in being authentic, and the kinds of challenges many people believe are barriers to happiness can be the sort of adversity compatible with, and perhaps necessary for, happiness and authentic being. Jonathan Haidt believes that happiness also happens "in between," where what is internal joins with what comes from society and culture, thus locating happiness at the same juncture as I situate authenticity, and in the end these closely-related phenomena are about meaning and purpose, which in turn are about stories or frameworks of interpretive meaning. Our identities are tied up with the stories of our lives which means that not only is it critical to live intimately with nature and other humans, but that how we interpret our lives also plays a vital role in determining, e.g., whether the suffering we experience is debilitating or transformative.

I find that the perspective given by positive psychologists like Haidt helps to break the logjam created by the either/or of essentialism or the postmodern no-self. A large portion of the ingredients of the self are given by our DNA (Haidt calls the given of our biological nature the "elephant," in contrast to the "rider" of our consciousness, to emphasize how large this source is), but through a variety of strategies we can change our lives in ways that improve our happiness or authenticity. Based on a half century of research by a wide variety of social scientists, Haidt asserts that we can influence significantly the conditions affecting our happiness. Improving our relationships is fundamental, whether we work to create happy marriages or flowering communities. Positive psychologists contend that being more grateful and adopting the kinds of stories and practices found in religion can also help people live happier and longer lives.

In chapter six I will explore several such strategies within the traditional religious metaphor of *calling*. On the one hand this rather vague metaphor emphasizes a proper fit between what we do and who we are (between our social identities and our subjective identifications), for if our work or leisure activities do not suit us we can become lost and often harmed. On the other hand, the category of calling reminds us that much of how we are depends on luck or grace, on forces beyond our ken and control. The metaphor of calling also emphasizes our response to what we discern. Sometimes we are fortunate to go it alone and find our way. More often those who succeed are given an adequate set of stories, or interpretive tools, by a guide, which means we need a special kind of education if authenticity is to occur. Thus part of what I will recommend, as you continue on your path to becoming more authentic, is a set of personal and social practices that will make it easier for you to find your way. For contrary to what I learned as a child, you can be too independent just as you can be too dependent and other-directed. Great balance is needed, over and over again. I hope that this conceptual journey I am inviting you to take with me is of value on your personal path to authenticity and perhaps to happiness as well.

CHAPTER ONE
WORK

Work and Authenticity

> *"All too many of us are blind to a world charged with the glory of God, preoccupied with the business of money-making, money-having, money-spending and the pursuit of power and pleasure, distracted by distraction from distraction."*
> —*D.H. Lawrence*

I always begin my class called Working in America[1] with what seems to students a stupid question: *why* work? Once past their incredulity, their answers flow. Everyone knows we must work to make a living, to put bread on the table and gas in the tank; work is the necessary evil that can, if you're lucky, lead to the good life; or, at least life won't be so boring if you work. Eventually, after much discussion, reading,

---

1 The humanities faculty at Kirkwood Community College where I have taught for twenty-six years, in conjunction with a set of faculty colleagues from various vocational programs, developed this unique course in 1986—an interdisciplinary humanities course that focuses on work and is designed to be especially valuable to students in vocational programs. A colleague and I put together a textbook for this class, *Working in America: A Humanities Reader,* and subsequently I edited a companion volume *Working in America: Supplemental Readings.*

and reflective exercises, they begin to realize that work, whether paid or unpaid, does more than allow you to enter, more or less successfully, the cycle of acquiring money and consuming goods and services. Work is also where you form long-term relationships; it shapes (and misshapes) you; work, like school, can be a place where you discover, develop, and express your self; and work is a major venue where you join and contribute to your community.

Once we have established that people have always worked and must work, and once they begin to realize that work is no minor force in anyone's life, we begin to explore another seemingly naïve question (alas, the stock and trade of philosophers), *how* should we work? I often begin this equally complex exercise with the distinction between good and bad work—what makes work good and what makes it bad? I have seen many changes over the years in how each successive generation of students initially answers this question. At one time students tended to prize adventure; during a different era they favored work that was most lucrative; while yet another generation most desired work that was easy. I ask students to keep a running list of good- and bad-making characteristics as we explore a variety of accounts of and reflections on work. Last year I was disturbed to have a class wherein every student viewed physical labor as the most prominent feature that made work bad. Generational shifts are not always for the better, as we will discuss shortly.

Again, their comprehension deepens as they realize that the quality of people's work is relative to their interests, attitudes, talents, social and cultural traditions, fellow workers and supervisors, how well work meshes with their non-work life, and so on. Probing still deeper, at a level of generalization one step beyond the great variations in why work is good or bad for people, we discover some patterns and perhaps even universal features of good and bad work. Of course good work helps people make a living, but work doesn't necessarily become ever-better the more income it generates. For good work must also challenge people without degrading them, it must not be boring and it needs to help or allow people to grow and learn. Good work contributes positively to the community, it provides the opportunity for people to be a part of something important that is larger than themselves and their individual lives, and it helps, of course, if one's fellow workers are compatible. Bad morale makes for bad work, and bad morale is a function of poor leadership and poor relations with one's compatriots. Good work is also work that "fits" the worker—even if someone else might thrive doing a particular job or task, if the work doesn't match your profile in requisite ways, it won't be good for you.

While there are yet other things that can make work good or bad for an individual or in general, what this short list indicates is that work is a major context (the others perhaps being family, school, religious, and community life) wherein people discover, become, and play out who they are. If I am correct in believing that authenticity is about identity, then work affects our authenticity in profound ways. It is small wonder that Freud believed that besides food, clothing, and shelter, the most important human needs are love and work.

Encountering My Self in Work

In the late 1960s when the Civil Rights movement and Vietnam War protests were at fever pitch, on appeal of the local draft board's decision I was granted conscientious objector status and found a two-year job in Alaska working with disturbed teenagers. My job as counselor was to help keep order in our cottage, deal with conflicts, and provide meaningful recreational activities for fifteen troubled boys. Basically I was to try to help them grow and mature to the point where they were no longer a danger to themselves or others. I had avoided going to war, but I did not avoid the most challenging job I have ever had in 50 years of working.

In college and graduate school I was a student of human nature, majoring in psychology and philosophy with an emphasis on morality and choice. It was in that home for disturbed teenagers, however, where I learned the most about human beings, especially myself. If not daily, at least several times each week, I was confronted with situations where I had to discover my strengths and weaknesses, where I had to act decisively, and where I had to grow and adapt or fail.

While my pacifism has mellowed (if not matured) since then, at that point in my life it was pretty absolute. After all, I had just managed to convince a state draft board in a conservative Republican state (South Dakota) that a mere Methodist (as compared to members of "peace" traditions such as Quakers or Mennonites who were routinely granted conscientious objector status) was morally opposed to war and not just to the current one. I had gotten this unforgettable job by being a strong pacifist, but I learned I wouldn't be able to do the job I had chosen for my CO work if I maintained the same outlook.

I will never forget the winter day on the ice rink when Bobby Fee confronted me about something and began punching me when I refused to respond in kind and held fast to my pacifism. After many rounds of his physical attacks and my attempting to talk him out of his behavior, in defeat I called for reinforcements. Often we had to rely on fellow counselors or other employees to help us restrain a young person who had lost control, which was wise, because of the potential for great harm that such "blows," as we called them, could wreak. I had ample opportunities to discover the power of adrenaline as an out-of-control 100-pound 12-year old took two or three full-sized adults to contain. But my needing help with Bobby was different—he was not out of control, nor was he harming me badly; rather, he wanted me to show him that I cared enough about him to put my strong commitment to non-violence aside and respond in kind. Bobby wanted me to deck him, and because I did not, the respect he lost for me in that moment took months to re-form.

Was I being authentic in how I responded to Bobby Fee? Or would I have been more authentic if I had responded in kind? Usually we think of being authentic as a matter of being true to how we feel, to our true desires, and a major reason why so many people feel disconnected at work is because they are not able to be genuine in this way, to act on their personal feelings and desires. While there is little doubt most people probably experience this frustration on the job, and while many people probably would claim, thereby, that their jobs require them to be inauthentic, I believe that this description does not fit my experience in this situation. I acted on what I believed—that is, that it is wrong for humans to be violent to other humans. Period. Nevertheless, setting aside the issue of my failure, I was not (fully?) authentic. The reason for my lack of genuineness is that the self I was did not fit the occasion. At the very least, acting on my desire to be pacific was not enough to make me authentic.

As it often happens with seminal moments in our lives, it took me a long time to sort out what did occur that dark winter night in Anchorage. At first I thought that the problem was simply that Bobby did not understand the alternative to violence I was trying to model. While that was true to some extent, eventually I realized that my failure was also due to my own inauthenticity. I was being true to my beliefs and commitments, but I was not being a good counselor, and authenticity has as much to do with the realities around us as the psychological realities within us.

The job of counselors is to respond effectively and appropriately to their charges. Most centrally, this responsibility requires you to know your clientele well and to "speak" a language that communicates most clearly. My first mistake was not to understand what this young man was expressing in his attack against me. I thought he was simply acting out some frustrations aggressively, and if that had been the case, refusing to respond in kind might well have been precisely the antidote he needed. But if what he wanted was help dealing with frustrations in an appropriate manner, or if he simply wanted to vent, he wouldn't have been so alienated from me for months to come. In retrospect, it was clear that Bobby had a different message, one to which my predilection to non-violence blinded me. He wanted to know if I cared enough about him to compromise my pacifism, to speak *his* language rather than the unfamiliar and abstract one I had chosen.

In his marvelous poem about good work, "Two Tramps in Mud Time," Robert Frost says of the two "tramps" (woodcutters) who stare him down and tacitly appropriate his avocation of splitting wood on an April day, "They thought all chopping was theirs of right./Men of the woods and lumberjacks,/They judged me by the appropriate tool." Bobby Fee was a tough, abused child of military parents who, like most of our troubled teens, spoke street language that included violence of many kinds. He, too, "judged me by the appropriate tool." Over several months he had seen that we were trying to get him to change, to forsake his familiar, if ultimately counter-productive, behaviors and adopt the non- (or at least less-) violent and more civil speech and actions we knew would serve him better. During his three years at the institution Bobby would warm to this transformation. He became one of our great success stories, eventually becoming a soldier who went on to a distinguished career. I am convinced, though, that if I had understood and responded properly to his challenge that night his stay with us might have been shortened significantly. Thus I failed. For what Bobby wanted was for me to show that I cared enough for him to forsake, for a moment, my cherished ideal, to choose his "language" rather than mine. To punch him back.

To Be Authentic Is To Play Our Roles Well

What does my story have to do with work and authenticity? My job as counselor at that point in my life was more dramatically and thoroughly formative than many people may experience. Whether or not people know it, however, work shapes them in profound ways. Everyone works. Everyone is shaped by work. Therefore the question is not whether work affects our identities, but in what ways and to what extent. And if authenticity has to do, at least significantly, with acting from our identities, then work not only can lead us to be inauthentic, but it can set the very conditions of our authenticity.

Think of my example this way: my struggle with Bobby Fee not only revealed a conflict between my chosen stance of non-violence and what my job required, but the job required me to change if I was to truly *be* a counselor and not just play at it. Perhaps this sounds a little harsh or overly dramatic, but the point I am trying to make is that to a great extent *our roles define us* and to be authentic is to play our roles with excellence in such a way that over time we become that role. Thus while being authentic involves being true to our beliefs and desires rather than capitulating to others' opinions or desires, that is not enough. I was swimming against a rather stiff tide not only opposing the war but being willing to go to jail (or cross the border into Canada—happily I didn't have to make that decision) to avoid being drafted into fighting in a war I so vehemently opposed. If I had not found myself working with disturbed teenagers perhaps my commitment to pacifism eventually would have been enough for me to be authentic, but as it always seems to happen, the world had other ideas.

Selves Evolve as Roles Evolve

Part of what we can take from my Alaskan story is that identity and authenticity *evolve*. If your identity is not clearly and thoroughly formed, you can act consistently with and from it and yet not be authentic. Why? Because half of the equation is that to be authentic you must be an authentic *something*—parent, child, employee, boss, lover, vegetarian, citizen. Furthermore, the shape of your identity is conditioned precisely by the roles you play and how you play them, and if you are not well-versed and very comfortable in your respective roles, you cannot be fully authentic.

Consider another example from my personal history. I grew up a veterinarian's son in rural South Dakota during the 1950s and 1960s. Life was hard and often my father was paid in the only fungible available to struggling farmers, produce, most usually meat. Thus, while our family's bank account was often low, our freezer was usually full, and I came to view a meat-based diet as normal. When I encountered strong examples and arguments for vegetarianism and decided to give up my more common omnivore diet, I was bucking personal habit and taste as well as social norms. During the first months and years of my sojourn into a meatless diet, my forays into vegetarian cuisine and nutrition were accompanied by uncertainties and insecurities that often took the form of confronting others about their "immoral" diets, or at least broadcasting my own dietary virtues. I am sure I was obnoxious to more than one person on more than one occasion as I struggled to become a vegetarian as distinct from simply not eating meat. From the start, technically I was a vegetarian, and being meatless was a strong desire; but I wasn't an authentic vegetarian until years into my 15-year meat-abstinence.

In the famous "Ox-Herding" visual parable from ancient China, a young seeker is depicted going through a series of stages in his quest to become enlightened. At first he is living in the blissful ignorance of childhood; but then he discovers the tracks of the ox and thus begins his quest to discover, understand, master, and finally become at one with the way of the "ox." In a third image the youth has the proverbial ox (tiger) by the tail as he is nearly overwhelmed by this strange and powerful creature. This picture reminds me of my experiences in my first year of struggling to be a vegetarian or my first decade with the enterprise of philosophy I discovered in college. It takes a very long time to become familiar with the language, style, assumptions, beliefs, dogmas, strategies, and standard issues of any new discipline. The more complex and numerous these aspects, the longer it takes. And the more it can throw you for a loop!

After the initial struggle to "herd" (makes sense of) the ox, the boy "domesticates" his chosen discipline and begins to lead it around. Eventually, two pictures later, he sits astride the ox, finally quite comfortable with his chosen[2] path. At what point is he an authentic ox-herder (vegetarian, philosopher, Daoist, etc.)? Part of the message of this lovely visual parable is that there is no magic moment when this occurs, but certainly it has occurred by the seventh frame where we see the man, now clearly older, sitting beside a pond with no ox in sight. He has now internalized the discipline so much that he is finally a master of it—he is a woodcarver/poet/plumber/etc.—and he is so much at home with the language, assumptions, style, and so forth of this "way" that it no longer "shows." When I finally became a genuine vegetarian, I thought, acted, and spoke like a vegetarian, un-self-

2 Or does it choose him? We will explore this critical question in chapter six, on Calling.

consciously and naturally. I had long-since moved beyond the initial stage where I had to prove to everyone, including myself, that I was a vegetarian. Authenticity is too vague a concept to determine how close of a fit there must be between the role and the person before one becomes that role, but clearly it is not a mantle one learns to wear seamlessly overnight.

To make this same point from the other end, someone who is not following the path of a particular ox is not an inauthentic ox-herder; only someone who is "playing at" a role, who has begun to take on the trappings of that discipline, can be inauthentic in it.[3] Earnestness of intent initially only highlights one's inauthenticity rather than sufficing to render one authentic.

Workers Who Are Real

> *We seek a real world to find a real self.*
> —*Richard Todd*

Author Marge Piercy has a wonderful short poem that captures this somewhat counter-cultural aspect of authenticity and leads us to a further point; I quote the entirety of this lovely poem about genuine workers:

The People I Love the Best

The people I love the best
jump into work head first
without dallying in the shadows
and swim off with sure strokes almost out of sight.
They seem to become natives of that element,

---

3 This is a tricky point, for while sometimes we say she is an inauthentic poet or teacher (i.e., she is inauthentic with regard to a particular role), sometimes people use the word in a broader sense to refer to a pervasive feeling of rootlessness, of being unreal in general. We will turn to this more pervasive sense of inauthenticity in chapter four.

the black sleek heads of seals
bounding like half-submerged balls.

I love people who harness themselves, an ox to a
    heavy cart,
who pull like water buffalo, with massive patience,
who strain in the mud and muck to move things
    forward,
who do what has to be done, again and again.

I want to be with people who submerge
in the task, who go into the fields to harvest
and work in a row and pass the bags along,
who stand in the line and haul in their places,
who are not parlor generals and field deserters
but move in a common rhythm
when the food must come in or the fire be put out.

The work of the world is common as mud.
Botched, it smears the hands, crumbles to dust.
But the thing worth doing well
has a shape that satisfies, clean and evident.
Greek amphoras for wine or oil,
Hopi vases that held corn, are put in museums,
but you know they were made to be used.
The pitcher cries for water to carry
and a person for work that is real.[4]

Piercy celebrates people who dive into their work, who are willing to do what it takes to get the job done and done well, and she recognizes that those who are able to do so tend to be people who are as at home in their element (with their ox) as seals in the ocean. They are masters of their crafts. When my students who shun physical labor

---

4 From *Circles on the Water* by Marge Piercy.

read this poem they are stymied, for they know exactly what she is talking about yet they have preordained that the very work they, with Piercy and the rest of us, now admire is automatically bad work. Philosopher Matthew Crawford[5] delves into this paradox and contends that much of the degradation of manual labor results from our identification of "white collar" work as conceptual and challenging while we associate "blue collar" work as mindless and menial. Using motorcycle repair as his example, Crawford contends that much manual work requires a great deal of conceptual sophistication and problem-solving. Another piece of this puzzle, of course, is that the white/blue distinction is quite unhelpful as many so-called white collar jobs are menial and mind-numbing rather than being mentally stimulating.

So what is it that we admire in workers who get the job done without complaining, pretense or preening self-consciousness? To use Piercy's word, they are *real*. If I was correct in the introduction to this book, people today have a deep and gnawing desire to be real; but many people believe it is precisely in avoiding "work as common as mud" or other everyday roles that authenticity is to be found. Potter attributes such unfortunate results to "our modern religion," the pursuit of authenticity. I contend that pursuing the wrong version of authenticity is the problem. The mistake is not to want to be real, it is to pursue being real in the wrong ways. In Piercy's metaphor, real people are those who are willing to do what they are cut out for, often at great cost (they harness themselves like ox or pull like buffalo) and become part of a work team (work in a row and move to common rhythms) where they don't necessarily stand out. Many people today (such as my students who shun physical labor) seem to believe that being authentic is about standing out, being unique or at least unusual, and doing things that are not mundane, ordinary, or repetitive. As

---

5 Matthew Crawford, *Shop Class as Soulcraft: An Inquiry into the Value of Work.*

Crawford argues, becoming real might just lie in the opposite direction from where many people are searching, and coming up short.

Contributing to the Community

I think that we may feel real in direct proportion to the
reality that we can grant to others.
—Richard Todd

Probably the most successful assignment I give in my class on work is to have students interview someone who has worked at least 25 years. They often choose someone close to them (a parent or other relative, their current boss, a lifelong friend) and the simple fact of asking about and listening to their interviewee's story regularly improves their relationship with that person. Over the years these simple interviews have revealed or helped to create reconciliation, deepened understanding, or allowed a recognition of the student as an adult by their relative or friend, and significant progress in my students' appreciation for and understanding of the power and importance of work. This assignment is due about a third of the way through the course and I ask them to apply what they have learned: how work is about much more than a paycheck, what makes some work good and some bad, how work shapes people's identities, how social class weaves through the workplace, how people become enmeshed in their communities through work, and so on. All of a sudden most students realize that the ideas we have been talking about have real world applicability, as their parent tells of dreams lost because of a bad job, or a grandparent reflects on how meaningful they found working as a teacher or a farmer. One semester I had a classroom full of young men who were angry at their fathers until their interviews revealed that their fathers had been absent during their teen years because they had been trying to save the family farm (and often the family!) during the farm crisis in Iowa during the early 1980s.

One memorable interview was with a student's small town grade school janitor who after 40 years of cleaning up after children teared up when he spoke of how much it meant to him to be able to give so much to his community through his work. He felt he was doing invaluable work that no one else wanted to do or could do as well, and he swelled with pride as he talked about what he had helped do, in his small and inconspicuous way, as one child went on to become a doctor, another a farmer, one a mother of five, and so on. I remember the student who interviewed this memorable character being at a loss to explain why someone would find cleaning toilets, classrooms, and lunchrooms for 40 years so meaningful, finally settling on the description, "he is so real."

We say the same thing in many ways: she is so at home in her role, he is the quintessential businessman, you can tell he is a craftsman by how he carries himself, she is so genuine, that athlete embodies her sport, he is authentic through and through … he is so real. I am very grateful to live in Iowa where so many "salt of the earth" people reside, where people enjoy good, hard work, where so many people feel connected to their communities, and where craftsmanship is still prized. Unfortunately, Iowa is also becoming a place where the webs of relationships that bind people in small, rural communities are unraveling. My students' interview papers continue to reveal the lives of people who are as Piercy describes, women and men who labor long hours as nurses, business people, daycare workers, or teachers and who then continue to contribute to the community in their leisure time. Increasingly, though, I also hear stories of pain and desperation as factory "farms" replace family farms and local businesses are shoved out by agribusinesses and big box stores. *Methland*[6] is a chilling account of how people without hope in rural Iowa turn to the local drug of choice, methamphetamine, and in the process the fabric of their community, as well as their personal health and lives, is torn asunder. If you know, as the residents of "methland" must, how this drug affects people, including how addictive it is, something very strong must drive these sensible, practical people to it. That something is the lack of good work.

Money and Authenticity

When I ask 18-year olds what they seek in work, what would make their current work better, or what they most think about as they choose and prepare for careers, by far the most common response is "money." When they interview people who have worked for a long time, money is rarely mentioned. Experienced workers, at least in Iowa, do not put money near the top of their list of things that they find most important in their work. Instead, they talk about copasetic fellow workers, interesting or challenging work, the opportunity to work with a team, the ability to determine when and how they will work on what, a boss who listens and understands, the sense that what they are doing is important, recognition, and finally, "a decent living."

Part of why young people have a different set of priorities for work and careers is that they are just beginning and most have not had much money or the things it can buy—automobiles, houses and things to fill it, travel…all the things necessary to have the life they desire. Their version of The American Dream. Older workers who don't have enough money to meet their material needs and desires also tend

---

6 Nick Reding, *Methland: The Death and Life of an American Small Town.*

to put money at or near the top of their lists. Those who are relatively satisfied materially and are secure in their incomes, however, emphasize other values they want from their work, and it is this discrepancy of priorities that I want to examine.

If money is so critical for becoming the person you want to be, as the vast majority of my students believe, why wouldn't ever-more money help in your lifelong quest for identity and authenticity? This question brings us to a central issue in this chapter and in this book: many people in today's culture are confused about the relationships between money (and the things it can buy) and authenticity. In a nutshell, with authenticity as with love or happiness, money can't buy it.

As is typical, though, nutshells tend to be clichés and rather empty abstractions, so let us move to another abstraction that is more informative, the nature of money. Teachers of poetry and religion decry the literalism of their students when deciphering poems or myths, and oddly a kind of literalism also occurs with money. Everyone knows that the paper or metal out of which money is made is nearly worthless in itself (just as everyone knows the ink on the page is not the poem), but many people tend to act as if the value of something is strictly determined by how much money it costs. Hermeneutic literalism, reading a symbolic utterance as if it were not symbolic but literal (the messenger Hermes flies between humans and the gods) is a kind of reduction, a draining of the symbolic meaning leaving only the residue of the material from which the metaphor is formed. Money is a very malleable symbol that can be used to purchase a wide variety of valuable items (including non-material goods such as experiences or other symbols), but to value a work of art, an experience, an education, a wedding ring, or a wig for a cancer patient simply in terms of how much it costs or can be sold for is to make a similar mistake. Money is not the thing itself, nor does it tell you much about its values.

What does money symbolize? At bottom, it symbolizes work. The money you earn symbolizes your effort, the toil you put in to gain the symbolic power the money represents. Even if someone inherits money, it represents someone's work. In our culture we tend to overvalue *and* undervalue money and what it buys. The overvaluing critique is most familiar—Americans are too materialistic, we tend to have too much stuff, consumerism runs rampant in people's lives, we worship the rich and famous, and so on. (We will return to this theme momentarily.) Given our obvious obsession with money, what could it mean to assert that we undervalue money and what it can buy? Jacob Needleman[7] makes the startling claim that Americans tend not to be materialistic enough. He contends that by forgetting that money symbolizes our effort (it is, symbolically, our essence squeezed into the coin or bill or what is even more abstract, the electrons in our accounts), we squander it on trivia thus simultaneously denigrating our selves and the world we are wasting. If we were truly materialistic in the sense that we cared deeply about the material world, including our bodies and minds working in that world, we would spend our money on what really mattered, on what could make a real difference. I believe that the all-too-common temptations in our consumer culture to spend our selves (our money) on trivia is a major distraction that keeps us from being authentic because how we spend our money is a major way we have of connecting with reality.

Take the simple example of a bottle of water. Around here they cost about a dollar and a quarter. Many of my students, most of whom complain they do not have enough money, regularly purchase one or another of the many brands of bottled water. When I point out that

---

7 *Money and the Meaning of Life.*

tap water is as good as or better than bottled water and it is free, they say they buy it because it is convenient. A tricky word, convenience. In every hallway at our school is a drinking fountain where cold water is always available. Refillable containers are no less convenient than throw-away ones because either kind must be carried. More importantly, the trivial convenience of bottled water pales at the inconveniences of the purchase for people and the environment. Four or five bottles of water cost my students an hour of labor, often at a job they dislike. An hour of sweat or boredom or even enjoyable work in exchange for something that is otherwise free? Convenient? This simple example can highlight an array of everyday purchases where we (inconveniently) spend our essence, the best part of ourselves squeezed into our money, on unimportant things...and then throw them away. To trace the life of a bottle of water is to see how terribly inconvenient our purchases can be for the environment: the processing of the oil to make the plastic bottle uses up an increasingly precious commodity while adding to greenhouse gasses, as does the transportation to and from the bottling plant, as does the water "purification" and bottling, as does the disposal of the bottle. Each bottle of water has a heavy footprint that is totally avoidable by getting that drink from the convenient fountain down the hall.

The point of this small example is not to exaggerate the hidden costs of drinking bottled water, but to illustrate Needleman's seemingly counter-intuitive point that we are not materialistic enough in a way that shows how important his point is in relation to authenticity. In far too many ways we tend to treat our selves and our world with wanton disregard for the values that are most important. One of the most powerful exercises I have had students practice over the years is to do the simple cost accounting Joe Dominguez and Vicki Robin outline in their little book, *Your Money or Your Life*,[8] and few of them come away from this experience without improved clarity about their priorities and how little their current spending habits reflect their values. Students have realized, for example, that they are spending $9000 per year on transportation out of their $25,000 budget, or that their weekly entertainment bill is much higher than they knew which is why they could never seem to make ends meet no matter how many hours they worked each week. Through this cost-accounting activity my students begin to discover that to be distracted from spending their selves wisely is to be disconnected from reality.

There is no doubt that the factors contributing to authenticity my students find when they interview long-time workers are crucial—a sense of contributing to the community, work that is important, recognition, flow, camaraderie, and so on—but surely money is also important. Money is important for survival, of course, but also for being authentic, for it is very difficult to be real without aspects of what money can buy. Again, we need to be very clear on how money affects authenticity because it can be, and often is, a major ingredient in the rampant *inauthenticity* we find in our society.

While we are discussing money and authenticity, let me mention one more point that we will take up in detail in chapter four where I offer my narrative and communitarian alternative to common individualist theories of authenticity. When I was in graduate school my father aggravated me greatly when he implied that I was not yet real (he said "a full-fledged adult") even though I was financially independent from him and had long paid my own way through a combination

---

8 *Your Money or Your Life: Transforming Your Relationship With Money and Achieving Financial Independence.*

of scholarships and part-time jobs. He said that I would realize the truth of his claim when I finally got a real job. Although it was hard to admit at the time, when I got that first teaching job I realized the accuracy of his statement—there was something qualitatively different in my identity once I had a job in the career for which I had been preparing; and part of the symbolism that marked my having arrived was money—a salary and benefits. Was I thus authentic overnight? Of course not—as we discussed earlier, becoming fully identified with a role can take years. And the point isn't that not depending on one's parents for support is what is important. What is crucial is to see that roles, and thus one's identity and thus one's authenticity, are socially determined. Both the career, in this case, and the things symbolizing that I had arrived, were set by social convention and were not of my choosing. Much of why I chaffed at my father's remark was due to my wanting control of aspects of my identity I couldn't have.

At the most basic level, money can symbolize that you are capable of making your own way in the world, that you are financially independent. For this you do not even need to have bought anything. It is enough that you *can* buy what you need to live on your own. The valence of money in being authentic is tricky, though. Clearly simply having money is not enough to render a person authentic as a host of ready-to-hand examples of rich but fake people shows. And on the other hand, there have been plenty of authentic people with little or no money, for surely many, if not most, pre-modern people had little difficulty being authentic and many of them had little money or lived in basically non-moneyed societies. In modern moneyed societies, the symbolic power of money can be important in marking your being authentic, or not, precisely because money for us is such a powerful symbolic system. But the trick is not to gauge a person's authenticity by how much money they have. Instead, it is how the person uses their money and the things it buys that connects authenticity to money. It is the quality of their relationship to money and what it can bring that counts.

Authenticity and the Quality of Experience

Several years ago my wife, Lori, and I had an eye-opening experience leading a seminar on simple living. We were taken aback when more than 40 people showed up for the first of four, two-hour sessions, most of them professors, doctors, lawyers, and other professionals from our church and community, all of whom were well off financially. We wondered why these incredibly busy and capable people, who epitomize well-ordered and successful lives, would take the time to discuss at length the rather simple ideas I was used to discussing with my normally disorganized students who had not thought much about how to bring order to the chaos of their lives. The answer to our puzzlement came as one after another these pillars of their departments and institutions told, with tears in their eyes, of how, in the words of one participant, their "lives were running them rather than they running their lives." Nearly every person there had achieved their professional and personal goals, yet they were exhausted, frustrated, and almost desperate. Desperate for time with family, for relaxation, for spontaneity and the ability to respond to serendipity, for fun. Their accomplished busyness required significant disconnects from reality. Perhaps it also was a result of their anxieties about fully engaging with reality.

How does this happen? Why are so many people in modern societies, perhaps especially professionals who "have everything," so hungry to reclaim their lives? At least part of the answer is Needleman's first point, which is that we have become caught in the whirlwind of consumerism. But before we turn to this over-trodden field, let us consider how this example relates to authenticity. For it seems that our seminar participants are quite authentic based on our discussion of the centrality of playing one's roles well for being authentic. These doctors and professors and librarians and administrators are, if anything, over-identified with their roles, spending 60 to 80 (or more!) hours weekly plying their crafts, and many of them are also very involved with their children, their churches, and their communities in impressive ways. Perhaps they suffer from time famine, but surely they are not inauthentic?

Perhaps. But remember that authenticity has to do with feeling and being real, and their laments that they felt disconnected from their lives, that they had turned into automatons who were just going through the motions indicates a separation from reality of significant magnitude (Norris says that *acedia* is like sleepwalking through one's life). I believe there is an important lesson here: the *quality* of experience and accomplishment is as important as being in the right place doing the right things. This quality is at the core of Mihalyi Csikszentmihalyi's idea of flow.[9] As we will discuss at some length in chapter three, you are in flow if time flies and you lose yourself in the experience. The experience of flow is often described as when you and the object of your experience "become one" (it can be a physical object, a task, a thought, nature—most anything in the world). If you are so busy and stressed from doing a job, even one that you are cut out for and doing well, the experience can be, and obviously often is, one of a kind of alienation rather than identification with that work—the work is in charge, not you. Being authentic requires time, time to prepare, time to square one's psychology with the task at hand, time to become attuned with the thing with which you are working, time

---

9 *Flow: The Psychology of Optimal Experience.*

to lose your self in the work rather than to have that self be an alien in what should be its natural setting, a setting where the self is so at home that self-consciousness disappears into flow.

If Norris is correct, there is a deeper problem for many people who are busy, busy, busy—they have succumbed to that subtle but powerful noonday demon, *acedia*. Remember, the essence of acedia is not-caring. Thus even if a busy person wants to care, they simply do not have the time to care well. Behind the simple mathematics of the 24-hour day, though, Norris believes many people *choose* to be insanely busy to avoid something—they live incredibly full lives to avoid living up to their full potential.[10] What does she mean? It is clear to see that if you are too busy it is difficult to do something, and sometimes anything, well. But surely no one lives this way on purpose?

Sometimes Norris seems insensitive to the forced busyness many people have because of their jobs. I know many residents and doctors at the University of Iowa's marvelous hospital who have to spend insane hours at work if they wish to have their jobs. Perhaps the hospital should change its labor practices, but it is unreasonable to expect individual people singlehandedly to change a major institution. The same could be said for many of the lawyers, professors, and business-people at our seminar who wept for their lost lives. We should not blame people for institutional practices they cannot change. However, there are people in high-powered jobs who do not seem to suffer in this way from the work demanded of them. They somehow manage to live their lives, on and off the job, at a pace that allows them to engage fully with their patients or clients or customers, to spend significant quality time with their families, to take time for themselves, and to

---

10 Norris takes up this theme in a section called "Industrial Acedia" (121-28) and again in a section about the importance of everyday activities, "Mysteries Great and Small" (188-95).

enjoy significant community involvement. Such examples lead us to wonder, with Norris, if breaking away from the tyranny of a life too full isn't possible for us all...if we really wanted to.

I believe the philosopher Martin Heidegger can help us understand something important about this puzzling phenomenon. For Heidegger to be human is to be *thrust* into a world only partially of our own making where we must respond. In agreement with Norris, he contends that ordinarily our fundamental response is *Sorge*, to care. However, *Sorge* has a second meaning, *anxiety*. To care is to open ourselves to the possibilities of failure, disappointment, tragedy, and suffering. Thus underlying every act of care is the anxiety that something might go wrong, sometimes terribly. Nevertheless, most of us proceed to fall in love, have children, go whitewater rafting, move to a new city, or change jobs despite the negative possibilities because our care outweighs our anxiety. Nagging existential anxiety can become fear of flying, though, and we can find ourselves hedging our bets, pulling in our compassionate tentacles, or otherwise playing it safe. One strategy might be to guard against our fears by being busy.

Undoubtedly you are familiar with stories of people who spend endless hours on the job to avoid going home to a bad relationship or to no relationship at all. A variation on this story is the person who tries to get too much from his job—his social life, the majority of his community status, his meaning in life. There are also people who care less because they are so busy in their non-work lives. There are even people who are so incredibly busy in their non-work time doing good things for other people that they never have (take) time to be alone or engage in spiritual activities. A common result of such busyness can be expressions of unaccountable anger, resentment, and depression that seem to indicate the same frustration with a life out of control we witnessed among the participants in our seminar on simple living. When we have strong designs on the world and when others don't behave the way we expect, we become frustrated. This frustration often spawns anger and resentment, emotions that Sartre rightly sees as magical tools we wave at a world out of our control to try to bend it to our will.[11]

The world is a messy place, and perhaps people are the messiest of beings in our unpredictability, irrationality, and endless complexity. To care for people requires time, much more time than we usually allocate, and it requires that we listen deeply and long in order to know how to care best. If we gave up our designs on the world and lived more in the realities of the unpredictable moment—at least by building time for unpredictability (serendipity) into our schedules—we could care more and better.

In the next chapter we will discuss some of the roles technologies play in enhancing and degrading our authenticity, but I think it is relevant here to give a technology-aided example of what appears to be a similar situation for many young people today. I am talking about the remarkable shift away from actually talking on cell phones to texting. Sociologists tell us that in this age of ever-more ways of not communicating face-to-face, recently there has been a dramatic drop in the number of talking phone calls, especially among young people.[12] Apparently those missing calls are being replaced by texting. But why?

---

11 Sartre contends that we use many emotions to manipulate our worlds. We might use anger, e.g., to get people to bend to our wills, or tears to soften them for a favor. Emotions can and do function as magic wands. See his *Existentialism and Human Emotions*.

12 MIT sociologist Sherry Turkle has studied this and many other technology related social and psychological phenomenon, especially among young people. See her *Alone Together: Why We've Started Expecting More From Technology and Less From Each Other*.

Why would teens, who love to talk with friends, replace conversation with asynchronous, brief bits of text? This downgrading of quality of communication almost seems like a return to sending smoke signals! Perhaps that is precisely the reason. When I ask my sons and their friends, as well as my students, about this dramatic trend, they say that they want to avoid interrupting their friends, but I don't buy this rationale. They are constantly interrupted by text messages, which they quickly answer, often, in turn interrupting classes, conversations, and (horrors!) driving (or walking) concentration. What does make sense is a second response, which is that texting is easier and more efficient because you don't have to become involved with the other people. This strikes me as a clear recognition that engagement with others is messy and interferes with one's (fleeting) control over one's life. It seems ironic that this latest tool of communication not only contains far less information than even a phone call (voices carry emotion), but that it provides a convenient cover for caring less.

Norris discusses another dimension of *acedia* that sheds light on our busyness. She says that busyness is a strategy not only for avoiding full engagement with others, but it can be a way of avoiding full engagement with our selves. The paradigm of this avoidance, Norris contends, is the way busyness can function to convince ourselves that we are too important to die (our ultimate anxiety). For Heidegger the paradigm of the anxiety side of our *Sorge* is, to use Kierkegaard's phrase, a "sickness unto death." In less dramatic language, these and many other thinkers note that spending real time getting to know, evaluate, and develop ourselves can be the most difficult and frightening enterprise we face. One marker of how strong this anxiety is can be our tendencies to be hyper-busy. Another way to talk about the dimensions of life that many of us try to avoid by being busy is to say we are avoiding our calling, a theme to which we will turn in detail in chapter six.

A Derivative Take on Consumerism and Authenticity

We harbor selves that go deeper than masks.
—*Richard Todd*

What, finally, are we to make of the relationships between material-ism in the common sense—consumerism—and authenticity? On one hand people's identities are, and always have been to some extent, tied up with the things we possess. Even poor nomads mark their sense of self and self importance by the number of camels or horses or yaks in their herds. Consumer societies, it seems, are simply expanding our options. Modern materialism can be linked to the problems of class and the competition for status, and surely no one can deny that our amazing capacities for consuming the bounty of the earth are wreak-ing havoc with whole ecosystems. But in an age that celebrates free-dom, diversity, and the emergence of the individual why is modern materialism also a problem for people being authentic? The common answer afforded by a great variety of critics is that authenticity has to do with who we *are* and not what we *have*: someone can have great wealth and possessions yet be a fake, while many authentic people have little. I believe this diagnosis is on the right track, and we will re-turn to this direct link (or its lack) between consumerism and authen-ticity in chapter five; but for a moment I want to look at materialism and authenticity in a more oblique way.

Rather than rehearse the familiar and lengthy litany of complaints of modern market economies offered by critics over the past two hun-dred years,[13] let us begin by returning to Richard Todd's book where

---

13 For a recent rehearsal of these views, along with sometimes salient criticisms of them, see Deirdre McCloskey's monumental four-volume work in progress touting the bourgeois virtues. Her first volume is *The Bourgeois Virtues: Ethics for an Age of Commerce.*

he makes a crucial distinction between the things of our lives. Todd begins with a claim not unlike that which is central to this book: contemporary Americans, if not citizens of all modern societies, have a great hunger to be real, to be authentic, and he also claims (what seems obvious) that we have been convinced that the way to satisfy this hunger is to consume. Rather than decry the failure of this strategy (which also seems obvious), Todd makes a distinction between pursuing and acquiring objects (and experiences) that are fake from ones that are genuine, with the unique proposition that if we consume what is genuine we have a much better chance of satisfying this existential hunger than if we accumulate what is simply new, expensive, in vogue, or cool.[14]

The chapters in the first two of the four parts of Todd's book are sorted according to kinds of consumer objects: antiques, experiences, hand-crafted objects, art, technologies, and so on. He explores what it means for each of these things to be genuine and in the process reveals a great deal about the materiality of human identity and authenticity. While he regularly gets sidetracked in interesting discussions, such as whether or not good fake art has a genuineness worth paying for and collecting, Todd makes a strong case that simply dismissing materialism as a path to authenticity is a mistake. At the very least, he contends, people realize in a deeply intuitive way, that things are parts of our identities. I believe this insight is an important addition to Taylor's lengthy discussion of the sources of modern selves. As Taylor powerfully shows, human selves are made up of the beliefs, values, meanings and other "mental" phenomena he laboriously catalogs; but humans also symbolize these ethereal phenomena in concrete ways. Thus pursuing concrete symbols in an attempt to become real is neither wrongheaded nor avoidable. The question is what things to pursue in what

---

14 In chapter two we discuss the failure of "cool" at length.

ways, not whether or not to be 'materialistic' in some sense, and this pursuit has become very complicated in our consumer society.

Failed Quests for the Real Through Symbols

As I write these words our country and the world are poised at the beginning of what might become (but hopefully not!) a global economic depression. By now the causes of this dramatic downturn in the fortunes of markets everywhere, and therefore a downturn in the fortunes of workers everywhere, are becoming clear—too many investors went too far into risky debt, whether in stocks or stock derivatives, houses or credit cards, durable goods or futures. One analyst said that it is as if people forgot that we are dealing with real things, real jobs, or real money and played the games of life as if we were playing Monopoly. A major Chinese investor, Gao Xiqing, in an interview with James Fowler in the *Atlantic*,[15] explained derivatives this way:

> First of all, you have this book to sell. This is worth something, because of all the labor and so on you put in it. But then someone says, "I don't have to sell the book itself! I have a mirror, and I can sell the mirror image of the book!" Okay. That's a stock certificate. And then someone else says, "I have another mirror—I can sell a mirror image of that mirror."

Gao goes on to say that what we need to do is to come back to reality, to making, buying, and selling real things rather than spending our time and wealth dealing with ever-more distant abstractions (10,000 mirrors). To do this he says Americans need to be humble in our dealing with other people and not become enamored by our abilities to

---

15 James Fallows, "Be Nice to the Countries that Lend You Money." *The Atlantic*, Dec., 2008, 62-65.

fool others (and ourselves) with mirrors, and we need to get more real in our economic activities.

My goal here is not to pretend to fully understand or to resolve the predicament in which we find ourselves (who can?). I do believe we can see, though, in the economic whirlwind that engulfs us today, a powerful source of the inauthenticity so many people feel. If our lives are preoccupied with and greatly influenced by abstractions such as derivatives and variable-rate mortgages, that means we are removed from everyday realities in dramatic ways. In such a world our abstractions can easily become more real than actual people or food or winter cold or watersheds that comprise the primary world in which we are embedded.

Working Americans understand work and its wages give us the power to buy the clothes we need to cover our bodies and keep us warm. However, while few people are caught up directly in the byzantine world of high finance, far too many ordinary people have succumbed to a similar abstract world, the symbolic world of fashion. After the third or fourth pair of shoes, the tenth shirt, or the fifth coat, something besides necessity or functionality has taken over, something that begins to separate people from reality occurs in subtle but powerful ways. We might be purchasing those items to salve a wound we experienced at work or school, to improve our sense of well-being in relation to a neighbor or friend, to advertise our social status or declare our moving out of bondage in a social or cultural niche; whatever the motivation (often unconscious), when we do such things we are operating at a level of abstraction which is disconnecting us from basic reality. I am not claiming any one of these symbolic gestures is bad in itself, but I do believe that when money and what it buys are removed to this secondary symbolic level, the accumulative effect can be to give us a growing sense of distance from reality.

Consider another example of how people can get lost in a "concrete symbol." Because my family and I usually visit my mother in Spearfish, South Dakota, during the first week in August I have witnessed the annual migration of hundreds of thousands of Harley Davidson motorcycle enthusiasts to the small South Dakota town of Sturgis. People flock from across America (some of them actually riding their motorcycles) to spend up to two weeks with other Harley enthusiasts admiring bikes, telling stories, partying, and exploring the Black Hills. In a large state geographically but with only 780,000 residents, the influx of between 200,000 and 500,000 outsiders presents monumental logistical challenges and often means various hardships for the visitors. Yet they come, year after year. Why? To a significant extent, because of the symbolic power of a technology. Harley Davidson motorcycles, with their patented and Congressionally-protected loud roar (aficionados would say "purr"), have come to symbolize the west, open spaces, independence, and defiance, all with the strong coloration of living beyond convention. In a nutshell, the Outlaw. But these riders are rarely the real outlaws of motorcycle gang fame. Instead, they are factory workers, waitresses, and clerks, but also lawyers, doctors, teachers, and corporate workers. This crowd, caught up for a week in races, gear, tattoos, beer, and a carnival atmosphere represent a cross-section of America. Many of their bikes, trailers, and gear together cost tens of thousands of dollars, and many of them are using their precious vacation days to attend. To be Outlaws for a few days. But why?

Few of them are anarchists or even libertarians. Most do not want to eliminate government or avoid paying taxes. They enjoy the amenities of life and appreciate the good roads and medical services South Dakotans and the Federal government provide. What they want is to identify with something real. Without having to put up with the hardships, the hunger, fear, loneliness, and public ostracism afforded real outlaws or even cowboys. And owning and riding their Harleys, at least for a few days each year, gives them the illusion of being the Outlaw they deem to be real.

I am not making fun of Harley riders. They represent but one example of many identities people seek through surface associations.[16] In Spearfish, South Dakota, I have also witnessed similar, though smaller, gatherings of groups who engage in the same kinds of rituals around their Corvettes, Impalas, and other vintage automobiles as you will see among Harley riders. In Nebraska and Wyoming I have seen roving bands of Airstream trailer owners behaving much like nomadic tribes seeking new campgrounds where they share their common interests; or visit any college campus on football game day and you will witness yet another variation on this theme—the fan who gains a fair amount of his or her identity by being part of an in-group crowd marked by a variety of rituals that often border on bacchanal. In Michigan every summer you can find a set of wild women in the woods gathering for their rituals—the list is nearly endless. On one hand, this remarkable variety of associations represents one of the great triumphs of modernism, especially in America—pluralism. On the other, there is something very sad and perhaps scary about the number of people who invest so much time and resources into what are often disappointing quests for identity. While some or perhaps even many of these seekers have healthy identities that they live out deeply involved in their communities back home, for many of them

---

16 See Robert D. Putnam's *Bowling Alone* for an extensive catalog of the many avenues Americans pursue to belong to an identity: airstream trailers, antique autos, butterfly collectors, clubs, leagues, etc. The list is nearly endless. The point, though, is not that these surface associations are in themselves problematic but rather that for many people these are the only or main associations upon which they rely for identities. See my discussion of "thin vs. thick" cultures in chapter four.

these fun-laden forays are a deadly serious quest for a reality they lack in their everyday lives.

Work (and Leisure) That is Real

One of the themes of my course on work is that leisure is the other side of the coin of work. If you wish to understand the meanings and impacts of work on someone look at what they do in their leisure time. If someone spends their non-work time watching television they probably are so worn out from work that all they can manage most of the time is to engage "the plug-in drug" of television. People who have meaningful and fulfilling work tend to be volunteers after work or after retirement. And those who are authentic in and through their work tend to be actively involved in building and maintaining their larger communities.

Richard Todd's point is not that no things are genuine or that we should not identify with things if we seek to be real; rather it is that mere possession of some thing, even if it is genuine, is not enough to grant authenticity. Things do not magically bestow authenticity, but they can symbolize someone's authenticity.[17]

In the fall of 2000 my family and I visited the home of James Herriot, the author of the wonderful book *All Creatures Great and Small*, and main character in a television series by the same title. The people of Thirsk in Yorkshire, England, where Herriot lived and worked, and where the television series was filmed, have done a marvelous job preserving his house, grounds, and the television set where his stories were brought to the screen. When we toured the modest house in which Herriot wrote and practiced veterinary medicine, we came upon a large set of drawers filled with the tools of veterinary trade in

---

17 We will discuss this salient idea in chapter two when we discuss Richard Stivers' ideas in *Technology as Magic: The Triumph of the Irrational*.

Herriot's era. As I began to examine these things used to vaccinate, immobilize, shear, clip, calm, and operate on animals large and small I was reminded powerfully of my father who had died earlier in the year and whose death I realized, at that moment, I had not fully mourned. He, like Herriot, was a skilled veterinarian during the same period, and the tools I was seeing and touching were the tools I had seen him use countless times as he ministered to animals in South Dakota many years ago. Especially when I was a teenager I often accompanied my father and helped him with many of the tasks of offering medical assistance to large and small animals, and I knew many of these tools intimately. It was these tools of his and Herriot's trade that finally opened up my wounded heart to remember and grieve for my dead father. So tied to his craft was "Doc Sessions" that his identity for me was carried by these "literal symbols," more so than by most aspects of his life I have explored either before or since that moment in Thirsk.

Matthew Crawford gives a different account of motorcycle riding than my critique of the outlaw mystique. He contends that some people ride and repair motorcycles because the technology many people have contact with calls forth their creativity, ingenuity, and applied intelligence. Crawford no doubt would agree that there are indeed many riders who merely want the easy symbolic aura I described. There are also many who find a deep connection with the material world in the process of customizing, repairing, and riding their cycles. They, like my father, find that technology can draw them into touch with the world that is more genuine than the ways in which most people's work abstracts them from reality.

In a brief chapter on "The Separation of Thinking from Doing,"[18] Crawford traces the history of industrialization in which craftsmanship was devalued to make way for a work system based on efficiency

_____

18 Chapter two.

and profit maximization rather than personal expression, genuine creation, or the satisfaction of having engaged intelligently with reality. In this new work system, the likes of which the world had never seen, workers were (and continue to be) abstracted from work, themselves, and their products with the only rewards being extrinsic to the work rather than the traditional intrinsic values of craftsmanship.

Crawford contends that what people desire, whether or not they can articulate it, is "To Be Master of [Their] Own Stuff" (the title of his third chapter). True lovers of life with motorcycles eschew comfort and convenience (if you've spent time fixing and riding motorcycles you'll agree with that!) pursuing self-reliance in relation to their own lives ("stuff"). This self-reliance, though, is not about not being independent from others (Crawford calls this the myth of "freedomism"). In fact, this relationship joins you intimately with the material world (that, he says, also "masters you") and with other motorcyclists upon whom you depend constantly for knowledge, tools, and friendship. The modern worker, he contends, whether white collar or blue, and as consumer as well as worker, has been turned into a passive consumer rather than an embodied agent.

I believe Matthew Crawford has his finger on the same pulse that I am trying to reveal. With the great material advances our new work system and the disburdening of difficulty and inconvenience consumer society has brought, we have also purchased a distancing from reality that we try to reverse through further purchases. We are caught in a work/consume cycle from which we cannot escape with more work or consumption,[19] but Crawford's writing and personal example give us hope that there are backwaters where people are resisting the relentless whirlwind of materialism gone awry. I hope to suggest fur-

---

19 For a brief overview of this endless and pernicious cycle, see Annie Leonard's visual parable, "The Story of Stuff," (www.storyofstuff.com).

ther aspects of working and living that hold promise of reweaving authentic lives.

We are materialistic beings. Stories abound about Native Americans living with and through their favorite horses, story tellers with their special staffs, and fishermen with a special pole or lure. Genuine things have a special place in our lives because of what they represent and because of inherent characteristics (have you ever seen an actual Rembrandt—his paintings have remarkable qualities?). Ordinary things, whether genuine or not, can and do enhance our lives in countless ways. But economists are surely correct in their law of diminishing returns—the more we have of something (or of things in general), the less value any individual thing has; and there is little connection between our personal authenticity and most things, even authentic ones. Consumerism can be a path to social status, comfort, and convenience, perhaps even some measure of happiness (see chapter five), but ever-more things won't make you real. Work can. But only if we follow the intuitions of dozens of ordinary Iowans my Working in America students have interviewed over the years who do work, whether paid or unpaid, in ways that connect us to others, accomplish something important, and give us the opportunity to explore, develop, and express our gifts. All this can occur, even if our work is "as common as mud," if we play our roles with excellence. Perhaps this is at least part of what Plato meant when he claimed, in *The Republic*, that a just (good) society is one where everyone is doing with excellence the work for which they were cut out.

CHAPTER TWO
TECHNOLOGY

The technological revolution of our times is the "decision"—collective, unconscious, incremental—to unbind ourselves from the soil.—Rosalind Williams

But lo! Men have become the tools of their tools.—Thoreau

The Magic of Television

In 1980 my first wife and I received a phone call from the educator and writer John Holt asking us to join him on the *Phil Donohue Show*. For several years we had been home schooling our three children and we had gained enough notoriety because of the resulting political and legal battles surrounding our case to attract the attention of someone as noted as Holt. After initial interviews with *Donohue* editors, we flew with two of our children to Chicago where we were escorted to the downtown studio in a limo to be guests on an hour-long daytime talk show that was the "Oprah" of its time. A few months later we did a repeat performance, this time sharing the hour with another home schooling family as well as with Holt.

I have many strong memories from those experiences. John Holt was one of the most democratic people I have ever met in that he treated everyone, regardless of social status or other distinguishing characteristics, with great and equal respect. Phil Donohue was a very down-to-earth guy whose gift was his ability to get his studio audience involved and for them to stand in for millions of viewers. It was fun, and rather overwhelming, for people from rural Iowa to stay in a fancy hotel and ride in a limo for the first time. But most of all I was struck by the magic of television. Anyone who visits or acts in a studio or upon a stage can tell you that the difference between what goes on backstage is mundane and everyday and bears little resemblance to what shows up on stage or screen. Playwrights and actors have long known this and have studiously learned how to create the illusions that help make stories come to life by sparking the imaginations of their audiences. Even Plato was concerned that the abilities to manipulate our minds by magical devices like these were so powerful that few people are capable of dealing with them, and he therefore proposed banning most art for the masses. I didn't comprehend the powerful magic of television or fully understand the wisdom in Plato's warning until we returned home after our *Donohue* appearances.

We had gained notoriety, in part, because we were in a school district where, unlike many places in Iowa and around the country, the superintendent was dead-set against home schooling and was willing to take us to court to get our children into his school. We also drew attention because of significant media coverage, including the *New York Times*, the *Los Angeles Times*, the *Chicago Tribune*, and even the major paper in Israel, as well as local, state, and regional broadcast and print media. Finally, because the time was right, significant and publicized concerns with public education caused many people to find it ironic that a school system would spend significant resources going after "truant" children who were being well educated while many children within the district's control were being poorly educated. Others, of course, agreed with the superintendent and felt our children should be in school.

In order to be selected to be on a national talk show like *Donohue* or *Oprah* people have to become noted, if not notorious. Two years before our television appearance, our case was covered in the local and state press, we met with the Iowa State Board of Education, and I had given talks and answered countless questions for hours in various venues throughout Iowa. After our television debut, I distinctly remember one man saying what many others articulated in their own ways: "The several times I have heard you discuss your beliefs and practices regarding home schooling I thought you were crazy and didn't understand what you are doing and why. Until I saw you on *Donohue*, and then I understood and agreed."

At first I did not understand what he was saying. I had watched the tapes of our *Donohue* appearances and I know that I was much more clear, thorough, and convincing in most of my local talks and discussions. (And this was a man who had a number of lengthy and direct conversations with me after several talks.) Yet I was more convincing to him in a shaky performance on national television! Why? Because television seems to have the power to grant a metaphysical reality that trumps face-to-face encounters. Psychologically, often things experienced on television (seem to) have greater reality than the same things experienced first-hand. This is magic.

No doubt you have seen the ads in a variety of stores or on many billboards, and you have heard them on the radio: *As seen on TV.* You are also probably familiar with a related and equally peculiar phenomenon wherein many people seem willing, even anxious, to appear on television where they often say things and act in ways before millions of people that they wouldn't consider for a moment saying or doing at home or in their communities. I have often heard people saying things such as: "Last night I saw a building on fire as I was driving home, but it didn't seem real until I saw it on the news." I am sure you could add your own examples of the peculiar power of the media, especially television, to give something an aura of legitimacy and importance it wouldn't otherwise possess. Certainly politicians long ago understood this power, and it has become a truism that even bad press is usually better than no press at all. Our media star system elevates ordinary people to super-human status. Many of them, of course, cannot handle the accompanying adulation and great wealth that come with celebrity.

In his book, *Technology as Magic*, Richard Stivers contends that this magic is especially powerful and dangerous today because we have the illusion that technology and its uses are the last places you will find superstition operating, and therefore we tend not to be on guard against the many forms of irrationality our relationships with technologies often involve. Similarly, people expect medicines, whether folk or prescriptions, and medical practices to perform magically: "If one of these pills might help, surely two will be twice as good"; or "This cure will reverse years of neglect that has resulted in my obesity, heart condition, or diabetes"; or "I want the doctor to prescribe an antibiotic to cure my cold." Stivers finds similar irrationalities in scientific management, his area of expertise, where employers are led to believe that one form of "humanistic" intervention or another will eliminate the worker alienation, stress or physical ailments created by work systems that by their very nature reduce humans to sub-human functionaries. As with many medical uses, such strategies typically treat symptoms but not the underlying causes or structural problems. But Stivers' paradigm case is the media.

We have already rehearsed one reason for the magical powers of the media: they are part of long traditions of staged events whose purposes have been to get people to believe what they ordinarily do not believe (some people define magic as the ability to alter someone's consciousness at will). Shamans and other traditional healers and therapists, writers, directors, actors, and story tellers of every description play with people's imaginations and beliefs, often with both good intentions and good results. It turns out that humans love to be transported, at least in their imaginations, to other realities. Well told, stories can teach while entertaining, and they can help cure a variety of ailments, whether physical, social, emotional, or spiritual. We humans have always loved a good story.

Brands

Unfortunately this natural orientation[1] is ripe for exploitation. Consider brands. It is well known that brands are powerful and valuable. Corporations sometimes go to absurd lengths (for example, suing individuals who in innocent ways use a corporate logo) to protect their brands. James Twitchell[2] says that brands are so powerful because they are "condensed stories" that encourage people to associate their own values, stories and identities with a brand: "I am a Chevy sort of person," "She is a Coke person," "He is manly because he drinks Jack Daniels." One of my favorite examples with students are Mountain Dew ads that show young people having fun at a swimming hole, on the beach, or at a picnic with the implied association that if you drink

---

1 There are a host of books and articles, especially in literary studies, but also in various psychological and sociological sub-disciplines, that link the development and nature of the self to stories. For example, James A. Holstein and Jaber F. Gubrium in *The Self We Live By: Narrative Identity in a Postmodern World* say that we have "narrative minds." Much of so-called postmodern thought contends that the self is (merely) its stories, while much psychotherapy involves changing or healing the self through stories. See, for example, Olav Bryant Smith, *Myths of the Self: Narrative Identity and Postmodern Metaphysics*, or Dan P. McAdams, *The Redemptive Self: Stories Americans Live By*

2 *Branded Nation: The Marketing of Mega Church, College Inc, and Museumworld.*

their brew you will be good looking and get the good looking guy/gal. Would anyone rationally believe that the mere act of driving a particular car, drinking a particular drink, wearing a shirt with a particular brand, or sporting a cell phone of a particular type would make you more sexually attractive to someone? Surely not. Yet advertisers are betting billions of dollars that we will do precisely that, and they are right. Why? Twitchell says it is because we are storied beings who naturally seek to make meanings and who associate the stories we find with characteristics of our own stories.

I won't quibble with Twitchell's logic of our illogicality, for surely he is pointing to something very powerful and pervasive. It is interesting that his focus is on institutions usually seen as residing near the margins of the marketplace—colleges, museums, and churches. Instead, I want to drill deeper into the psycho-social realities he and many others are exposing. First note that consumers are not entirely mistaken, for if they were in error the magic used in advertising, politics, religion, medicine and education would not work. Folk remedies often do have curative properties, albeit weak or vague. Believing an incantation or high tech intervention can cure often works, as indicted by studies of the placebo effect in a wide variety of circumstances including serious medical illnesses. Purchasing and using an item with a particular brand actually can be part of what attracts those other people, for the efficacy of brands lies in their symbolic powers.

Usually the primary and rational purpose of a technology is its functionality. Automobiles can take us from point A to point B more quickly and comfortably than walking, riding a bicycle, or using public transportation. Cell phones are communication devices. Clothes are for keeping us warm. However, many technologies are major consumer items and thus their functionality is married with, and can become secondary to, their meanings. This certainly is true with most clothing, but we should also not discount the symbolic importance of big-ticket items such as houses or cars. Driving a certain brand and model of car might very well be critical to gaining the attention and even affection of that desired person.

Often theorists suggest that the manipulation of people's minds involved in selling them something requires that the sellers know something about their potential customers that those people themselves don't know. However, with regard to the magic of selling, it seems that consumers must know that a given item has potent symbolic power, what the symbols represent, and how to use them. Otherwise there would be no power in the logo or advertisement. Consumers are willing to shop carefully and often to spend extra money to purchase the item with the symbolic messages they desire. How, then, can someone claim that magic—manipulation of consciousness—is at the root of much technology purchased and used?

While no doubt there is clandestine manipulation of people in advertising and other examples of using technologies magically, I believe that often what is occurring is what philosophers call self-deception. People know what is occurring but allow themselves to join in the illusory game that has them buying a technology (or other consumer products) with the hope they can use it to magically affect the world. Consider how many of us purchase any variety of over-the-counter medicines or herbal products with unproven healing properties that we hope will help ease our distress, or when we pay good money for the latest smart phone "apps" that promise far more than we know they can deliver because the very possession of more apps helps us feel more secure or that we are keeping abreast of progress. In such instances, the advertisers are not fooling us; we are fooling ourselves. How can this be? How can we be both the liar and the one being lied to? Existentialists long puzzled over this seeming paradox, and attempts to dissolve or explain self-deception spawned much of what is original in their thinking including their analyses of authenticity. For if humans nearly automatically engage in magical thinking and thereby consistently manage to deceive ourselves, how can anyone be genuine? With some exceptions, the Existentialists answers are very pessimistic, bordering on a kind of original sin or stain on the human character, resulting in the woeful metaphors of Sartre—bad faith and hell being other people—or the heroic but futile diagnoses and prescriptions of fellow Existentialist Albert Camus in much of his work.

If the Existentialists are correct, the situation is both better and worse than Stivers and many contemporary social scientists and students of advertising suggest. It is better because we are not mere pawns in the hands of master chess players who control our every move. Perhaps the young and naïve can be strongly manipulated by advertisers, but aware adults often (usually) know the symbolic appeal of consumer items and that is precisely why they purchase them. Granted, the goal of advertising to the young is to get them to form lifelong associations with a given brand, and thus perhaps there is justification for limiting advertising to them; but regardless of how deliberately branded children are, they quickly learn the "language" of brands and advertising.

Several years ago I taught a Boy Scout merit badge class where I flashed images of automobiles in front of a group of 10-12 year olds. I was not entirely surprised to discover that almost all of them could name the makes and models of dozens of new and older cars, but I was amazed when I asked them what kinds of people were driving which cars for what reasons and they did not hesitate in giving sociologically and symbolically astute answers. They could distinguish Volvos from Mustangs and knew that people in upper-middle class families were more likely to be driving the former than the latter. Four to six years away from being eligible to drive, these boys already knew the symbolic universe of automobiles in America, and no car companies had been targeting them with ads as had, perhaps, tobacco, clothing, or soft drink sellers. Furthermore, these boys knew, almost instinctively, that if the world remained the same in the coming decade (at least with respect to the roles and meanings of autos), they had better know this language if they wanted to succeed in various ways.

The situation seems worse, of course, because the Existentialist perspective says that we knowingly "enslave" ourselves. We buy into the games the sellers want us to play and then pretend (self-deception) that we don't realize we are playing. As I will attempt to show in chapter four, I believe the Existentialist analyses of authenticity given by Sartre and Camus (and to some extent Nietzsche and Heidegger) are mistaken, but I do believe their emphasis on choice, while sometimes too strong, helps to correct much of the "consumer as victim" perspective found among media critics. I believe that while the media does play a role in shaping our desires, we are not hapless pawns with no say in our consuming fates, and that there are also larger forces at work in our culture. Let us begin exploring this "mixed" perspective by examining self-deception more carefully.

Self-Deception

As we discussed briefly in the preceding chapter, currently we are on the front end of what might become a very long and deep economic trough. Large numbers of people, including bankers, economists, historians, and politicians who should have known and warned us, were surprised when the American housing market collapsed in 2008, precipitating a worldwide wrench in the basic financial institutions of most countries. But did the lenders and those purchasing houses not know their behavior was problematic? Probably few people anticipated the tidal wave that has engulfed us, but I believe that not many of those who over-reached on their loans, whether buyers or lenders, were unaware, at some level, that borrowing/lending that much by/to that person could be a problem. Being objective and honest with and about ourselves is notoriously difficult, and herein lays the crux of self-deception: we are not really lying to ourselves when we "deceive" ourselves. It is much more a refusal to be honest, to draw conclusions about our situation in the same way we more typically describe others' realities. It is as if these borrowers said to themselves, "If my friend, Joe, wanted to borrow this much to build or buy a big house, I would tell him he couldn't afford it; but I have better money habits and am more capable than Joe at managing such a large loan," knowing pretty well that they and Joe are alike in most relevant respects. The lenders, of course, *did* know the difference. They are trained in actuarial accounting, in being able to predict who can and who cannot afford what levels of economic risk, and because their dishonesty did not involve their own abilities to pay, their actions are probably better labeled greed than self-deception.

But leaving aside the economic system's downturn, why did so many people borrow so seriously beyond their means when they knew at some level it was a bad idea? In many instances, at least, I believe it is because they were guilty of what psychologists say is a common, if not universal, human trait: "we are all hypocrites."[3] We tend to attribute to ourselves characteristics that we would like to possess, even if we do not, and we tend not to judge ourselves as clearly, harshly, and objectively as we do others. Put differently, we have a strong bias that favors ourselves to the point of pretending, to ourselves as well as others, we are something we know, at some level, we are not. Freud

3 Haidt, xi.

created the theory of the unconsciousness, in great measure, to make sense of this "level" and its "secrets," while the existentialists, in their quest for honest and authentic being, refused to grant such control to an aspect of our psyche so out of our conscious control.

In other instances, I suspect something different from either depth or Existentialist psychology occurs. When I was going through a very difficult divorce I found myself walking many miles and often my path would lead through graveyards. I didn't comprehend what I had been doing until someone suggested that experiencing a divorce is like suffering the death of a loved one, and I naturally was drawn to a place of mourning in the throes of our breakup. Psychologically and socially, my wife had died even though the person who had been my wife was alive. People who have borrowed beyond their means and have triggered this worldwide financial crisis knew the facts of their wealth, income and debt incurrence, and they knew that people like themselves who had done likewise were going bankrupt, yet they simply didn't draw the conclusions that to others would seem obvious.

What the Existentialists had correct, then, is that when we engage in "self-deception," however we comprehend this too-common phenomenon, we cannot be authentic. For an object to be authentic is for it not to be a fake. For a human to be authentic at least includes that person not being dishonest about her/himself, and if the human tendency to be hypocritical is ubiquitous as psychologists claim, at the very least authenticity is a difficult accomplishment. To use Nietzsche's phrase, a great deal of "self-overcoming"[4] is required, which means we have much hard work to do, as we will see in detail in chapters four and five. History is filled with stories of religious heroes struggling for

---

4 Self-overcoming, for Nietzsche, involves discovering who and what we are, then seining out those aspects we find desirable and finally reconstructing the self. This is his famous camel-lion-child strategy of self development we will discuss in chapter four.

years mastering a wide variety of difficult techniques before achieving a clear-eyed self understanding and overcoming their natural proclivities to self-deception. It's no wonder that we take easier, if bound-to-fail, paths such as consuming technologies for their symbolic powers.

Being Cool

Perhaps the most revealing example of such failure is "cool." We use this word in many ways and contexts, of course: houses can be cool, as can movies, horses, cars, magazines, games, books, or shoes. Almost anything can be cool, or not. Including people. A common attribution of celebrities is that they are cool, and most of them spend inordinate time working to achieve and maintain this treasured moniker. Cool sells, cool is an asset, cool resolves conflicts and relieves tensions. Cool is very difficult to pin down, perhaps as beauty was when it was "cool," and this elusive quality is one of its main attractions. Cool is evanescent, it comes and goes like fog or a sound on the wind, and it is very difficult to know what will be cool tomorrow since predictable trends are precisely a way to kill cool. What is cool is faddish, at the mercy of complex cultural factors that lie, for the most part, beyond measure. And cool is lonely because the minute something becomes popular it no longer is cool.

The most common strategy in our culture for people becoming cool is through carefully groomed and customized consuming. Technologies are common items used in this process. Sometimes they are tools that help us acquire something cool, such as the tools and materials of tattooing. Sometimes they are automobiles, cell phones and other technologies whose meanings are fluid and can be transformed from a mere tool to a cool tool. Sometimes we wear the technology, and sometimes they become part of us—hair implants, gold teeth, botox, or even prosthetics can help a person become cool, given the proper conditions. We see most vividly with cool the many ways technologies become imbued with meaning, and how they grant meaning. For the ultimate technologies of cool are the media, as they provide the canvass on which cool is painted and communicated.

Young people, especially, desire to be cool, but the longing for reality and recognition that lies at the heart of cool comes from lifelong needs and desires and it is not surprising to find adults vying for position on some cool chart or another. Cool is a competitive sport with winners and losers and for cool to be meaningful there must be few winners and many losers. No one who is observant doubts cool can be cruel. Cool is a mass or group sport even for cool loners because you or I can be cool only if others recognize and admire our coolness.

So how can we become cool? (Well, maybe you; I'm hopelessly uncool! But maybe not—the gods of cool are notoriously fickle.) The secret is to work on your exterior, your look, your style, your impression. And work it is. You must wear that hat at just the right angle or those pants at just the right height, your cell phone must have the right ring or width or color or programs, your car needs the right sound and height and color and tint in the glass and seat covers. To discover what is cool requires experimentation. If you are just a tiny bit off your attempt falls flat, and often you look silly and can be subject to ridicule. Cool is a hard taskmaster and it can be unforgiving. Hopefully your audience is willing to give you a second chance, but often if you blow it once you aren't granted a second audition because what is cool is what is unique, new, and different, and if you fail to be cool once or twice why should they give you another chance—you clearly don't have "the touch." And of course, sometimes people choose cool strategies, such as tattoos, which if they fail can permanently mark you as un-cool.

The goal is to stand out, to offer a new look that will grant recognition and admiration. In some ways it is an easy strategy because it doesn't require years of study in college or endless hours of practice in the pool, in the music room, or on the court. Part of the appeal of cool is that it often is playful and fun, but the down side of the fun is that simultaneously it is deadly serious. We have all heard of young people being distressed, in need of counseling or even suicidal because of ridicule they have received for being un-cool. What about the few who succeed? If cool is the chosen path to authenticity the un-cool are inauthentic by definition. Are the cool authentic?

If to be authentic is to be unique, cool is one avenue to authenticity. Similar paths would include eccentricity, creativity, and one-of-a-kind characteristics or collections. One suspicion we should have about the pursuit of cool bringing authenticity is that cool is so fleeting. Doesn't it seem a bit odd to suggest that true authenticity has been achieved if it lasts but a moment and at best might be re-attained at a later moment with a different look? Unfortunately, the difficulties run way deeper. My example of becoming a vegetarian showed that getting to the point where I was a genuine vegetarian took years and there was no moment during those early, uneasy years when my not eating meat made me a full-fledged vegetarian. I was still practicing. Wearing a cowboy hat does not make you a cowboy any more than toting a gun makes you a sharpshooter. But that's the odd thing about cool—the goal is not to become anything or anyone; instead, it is to simply be cool, to be all style and no substance.

If what seekers of cool desire is recognition, this is a successful path—for some, sometimes, for a while. But if people desire substance, a deep sense of being real, of achieving a genuine identity, cool is the epitome of how *not* to behave. As Mark Crispin Miller argues in his introductory chapter to *Boxed In: The Culture of TV* titled "The

Hipness Unto Death," to spend endless hours on one's exterior requires ignoring one's interiority, which is to fail to develop the depths of character that would give one gravity, which I believe is at the heart of authenticity. Culture critics have long noticed that many people spend countless hours "customizing" themselves as if they were automobiles or homes. This, too, can be great fun, it is a crucial activity in capitalist economies, and it can be relatively benign (if you ignore the environmental and social justice implications of consumerism). The extent to which people pay great attention to their appearances is marked by statistics such as 63% of people living in the United States list shopping as their number one favorite leisure activity.

Problems With Cool

But what about people's inner lives? Franz Kafka's most famous short story, "The Metamorphosis," is an answer to this question. Gregor Samsa, Kafka's non-hero, awakes one day to find that he has become a human-sized insect (a dung beetle, to be precise). At first he and his family are distraught, but they quickly adapt and Gregor is confined (confines himself) to his bedroom. Gregor initially tries out his new powers but he soon tires of crawling on the walls. Mainly he is concerned about his boss and the job to which he cannot return, and with how his condition will affect his family's social standing. His family, too, quickly tires of Gregor's condition and eventually they forget to feed him even a few scraps as they forge new lives now that their former breadwinner is incapacitated. Eventually Gregor dies and eventually his family notices.

Think of Kafka's story as a kind of thought experiment: what would someone who is almost entirely focused on his exteriority do if he were suddenly transformed in a way that forced him to rely much more on his inner life? (Don't get lost in the insect metaphor. Kafka could have had his protagonist become paraplegic or blind or a cancer patient.) Gregor is in business and his life centers on his appearance—his attentiveness to the details of dress, orderliness, timeliness, and proper manners in the business hierarchy. If Kafka had written this story in the age of television and the modern media, he might well have had Gregor be a star, or at least someone cool. For his challenge is like my fear that if people spend most of their time indoors plugged into electronics they won't know or love nature (see chapter three). If the Gregor Samsas of the world were forced to rely on inner resources they would find little strength or ability to cope with adversity, let alone thrive.

Real life, as well as art, can provide us with powerful examples of how authenticity is not about one's surface. In 1995 French journalist Jean-Dominique Bauby was paralyzed by a stroke that left him captive in his body, only able to communicate using his left eye. In a beautiful movie, *The Diving Bell and the Butterfly,* based on the book by the same title, we see the world from the perspective of someone possessed of a rich inner life. Bauby goes from despair to painstakingly communicating by blinking "yes" or "no" to letters of the alphabet patiently repeated by his collaborator, eventually dictating an entire book about his inner life *one letter at a time.* In contrast to Kafka's pathetic little bourgeois functionary, Bauby's courage and character are truly inspirational.

All cultures lionize people who achieve great things and are models of various virtues, and you can learn much about a culture by looking at its heroes, at those whose stories get told and become legends, perhaps even rising to mythical status. Historically such people were noted for their inner as well as outer strengths, their abilities to weather great adversities and often then perform remarkable feats.

What happens when our cool icons suffer the inevitable difficulties life has to offer? The tabloids feed on stories of falling or fallen stars, and when we turn the page we often find that they are doing badly because they cannot cope with the adversity they face. The typical scenario is that a young, attractive, talented, cool star has difficulty dealing with the stress, adulation, wealth, or media intrusion and is driven to drink, drugs or other forms of escape because he lacks the support of community *and* the inner resources that would be required to live his often meteoric stardom with equanimity. We often say they lack the character to handle fame, and what we mean is that they lack the kind of practical wisdom that Aristotle or other ethicists tell us is central to being virtuous. My point is that they lack these needed strengths in great measure because they have been putting their attention elsewhere—their looks, their publicity, their presence, and their standing in the media. The kinds of exterior concerns that occupied Gregor Samsa.

I believe this same complex of concerns can be (and has been) put in religious language: pursuing cool too ardently, as one's most serious quest for identity, can, and often does, end in a spiritual crisis. Charles Taylor's image of the sources of the self is most helpful here. Think of the self, one's identity, as a set of building blocks which are composed of an amalgam of materials provided by a person's genetics, body chemistry, family, society and culture, place, and so on. The central pillars of the edifice of one's identity are virtues that, to a significant extent, are culturally given, but which also must be won or made one's own through practice. People who don't practice have weak pillars, and with enough stress the whole edifice can crumble.

If I say that a loom or painting or tractor or salve is genuine, I am saying that it is genuine, "of its kind." Our ability to determine whether a man-made object is authentic is relative to the stringency of criteria for determining what is involved in being of that kind, but generally we know pretty well when an object is a knock-up or real. When deciding whether a person is a real teacher or lawyer or vegetarian or parent we have in mind a similar list of characteristics that confer the status in question. I am claiming that at first I wasn't a real or full vegetarian because I was so clumsy, uncertain, and insecure about it, but someone could object and say that all that is required to deserve the vegetarian label is that they refrain from eating meat. Clearly all discussions of authenticity should begin with a clarification about what counts and what is not necessary for something or someone to be affirmed or denied this label of approbation. While the general title of being an authentic human, as compared to being a genuine plumber or monk, is more abstract and difficult to pin down, nevertheless there probably are "of its kind" criteria we have in mind. We will return to this set of philosophical concerns in the next chapter, but the reason for mentioning this point here is to reiterate that there is something conceptually odd about cool. A cool what? Not nurse or waiter—not that level of human authenticity. A cool, and thus authentic, human? But the goal of being cool is to avoid being judged by any "kind" criteria. The goal of being cool is to rise above any preconceived or traditional notions of humanity whatsoever.

An Empty Freedom Can't Produce Authenticity

> The bourgeoisie cannot exist without constantly revolution-izing the instruments of production...and with them the whole relations of society.—Karl Marx

We have reached a limit here, an absurdity that warns us something has gone awry. I am reminded of another Existentialist counter-hero, Dostoevsky's Underground Man.[5] This character is even less attrac-

---

5 Notes from Underground.

tive than Gregor Samsa. He not only hides from others, but he has a very unpleasant personality. While Gregor chaffed at not being able to continue his bourgeois existence where he was defined by his role and appearance, the underground man seeks to avoid any social definition whatsoever. The result is a kind of hyper 12-year old, a person obsessed with denying any influence in his life and identity in order to be able to say that he is free. I believe a very helpful way to read this powerful short novel is as a kind of *reductio ad absurdum*, a reduction to absurdity. Many people believe that to be free is to be uncaused or self-caused, and Dostoevsky is painting a vivid picture of what someone would be like who actually tried to live this ideal—a man miserable to himself and to others, whose misery is a result of the impossibility and nature of the project.

Joseph Heath and Andrew Potter[6] deliver a strong and surprising critique of the 1960s counterculture in America based on this point. They contend that rather than presenting a deep and true alternative to consumer culture, the so-called counterculture bought into the basic ideology and methodology of the very system it desired (but merely pretended) to overcome. The captains of business understood as far back as the 1920s that the goal of advertising is twofold: first to convince people to buy things they don't necessarily want or need, and second, to quickly render people dissatisfied with what they buy so that they will return to the market and obtain the latest version (or more) of the same or similar products. Forty years before 1960s radicals preached rebellion the market was using the psycho-logic of rebellion to sell products: if you want to be cool, you will rebel against

---

6 *Nation of Rebels: Why counterculture Became Consumer Culture.* Also see several books by Thomas Frank, *The Conquest of Cool: Business Culture, Counterculture, and the Rise of Hip Consumerism; One Market Under God: Extreme Capitalist Market Populism and the End of Economic Democracy;* and *What's the Matter with Kansas?: How Conservatives Won the Heart of America.*

today's fashions by taking on trappings that are *not*—that are new, unique, contrary, and so on. While I believe that Heath and Potter overstate their case and ignore the deeper and more successful attempts at revolutionary change begun during that era, their critique certainly helps to make sense of why so many attempts at serious change are swallowed up in the "blob" of consumerism. It is not just that the blob is ubiquitous, powerful, and alluring. You also need a deep understanding of its values and logic, you must have a serious, well-thought-out alternative, and you must be capable of becoming true outsiders like the Amish. In chapter four I will argue that a fundamental failure of much of the counterculture movement is that people operated with an individualistic understanding of authenticity and therefore were unable to create the kinds of rich, supportive communities and culture necessary for a substantially different way of life from the consumer culture they rightly criticized.

The idea that freedom means living beyond causation, or that somehow being impervious to nature or society and only subject to one's free choices runs counter to science and common sense. Of course we are caused. We are physical, biological, social, cultural beings whose selves and wills, like the rest of what we do and are, are determined by a rich combination of these same factors that provide the limits and materials for our habits, our metabolism, our susceptibility to cancer, our personalities, and our values. Of course the underground man is frustrated. His project flies in the face of all we know and believe. But worse than the impossibility of his life's goal is that he is rejecting the very building blocks of the self we all need and rely on. If you turn away from all traditions, if you deny your class, language, religious upbringing, family traits, cultural values, body, or native abilities, what is left from which an identifiable self can be built?

Is a cool person really so different from Dostoevsky's singularly un-attractive character? In some ways cool people are different, of course, but I submit that this is due mainly to their inabilities to remain true to the ideal of being uninfluenced or unpredictable, an ideal the fictional Underground Man came closer to achieving. Like the Underground Man, cool people want to be unique, and they do so by trying to be unpredictable. Like the Underground Man they act like the proverbial 12-year old by rebelling against whatever convention they can identify. But as we all know, in rebelling against a rule or value of their culture these rebels actions are defined by the very culture they are trying to transcend. (Remember the use of the negative, "not," to highlight, ironically, someone's failure to be convincing?) Furthermore, those supposedly most free of cultural icons, the cool ones, are more subject to fads and fashion than those who seem so mundane and predictable, for they must study fashion closely and tweak some aspect just right in order to create a new look that will get others to recognize them as rebels. If they go too far they will not gain the recognition they seek. If they don't go far enough, or if they are off a half note, they will be seen as one more ordinary person with a hole in her pants or his hat ajar. The desire for recognition, then, is the Achilles heel of cool. In seeking recognition the cool person is trapped in a never-ending charade of morphing images that require all her efforts and leave her exhausted and perpetually insecure.

Is Uniqueness Crucial to Being Authentic?

Authenticity, in contrast, seems to be about being secure in a typically quite predictable identity and set of actions. However, is there nothing to the idea that authentic people are unique? Of course there is. At the very least authentic people are unique in the sense that they are fairly rare. Becoming authentic is a long, arduous path, as we will discuss in chapter six, and few people manage to go far down it. And in keeping with Nietzsche's *Übermensch* (the person who is self-overcoming), each authentic person will be very different from the others (Nietzsche says that each *Übermensch* will be as different from the others as apes are from humans). But their uniqueness does not lie in their being unpredictable or in rebelling against all conventions. It lies in their positive accomplishments, in their efforts and abilities to set new standards or models for what humans might become.

Perhaps one brief example will make this point clearer before we move on and leave this rich suggestion until our final chapters. People often hold up creative artists as models of uniqueness, of transcending conventions to create something new, and indeed they are. But if you examine the biographies and autobiographies of great artists from across history and cultures, you will find two seemingly contradictory, but in the end complementary, characteristics. First, great artists tend to be steeped in tradition, in their culturally inherited tools, concepts, aesthetics and knowledge. They know in great detail what has preceded them. Second, their contribution is to play with that inheritance, to change a tone, a style, a method, a concept in a way that creates, as Merleau-Ponty says[7] about Cezanne, a new way of seeing. One way to put this critical point is to say that instead of saying "not," the great creative artists we remember, because they changed history, are saying "but," or "in addition to," or "try it this way instead," or "as well." Their transcendence is based in affirmation rather than denial. As Hegel, and Nietzsche after him explained, the creation of something new is a synthesis that incorporates the old yet moves beyond it.

---

7 Maurice Merleau-Ponty, "Cezanne's Doubt," in *Sense and Nonsense.*

Being Authentic in a Mediated World

In a 1954 poem titled "Not Ideas about the Thing but the Thing Itself," one of America's preeminent metaphysical poets emphasizes our concerns about how so many forces and features of our lives abstract and distance us from reality. In a brief for metaphysical realism Stevens says "It was not from the vast ventriloquism/Of sleep's faded papier-mache.../The Sun was coming from the outside." He hears a calling from outside that awakens him to "A new knowledge of reality." The media are one set of forces that increasingly keep us "indoors," away from the unmediated thing itself.

And cool is a mediated phenomenon. Though we seem to have strayed far from the supposed topic of this chapter, technology and authenticity, a moment's reflection reveals that cool has everything to do with technology, both as materials from which to construct a cool identity and as the source and purveyor of that identity. Thomas DeZengotita[8] contends that we all live mediated lives. He contends that the media affects us in countless ways but especially in making us all postmodernists, citizens of a world colored with irony and dedicated to the proposition that no one has access to reality or to the truth about it. DeZengotita says that because we all get the world through a media dedicated to commercial interests and especially to increasing the power of the media itself, we mainly experience the world they give us, a world as they want us to experience it.

No one who has reflected for a moment on the power of the media in our lives would disagree with many parts of DeZengotita's thesis: because of media concentration and the ideological biases of various channels and organizations we clearly learn about people and events through thick filters; the major goal of media programming is to at-

---

8 *Mediated: How the Media Shapes Your World and the Way You Live In It.*

tract viewers/listeners and deliver them up to the advertisers; television, and now the internet, are having profound effects on children, on their imaginations, their development, their bodies (including shaping their brain functioning!) and their social lives; and nature is distorted to where a viewer might come to believe that lions, e.g., are constantly hunting and killing rather than sleeping 22 of 24 hours per day. Sleeping lions make for programs with low ratings. DeZengotita's goal is not only to convince us that we are postmodernists, but to make this condition palatable by painting it as inevitable and ubiquitous. He contends we are all stuck with having to experience the world through the media, with having to accept the world and the judgments about it served up by our satellite dishes.

It is small wonder that people today are hungry for what is real, genuine, and authentic. The renaissance of the local—be it music, food, athletics, gaming, or worship—is a response to the packaged, imported, inauthentic goods, culture, and lives the media try to convince us to buy. Critiques of consumerism and strategies to downsize and live simpler lives abound. Indeed, some people seem to be managing to divorce themselves from viewing the good life as a quest for more. Yet the very existence of this mountain of materials, movements and people struggling to live more genuine and down-to-earth lives is testimony to the truth of DeZengotita's thesis. For the transition to a different way of life is fraught with difficulties and only a very small minority of people have tried, let alone succeeded, in their attempts to cut the cords attaching us to the media. And even those who have weaned themselves from television or video games must still get their news through the media. Finally, whether or not you believe in the relativism[9] of postmodernism, you must accept someone's view of reality if you want to avoid paralysis.

Alienation Through Technology

Whether or not you accept DeZengotita's near-celebratory capitulation to postmodernism, his examples and analyses help us get to the heart of why authenticity is such a strong desire in today's world. In a word, the forces dominating our lives that DeZengotita and others bring into the open leave us with a sense of loss. Sartre calls our turn to the past, to nostalgia or other attempts to find something genuine in tradition, *bad faith*, which he attributes to our lack of willingness and courage to face the fact that we alone have to define ourselves and create whatever meaning there is to be had in the world. As I will attempt to show in chapter four, I believe Sartre is too harsh in his judgment because he misunderstands the self and its development, but in his own way he points to this same sense of loss that other cultural critics recognize. I believe the heart of this postmodern malaise is what Heidegger[10] discusses, however obliquely, in his writings on technology. He contends that the tools we have available to form an identity, including many technologies, create a distance between us and the worlds we inhabit, a metaphysical alienation. Marx, of course, is famous for his critique of the dramatic alienation brought by industrialization, and the Heideggerians are continuing this important as-

---

9 I often call it "absolute relativism" in that its proponents often insist, with strong conviction, that relativism is true, that they know that we can know nothing with certainty. Right!

10 See Heidegger's famous book, *The Question Concerning Technology*. Several Heideggerians have followed his sketchy and parochial suggestions about how modern technologies alienate us from nature (including human nature). See, for example, Albert Borgmann *Technology and the Character of Contemporary Life*, or *Crossing the Postmodern Divide*. See also David Strong, *Crazy Mountain: Learning from Wilderness to Weigh Technology*.

sessment of our brave new world of ever-increasing reliance on ever-more-powerful and evolving technologies.

Over the years we have had fewer and fewer "farm kids" cross our community college threshold, while an ever-increasing percentage of our students are urban or suburban dwellers. The differences between these two broad categories of students are palpable. They differ in their work ethics and habits, priorities, how they walk and talk, their body shapes, and how they approach leisure. While many of the farm kids have been facing serious career anxieties in a world of diminished need for farmers, their sense of loss has been different from their urban counterparts. While they have questioned their "fit" for many non-farm jobs and lives, they come to class with a deep sense that they know reality and are able to detect what is fake, at least in the world they knew, without the need for mediation. Their "citified" counterparts rely, more and more, on media instructions and affirmation for their sense of who they are, what is real, good, true, and beautiful.

Let me be more specific. There are infinite ways young people today get their "original instructions" from ubiquitous and many technologies. Cell phones are quickly morphing into powerful computers that allow a multitude of communication modes—voice, text, internet (including countless social sites, games, email, searches, and so on), and pictures. Through cell phones people are *connected*—to and through technologies, and to other people. But we are less and less connected directly to the physical world of flesh and blood. While we are interacting on our cell phones, the physical world of nature, humans, and human creation fade and become background. The same could be said of travelling in most transport technologies: we are missing much of what is passing by as we sit in automobiles, trains, busses and planes. Children viewing endless hours of television or playing endless hours of video games are not playing outside or directly with each other. Even if the media were not directly or intentionally trying to shape our desires, perceptions, thoughts, and emotions—our minds—they still affect us simply by becoming major components of our worlds and thus crowding out what is "outside" the electronic bubbles we inhabit.[11]

One indication of how powerful technological distractions have become is the growing use of technological strategies to help people avoid the distractions of other technologies. Office workers and students alike are using technological blockers to shut down their email or cell phones for periods of time so that they can concentrate on their work. For some time parents have been using technological censors to prevent their children from viewing undesirable programming on television. Information technology training often includes instructions on how to disable or block undesirable interruptions, and individuals are applying those principles to their own cell phone uses. The good news is that people are recognizing some of the ways technologies can distract us from doing what we want to do or being whom we want to be. The bad news is that people have to rely on technical fixes to solve problems where self discipline probably would have been preferable. I am not asserting that all technical fixes are problematic. However, if the goal is to develop the strengths of character that are involved in authenticity, this lack of self-discipline seems problematic.

In 2009, for the fifth time, a colleague and I took a group of students to Costa Rica for a vigorous and fascinating study in the Costa Rican outback. Even in the decade since we first took a group of stu-

---

11 In chapter four we will discuss these differences in anthropological terms, as I will contend that a deep challenge to becoming authentic in postmodern culture is how "thin" this culture is compared to the much "thicker" cultures found in other cultures or in earlier times in America. Authenticity involves coherence or integration of identity as well as strong building blocks, and both of these characteristics are difficult to achieve in a thin culture.

dents to experience the rainforest, ancient turtles, coral reefs, volca-
noes, and plantation villages, I have detected some subtle but powerful changes in students on our excursions to this tropical land. While
most students are still game for the middle of the night turtle patrols
along black sand beaches looking for giant leatherback turtles, for long
hikes in the jungle over rugged terrain in the rain, or for early morning
bird watching, their waning sense of awe at the natural wonders, and
their increased desire to spend time in the cities shopping and in bars,
are noticeable. It is difficult to appreciate something you're unfamiliar
with, and it is doubly difficult to appreciate it if your previous experience with it has been mediated. But it isn't just that our students have
never experienced leatherback turtles in the wild—that was true of
me as well. What is lacking for increasing numbers of young people
seems to be unmediated experiences of nature in general. On the one
hand they are used to the nature they see on screens, nature that has
been edited heavily to make it interesting in a two-dimensional world.
On the other hand, because such a preponderance of their experiences have been in man-made environments, they simply aren't familiar
with nature and don't know how to experience and appreciate it.

Yet these community college students, who usually have modest
material means, are willing to raise what to them is a large sum of
money for our 11-day program. They are willing to risk scorpion, snake,
spider, or bullet ant bites, to suffer tropical heat and humidity, or to
get caught in a flash flood while traversing a quiet mountain stream-
bed. Why? I believe it is for the same reason that people are doing extreme sports or, as we discussed earlier, going to motorcycle rallies or
using mind-altering drugs. They sense that something is missing from
their heavily-mediated lives and they want to be connected directly to
the world rather than through the media or other technologies. The
Heideggerians transcend Marx's critique of alienated labor in an im-

portant way. In many ways the conditions Marx criticized in his analysis of alienated labor have been reduced or eliminated as workplaces have adopted changes to ameliorate the degrading features Marx catalogued. Nevertheless, these contemporary students of Heidegger tell us, because the fruits of a century and a half of industrialization have spread to every corner of our lives, our distance from our worlds, even from our very selves,[12] has increased. But because this condition has become the norm and because the artificial worlds we have created are so attractive, unlike the heavy alienation Marx describes, we fail to even notice the alienating features of our new dispensation.

But why have so few people noticed, or why do so few people seem to care? Even (or perhaps especially) in strong capitalist economies people did not need much prompting from Marxists to realize that worker alienation is very real. In fact, the people today who are paying the most attention are corporate managers who are concerned with having to avoid alienated workers because of the effects of what Marx called a "reduction of humans to their animal natures" also reduces the economic bottom line. As a result, office and factory managers regularly implement strategies designed to humanize the workplace and minimize, as much as possible, the inevitable alienation such work creates. David Orr[13] answers this crucial question as to why people don't seem to care quite bluntly: conditioning us to settle for mere consumption keeps us content enough to stay in the work/consume/work/consume... squirrel cage. This conditioning, Orr claims, results from four forces: "[A] body of ideas that the earth is ours for the taking; the rise of modern capitalism; technological cleverness; and the

---

12 One aspect of Marx's critique of alienation is that in modern work people are alienated *from themselves*.

13 David W. Orr, "The Ecology of Giving and Consuming." In Roger Rosenblatt, ed., *Consuming Desires: Consumption, Culture, and the Pursuit of Happiness*, 137-54.

extraordinary bounty of North America, where the model of mass consumption first took root".[14] He continues:

> "More directly, our consumptive behavior is the result of seductive advertising, entrapment by easy credit, prices that do not tell the truth about the full costs of what we consume, ignorance about the hazardous content of much of what we consume, the breakdown of community, a disregard for the future, political corruption, and the atrophy of alternative means by which we might provision ourselves. The consumer society, furthermore, required that human contact with nature, once direct, frequent, and intense, be mediated by technology and organization."

We have, Orr is claiming, been so placated by the great consumer machine that we have not noticed, or have ceased to care, that, as he contends, "our use of the world has been transformed from sacrament to desecration."[15] I believe that increasing numbers of people are noticing and do care as evidenced, among other signs, by a growing desire for authenticity. However, going from noticing and caring to acting requires even more than Sartre's courage, it takes a sense that others are willing to act with us, a pretty good idea of what the alternative(s) is (are) and a belief that we will be better off if we follow a new path. The good news is that help is available on each of these fronts; the bad news is that the countervailing forces are strong, if not subtle.

Beyond Domination by Technology?

> It is a question whether without restoring the category of the sacred, the category most thoroughly destroyed by the scientific enlightenment, we can have an ethics able to cope with

---

14 ibid., 141
15 ibid., 144

the extreme powers which we possess today and constantly increase and are almost compelled to use.—Hans Jonas

Recently our oldest son, Owen, who through high school played far too many video games despite our pleas and cajoling that he do something more constructive with his time, announced that though he is living on the engineering floor of his dormitory where most everyone spends a lot of time gaming, he is not playing much. He said he not only has too much studying to do, but that seeing how gaming keeps his friends from experiencing the rich possibilities of college made him realize that spending all his spare time in front of a video screen is stupid. Needless to say, we were very pleased by his realization and we hope he sticks to his resolve. His example highlights several important points about the process of getting people uncoupled from consumerism. First, he had to come to this realization himself, or at the very least his parents could not convince him. Second, he had to see that gaming was second-rate compared to the flesh-and-blood living. Third, the social conditions had to be right, as he not only saw his friends wasting their time but the young women in his social group expressed their disgust with the overindulgence in video games and Owen found socializing with them to be a far better choice.

In contrast to fears about gaming addiction, our granddaughter, Meg, illustrates a point that sociologist Sherry Turkle[16] has been emphasizing for two decades. Meg has learned to cope with her pre-teen shyness by supplementing her face-to-face encounters with email exchanges. We have already seen the fruits of her efforts in more comfortable face-to-face exchanges. As Turkle warns, electronic communication can replace or reduce physical relations, but it can also enhance them.

16 *Alone Together*

There are tens of thousands of people in the United States awakening from their consumerist hypnotic states wherein they had been playing an endless game of pursuing "the endless more" as Bill McKibben calls it. They, like Owen, have come to realize that this pursuit makes for a second-rate life, one at a distance from reality, one that is endlessly enticing and never ending, but one that lacks authenticity.

Much hardship and suffering is occurring today because of the global economic crisis, and no one should downplay the harm that is washing over people's lives as wave after wave of economic bad news is blown onto "Main Street" by this perfect banking-credit-liquidity storm. Nevertheless, there could be much good news in this dark cloud of economic despair. When times are good, it is easy for the marketers to sell us most anything through a little flattery (which DeZengotita believes is the main fuel of consumer society). In one way or another, all of the ads say, "It's all about you (me!)", or "if you just purchase and use (consume) this product, you will be better off in some (magical) way", or "you will be wonderful (or at least more attractive) if you have or use brand X." But in economic hard times people don't have the extra cash (or credit) to purchase brand X and they realize that nothing has changed, except that they don't have brand X in their lives. Furthermore, when people lack the wealth to pretend that they are independent because they can buy one (or more!) of everything, they often turn to interdependencies that enrich their lives more than brand X ever did. As we will see in chapter five, social scientists who study happiness are not surprised when people derive more meaning, and thus more happiness, from stronger relationships as compared to more things. A major conceptual stumbling block for many people, though, as they struggle to forge new lives that are not simply holding or survival strategies until economic good times return, is the belief that authenticity is to be purchased at the market place of independence and uniqueness. For even if people are hungry for what is real, and even if current conditions offer a striking opportunity to set out on a path that could satisfy this deep yearning, if they misunderstand this path they can easily end up back where they started—in the limbo of life at a distance.

Technologies Can Distract Us, But They Can't Make Us Authentic

Often my students believe that our course on technology (Culture and Technology) is anti-technology, but after a few weeks they are even more confused as we simultaneously celebrate technological innovations and critique what they bring. Our main goal in this increasingly important course is what I call "technological literacy," the ability to comprehend the complex and often subtle meanings and implications of our technologies. Every technology people adopt brings with it changes and benefits, as well as losses and costs. The issue of technology assessment and use is not whether to be pro- or anti-technology. Rather it is to comprehend as clearly and thoroughly as possible what adopting a new technological system (no item of technology can be separated from the many systems in which it is embedded, including the social, political, economic, and ecological dimensions) will mean for life on earth. I will argue in chapter four that Heideggerians such as David Strong paint with too broad a brush when they claim that any technology, except simple tools, distances us from nature and our selves. However, I believe Strong and others in this tradition are correct when they address the following questions: whether, how, and to what extent will adopting a technological system alienate us from the world? What crucial values should we use in deciding whether and how to use that technology?

I remember hearing, in the 1950s and 1960s, discussions about the wondrous educational possibilities of television, but by the 1970s few people held out any hope that television would ever be anything except a powerful tool for selling (the purpose of the programs is to deliver the viewing audience to the sellers). With the help of perceptive critics such as DeZengotita,[17] as we have discussed, we now realize that the media does much more than sell us products. Our concern in this chapter has been to explore how media technologies, especially, prevent us from achieving authenticity by cocooning us from reality. They create ever-more fanciful, self-contained, and all-encompassing images, activities and artificial lives. If becoming real is our goal, then taking the path through technological enhancement, whether it is to become cool or to link with realities through electronics, is not the way. That way might bring recognition, wealth, knowledge, or connectivity, but authentic being lies in a different direction.

But wait! Am I saying that people who play video games, especially those who are serious players and spend dozens of hours each week gaming, cannot be authentic? Surely if someone can be an authentic carpenter or doctor or student, they can be an authentic gamer (or member of a virtual community)? Well...yes, and no. When it comes to playing video games someone can become an excellent player who embodies "of its kind" virtues, just as, I suppose, someone can become an excellent thief or drunk. In that sense, the road to gamer authenticity follows the same kind of arc from novice to apprentice to master that is involved in acquiring a deep identity as an embodiment of a

---

17 Other perceptive and by now classic media critics include Mark Crispin Miller, *Boxed In: The Culture of TV*; Stewart Ewen, *All-Consuming Images: The Politics of Style in Contemporary Culture*; Herbert Schiller, *Culture, Inc.: The Corporate Take-Over of Public Expression*; Bill McKibben, *The Age of Missing Information*; and Neil Postman, *Amusing Ourselves to Death: Public Discourse in the Age of Show Business*.

kind. In this sense, authenticity is not necessarily a label of moral or aesthetic approbation.

As a label for someone who has achieved full humanity, a much stronger normative judgment, and much closer to our quest, gamers, just as teachers, judges or scientists are not thereby authentic as a result of achieving excellent gamer (teacher, etc.) status. Authenticity at this level of abstraction is a much more daunting achievement, both conceptually and practically. In the remainder of this book I will contend that while living in an age of great and shifting diversity makes it very difficult to maintain any kind of innate view of human nature, nevertheless any path to authenticity must take seriously a set of inborn characteristics of human beings. In chapter three we will take up a serious challenge to the view that having strong ties to nature is essential to being authentic. As we shift from living our lives in constant contact with nature to living in human-made environments it might be that human nature itself is changing based on our amazing capacities to adapt to an endless variety of habitats.

We will turn our focus squarely on views of authenticity in the Existentialist tradition and in the so-called counter-cultural movement of the 1960s in chapter four. I believe that while we can learn a great deal about this elusive ideal from thinkers like Kierkegaard, Dostoevsky, Nietzsche, Sartre, Heidegger, and their followers, there are fundamental flaws in their views of human nature and authenticity that are corrected by western philosophers such as Aristotle, MacIntyre, Bugbee, Taylor, and also by Daoist philosophers. This will be the most conceptually challenging chapter in this book, but hopefully the groundwork we have established to this point will provide a gateway to understanding this more philosophical discussion.

Taking a lead from positive psychologists such as Jonathan Haidt, our goal in chapter five will be to bring together philosophers' insights about human nature with the empirical work of social scientists who have been studying happiness for half a century. While I believe that the relations between happiness and authenticity are complex, for the most part people who learn to be happy also have acquired much of what it takes to be authentic humans. Our travels in this chapter will mainly be in the land of virtue and character, but they will take us from evil and despair to transcendence and spirituality, which will lead us to a final chapter on Calling. You would think that authenticity, that the forging of a strong and clear identity in the midst of a chaotically diverse and confusing world, would be, as so many Existentialists seem to insist, a singularly individualist accomplishment, a radical set of choices. Yet ironically, as Bugbee says so powerfully, the path to becoming an authentic human is to know when to say, "This I must do." We come to ourselves obliquely, as a response to a set of possibilities we did not create, as in a response to a call.

CHAPTER THREE
NATURE

The Experience of Authenticity in Nature

> *There is wild comfort in the cycles and the intersecting circles,*
> *the rotations and revolutions, the growing and ebbing of this*
> *beautiful and strangely trustworthy world.*
> —Kathleen Dean Moore, *Wild Comfort: The Solace*
> *of Nature*

I can remember the experience as if it happened yesterday. We were camping in Montana, up a side road from Paradise Valley. I'm an early riser and I love sunrises, especially in the American west. As I was walking with Merlin, our ever-eager border-collie mix, on the quiet road next to our campsite, the sky began to lighten and turn, in succession, the rainbow shades of orange and red. I was in an especially peaceful and joyful mood when "I" disappeared—all ego thoughts were suspended and the sunrise filled my consciousness.

Afterwards, I remember thinking to myself, "that was a mystical experience." No gods, no voices, no divine light. Just me experiencing the sunrise. But not my ordinary consciousness which is filled with thoughts and words and memories and desires and concerns and images of other times and places. Just me and the sunrise.

Nearly all of my experiences of "being here now," in union with the world in the moment, have happened outside, in the natural world and often away from other people. Once, upon Bear Butte, the holy mountain on the northeastern edge of the Black Hills, I was pulled out of myself and took flight with a falcon soaring on the currents above the sleeping bear's shoulder. Another time I was shocked out of my everydayness when tens of thousands of Sandhill Cranes roared from their early morning slumber along the Platte River in central Nebraska when something downstream frightened them skyward in a cacophony my wife described as like a freight train roaring through your head. I recall vividly the ecstasy of becoming one with the flaming sky of a sunset at yet another Native American holy site, Vedauwoo in southeast Wyoming.

But the quiet moment on that narrow canyon road in Montana best suits my purposes here. No roaring flocks, no grand wings of flight or skies of fire; just a change of consciousness that brought with it the feeling of being fully alive, at home, and secure in being simply a part of that moment. I felt fully alive, but was I authentic in that moment when my ego disappeared?

We are used to thinking of authenticity in terms of separation—as standing apart from the crowd, being unique, not settling for the mediocrity of convention. An authentic person is autonomous, independent. My examples of experiences in the wild seem to resonate with this longstanding and yet modern Western sense of and quest for authenticity, I was alone, separated from the social forces that keep us from being who we really are, and in that moment of reverie I was free from typical internalized restrictions as well. The problem is, authenticity is quintessentially about the self, who we are, and our selves are social through and through. While nature might be a place to re-treat from the crowd and do some soul-searching, it hardly seems like a place where we fully manifest our identities.

The initial question we must answer, to justify any further connections between authenticity and nature, is why begin with an experience that pulled me farther out of my ordinary self, that self which seems to be the locus of the quarry I stalk, authenticity? While I lay no claim to spiritual advancement, the brief times I have experienced reverie in the solitude of nature give me some sense for why the great spiritual heroes from every religious tradition retreat to some desert or other to commune with the holy. If these saints, gurus, shamans, and messiahs are our clearest examples of authentic being, then there must be a connection between nature and authenticity!

At the very least, retreat into nature provides relief from the relentless demands to present an acceptable social self. Philosopher Gordon Brittan, Jr.[1] says that the self is "forensic." Who we are in any given social situation is a self we are actively creating and projecting, whether consciously or unconsciously, in and for that context. Creation and maintenance of this ego self requires great effort and part of the wisdom the spiritual heroes impart is the simple lesson that we all need regular breaks from the demands of this rigor. We need "time out" in rest and relaxation, and we could all use the kind of re-energizing that comes through meditation or prayer. We need to put down the weight of the ego-self for short periods daily and most spiritual traditions also teach us to take a whole day each week (Sabbath) away from our normal ego-maintenance. Everyone is urged to take a yearly "retreat," and the examples of these spiritual heroes shows that we all need reg-

---

[1] "Autonomy and Authenticity," in Edward F. Mooney, *Wilderness and the Heart*, 129-49

ular extended times away (sabbaticals).[2] Usually the rationale for such spiritual practices is to come closer to the divine or to "recharge our batteries," but we should not overlook the simple fact that we need regularly to lay down our burden of the ego self.[3]

But why do American Plains Indians, seeking to leave their normal selves and experiences behind, commune with the still holy trek to natural sites such as Bear Butte, or Harney Peak in the Black Hills, or Devil's Tower in Wyoming? Why did Buddha sit under a tree in the forest, or Jesus disappear into the desert? Why not find a quiet place like Descartes' oven close by where you won't be disturbed? Rosalind Williams[4] contends that because of our dramatic increases in technological systems we have, in effect, created a new human habitat. If she is correct, it is likely that as people adapt to living in their human-made habitats, they might well find natural settings foreign places for their activities including spiritual retreats. Even in the past, people have found solitude in a great variety of places, and many spiritual voyagers have had profound experiences beyond the ego in cloistered cells or abandoned buildings or attics.

This, of course, is very good news for us all, as few people have time or access to natural places for daily or weekly quiet away from the demands of the social world. Yet nature still seems like the Cadillac of spiritual venues. Like many others, I have a much easier time shedding

---

2 My wife, Lori Erickson, and I argued for universal sabbaticals in an article titled "A Case for Sabbaticals," in a book edited by John DeGraaf, *Take Back Your Time*, 167-71.

3 In one of the most moving testimonials I know, Gerald G. May gives testimony to the healing powers of nature in coming to grips with his illness and impending death in *The Wisdom of Wilderness*.

4 Rosalind Williams, *Retooling: A Historian Confronts Technological Change*.

my everyday mind sitting near a stream, walking through the woods,[5] or gardening. If what we want is to lift the burden of being our selves, and if our selves are made up of the fibers and fabrics of social life, then being in a human-made place makes reprieve difficult, for every artifact of civilization we encounter has the ability to activate our social minds. As we walk by a row of houses we might dream of living in a particularly handsome place and all that might mean for our lives; in the quiet of our rooms we are surrounded by reminders of "things done or things left undone." Cars passing by make us wonder if it is time to "trade up" or change oil or abandon cars altogether because of their effects on the world's climate. Church/temple/mosque "sanctuaries" (from what? everyday ego) hold centuries of meaning that can enhance, but can as easily distract from, our attempts to lay our burdens down.

While I will sharply distinguish my understanding of authenticity from that of Existentialists such as Jean Paul Sartre,[6] his infamous view that "hell is other people" begins with the insight that "escaping" one's social being[7] is difficult indeed. In one of the famous scenarios in *Being and Nothingness* Sartre tries to articulate the source of this "hell" by describing the experience of walking down a street and meeting another person. He accurately notes that the mere presence of this other person shifts our consciousness. We become self-conscious and we naturally and automatically switch on our ego self, our social be-

---

5 Philosopher Henry Bugbee, a major inspiration for this book, follows Thoreau in recommending "sauntering," a kind of walking meditation long espoused by philosophers from many traditions. Socrates was "peripatetic" (walking about) in his philosophizing, and the greatest classical Daoist text by Zhiangzi, is titled *Wandering on the Way*. See Bugbee's *The Inward Morning*.

6 See especially Jean Paul Sartre, *Nausea, Being and Nothingness, The Imaginary: A Phenomenology of the Imagination*, and "No Exit."

7 Sartre never quite understood what I am calling the everyday forensic burden of ego self; and he seemed to have no sense for the kind of experience I had on that Montana mountainside, which I believe everyone needs and seeks.

ing. Even if we don't interact with or know the "other" we encounter, Sartre claims, we abandon, at least momentarily, our privacy.

I do not believe other people in general are hell (although encountering some people comes close), but I do think Sartre is correct in noticing how our consciousness is affected by another person. I am simply observing how the phenomena of civilization are extensions of humans not only because humans made them, but because they carry many meanings which we have a difficult time escaping and which can, like the actual other person, demand our attention and activate our social selves.

In his play, "No Exit," Sartre further describes his image of hell by depicting the labyrinthine entanglements in which we can become trapped, locked in perpetual encounters with other people. At the very least this dismal view of our sociality reinforces the perspective of the mystics: we need time away from others if we hope to avoid our relationships becoming a hell from which we have no exit. The mystics, however, usually return to society ready and able to serve others, to become intimate in ways Sartre doesn't seem to comprehend. What is there about their "desert"[8] experiences that help them not only be refreshed but more fully human than most of us?

Nature Deficit Disorder

Become a three-dimensional person. The totally urban (urbane!) life is one-dimensional. One needs experience of the urban, and the rural, and the wild. Otherwise you will be underprivileged.—Holmes Rolston III

---

8 Actual deserts, of course, were favorite places for spiritual retreats among many traditions, but many mystics sought "deserts" in other natural places. Celtic Christians, e.g., set off in rudderless boats across the "desert" of the sea to where they believed God led them. What such places must provide is solitude, preferably in a spare natural environment.

In a recent book, Richard Louv[9] coins an evocative label for the phenomenon of children in many contemporary societies today suffering from "nature deficit disorder." He, and a growing number of educators, psychologists, parents, and many others are increasingly concerned that children are missing something vital by spending so little time outdoors playing, exploring, being. Many physics teachers believe children who do not spend enough time actively manipulating the physical world lack an orientation crucial to comprehending basic physics. Environmentalists contend that because we tend to view as normal what we love and experience as children, people who lack immersion in nature when they are young tend to view the natural world as mere resource or as a place to fear and have a difficult time comprehending our fundamental membership in biotic communities. Epidemiologists fear that children's immune systems will not develop adequate vigor if they do not "eat their peck of dirt." Recent studies show that Americans are increasingly suffering from vitamin D deficiency because of lack of sun exposure And so on. The list is very long. My contention is that a nature deficit makes being authentic very difficult.

But if the authentic self is social, what else would retreating to nature be except an opportunity to relax from the rigors of being that self? As a beginning step consider the place of humans in classical Chinese landscape paintings where, on a large canvas, say three-feet square, humans might be an inch tall, perhaps in a corner or at the bottom, and non-human nature would fill the remainder. What time in nature gives one is perspective, an existential understanding of one's place in the cosmos, the realization that humans are but a small part of the diversity, complexity, and harmony of earth's ecosystems and their histories. And if this is true, then a major part of our identity, like it

9 *Last Child in the Woods: Saving Our Children from Nature-Deficit Disorder.*

or not, includes our place in nature. To be true to whom we truly are means that we must be aware of and in tune with our membership in earth's larger communities. Virtually all ecological ethics include the idea that we are "citizens" of communities that include, at least, all living beings, and that we will not cease our environmental destruction until we accept the implications of such citizenship.

As a marker of how far we are from this perspective, usually people today view as quaint Native American (choose your favorite premodern group) references to animals and plants as *relatives*. "Primitive animism," as this view often is called, is typically categorized as an early or "immature" form of religion practiced by people who had to be so familiar with other creatures in order to survive that they "anthropomorphized" them, dubbing them brothers, cousins, grandfathers, or aunts. People in aboriginal traditions around the world continue to feel they should treat nature and its beings as sacred, as members of their extended communities lest they fail to carry out their ritual obligations and bring disasters upon their families, clans, or tribes. They believe that to not follow the "original instructions"[10] is to transgress the sacred order of things and risk calamity. As V.F. Cordova, a Navajo whose philosophy has provided much guidance in my exploration of the "in-between" nature of the self and authenticity, and whose ideas we will explore at some length in chapter four, contends that "human beings are a part of a whole that is greater than the individual. A human is not something *apart from* the Earth and

---

10 In a striking article in *Native Universe*, the National Geographic Society publication issued in celebration of the opening of the Native American Museum in Washington, D.C., Gabrielle Tayac ("Keeping the Original Instructions") articulates that yet today Native Americans believe they have a deeply religious obligation to live as they were originally instructed in their foundational myths.

the rest of its creations, including rocks, trees, water, and air; he is a natural *part of* the Earth."[11]

Sometimes these traditions are full of superstition and magic in a world populated by spirits and sustained by wild metaphysical beliefs and outlandish rituals. The same could be said about the beliefs of many contemporary Christians, Muslims, Jews, Buddhists, etc.—it depends on the sophistication of the believer and the theology (stories) they have adopted. However, as many anthropologists and environmental philosophers have noted, there are far too many ways in which contemporary scientific views of ecology dovetail with features of Native American or other aboriginal beliefs and knowledge for their outlooks to simply be primitive superstition. We have reached the point today where a growing number of people realize that because we have been treating nature as a mere set of resources and ignoring the "original instructions" of most religions to take care of creation, we are indeed bringing calamities to our earth communities and therefore to ourselves.

What the anthropomorphizing strategies of aboriginal cultures have that the environmental sciences lack is a cultural understanding and set of practices for our larger community relations.[12] It is one thing for a modern, scientific perspective to tell us that if we keep fishing cod in the Outer Banks the way we have been we will fish them out (which, apparently, we have done!). It is quite another to feel such a bond with these "ancestors" that we would never consider taking more cod than we absolutely need or in a wasteful way. The genius of

---

11 Kathleen Dean Moore, et al., eds, *How It Is: The Native American Philosophy of V.F. Cordova*, 151.

12 For a detailed description of how such anthropomorphizing helps to create a community that includes nature, see Richard Nelson, *Make Prayers to the Raven: A Koyukon View of the Northern Forest*, a detailed study of the Koyukon of the far northwest Canada. David Abram, in *The Spell of the Sensuous*, explores at length ways in which our language and concepts have distanced us from our natural communities.

using human terms to relate to the creatures and systems[13] which are members of our extended communities is that we have a whole set of features built into our languages and practices that tell us to proceed in certain careful ways—we have *ethics* built into the basic terms and relations of our social communities.

If the search for authenticity is a journey only (or at least especially) for modern humans,[14] I believe it is quite likely that part of why this has happened is the growing alienation from nature that characterizes life in modern industrial societies. One of the main goals of this form of life is to achieve comfort and convenience *separate from* the inconveniences and discomforts of nature, and with more than half of people in the world now living in cities this has become a worldwide phenomenon. Furthermore, rural life in developed countries has nearly all the same comforts and conveniences (for example, you will find air conditioning in tractor or combine cabs or in barns, as well as in farmers' homes), with the result that few farmers are much closer to the land than their urban counterparts. In rural America the farms that produce the vast majority of the produce we consume are owned by corporations and run on previously unimaginable economies of scale are often called "factory farms" to highlight the fact that except for location these places of work and living are very much like where urban people live and work.

Rural Iowa is witnessing a dual shift in population and work, however. There is the sad and frightening emptying of the countryside, accompanied by great social and cultural loss described and decried by

---

13 Many traditions choose spider woman as one of the creator deities because she weaves webs, *systems*.

14 Charles Taylor has written extensively about this point. Taylor is the source of much of what I have to say about the causes of inauthenticity, but I disagree in several ways with his definition of authenticity and how to achieve it. I will take up this discussion in the next chapter.

Wendell Berry in his 1977 book, *The Unsettling of America*; but there is also a more recent return of people back to the countryside where they are establishing small farms to grow food for themselves and for the increasing number of farmers' markets. My eldest son, Erik, and his wife, Sara Peterson, have built a very successful community supported agriculture (CSA) operation in northeast Iowa that sells vegetables to subscribers, local restaurants and food co-op, as well as their farmers' market. Their three daughters, Meg, Mairi, and Nina do not suffer nature deficit disorder as they spend large amounts of time playing outside, roaming through nearby woods, and helping with their father's labor-intensive gardening operation. While I admit to being a biased grandfather, I find profound contrasts between these girls and young people brought up on a steady diet of indoor and urban activities. They are at home in and value the cycles and features of nature that surround them, and the "it's all about me" sense of entitlement borne by so many young people is at least muted in these girls who spend little time being entertained by electronics and much time making their own entertainment.

My point is not to decry, criticize or praise the ecological and social results and implications of the sweeping changes that have been brought by modernism and industrialization, but rather to explore a deep way in which we are at odds with ourselves. We cry for authenticity and yet the very way of life we have pursued might be a major cause of our inauthenticity. If mystics, whole cultures such as American Indians, or the classical Chinese painters are correct in believing that a major part of whom we are is members of more-than-human communities, then to separate ourselves from nature is to render being ourselves, being authentic, virtually impossible.

Cordova puts this powerfully ironic point in terms of alienation:

*European psychologies are predicated on the alienation of
the individual. Ironically, near total self-sufficiency and independence are methods developed to deal with the effects
of alienation. But since they are themselves also a cause of
alienation, their reinforcement serves merely to provide a
buffer for the individual against the inroads of others. These
methods do not eradicate alienation; they provide one with
the strength to accept, and live, with alienation* [15]

A Deeper Sense of Place

Place Studies is a new field of study that utilizes many disciplines
in calling our attention to the importance of place in the lives of all
beings.[16] Humans not only affect the world around us, but that world
also profoundly affects us. To demonstrate one powerful example of
this thesis, Kathleen Norris, in *Dakota*, is well-known for her detailed
description of how life in the short grass prairie of western South
Dakota shapes the people in the small town of Lemmon where, as an
adult, she returned to her grandparent's home to live out a portion
of her life with her ailing husband. She shows how the landscape,
seasons, weather, pace of life, sun, and wind conspire to give citizens
of this small town their outlooks, their senses of what life has to offer,
the way they walk and talk virtually everything about the very beings
of those who have lived there long. Author Barry Lopez talks about
the Spanish word *querencia*, which refers to a sense of belonging, of

---

15 Cordova, 123.

16 People in and across many disciplinary boundaries— Geography, history, art, creative writing, philosophy, psychology, anthropology and literature—have written about the
importance of place. Prominent Place Studies authors include Tim Creswell, *Place: A Short
Introduction*; Edward S. Casey, *The Fate of Place: A Philosophical History*; Paul Gruchow,
Grass Roots: The Universe of Home; Andrew Light, *Philosophies of Place*; William Vitek and
Wes Jackson, eds., *Rooted in the Land: Essays on Community and Place*; and Claudio Mauro,
ed., *In Praise of Fertile Land: An Anthology of Poetry, Parable, and Story*.

rootedness as "a place on the ground where one feels secure, a place from which one's strength of character is drawn—a place in which we know exactly who we are"[17] Such a place can be anywhere, but it is usually where one grew up. I, for example, feel most at home when I am in short-grass prairie country where the air and landscape have certain qualities unduplicated anywhere else in my experience.

One of the points many people have made is that a mistake we tend to make is to "set man apart,"[18] to define nature separately from humans, but in discussing nature in this chapter I in no way want to suggest that we can or should separate humans and nature. Rather, my point has been to show how important nature is for human identity and that a major reason so many people today experience alienation from authenticity is because we have *tried* to create such separations with the result that more and more people feel out of touch with a major part of the reality (nature) of which they are a part. Lopez has chosen the word *querencia* wisely, for the word comes from the verb *querer*, which means to desire, to want. We are deeply natural beings who desire connectedness with the vast realities of nature at a profoundly deep level. Ironically, though, because of the many barriers and distractions we have erected to discovering and being ourselves, we are not in touch with this need and desire. We will discuss this point in the final chapter of this book by examining Phil Cousineau's book on pilgrimage.[19] Cousineau claims that our desire for authenticity is the desire to be *in touch*, to touch what is sacred and real.

It is interesting that Cordova uses an ecological metaphor to make the point that we separate ourselves from nature at the risk of los-

17 Barry Lopez, *Rediscovery of North America*, p 123.

18 See Robinson Jeffers' famous discussion of this point in *Not Man Apart*.

19 Phil Cousineau, *The Art of Pilgrimage: The Seeker's Guide to Making Travel Sacred*. For a very helpful discussion of the power of stories to shape our lives, and thus our authenticity, see his *Once and Future Myths: The Power of Ancient Stories in Our Lives*.

ing touch with realities fundamental to our deepest being. Humans are, she claims, like any beings, in large measure defined by the *niche* they fill in the greater ecological community. We "are produced to fill a certain ecological niche and are therefore each different. Tolerance is built into the notion of different and separate 'creations.'"[20] She believes, in other words, that this sense of place, this story, not only gave Native Americans a deep ecological ethic but it also was/is responsible for their tolerance and respect for the wide array of other peoples. Each kind of being, including other tribal groups, has its place in the great tapestry of nature, and everything gains its strengths and identity from its place in this complex community.

In a striking image, in the process of exploring what "following the original instructions" means for contemporary Native Americans, Gabrielle Tayac[21] describes the explorations and ritual activities of urban Indians in New York City trying to reconnect with "the land" in the midst of this now concrete-laden island. They discover long-hidden waterways and ancestral rock paintings, they observe in wonder the remnants of once plentiful plants, insects and animals, and through rituals they rededicate themselves to doing their parts in preserving and resurrecting the ecosystem that once flourished there. Lest we think these remnants of a once-flourishing civilization are merely being romantic or nostalgic, consider the science-based understanding and imagination Alan Weisman[22] has given us of how quickly the other creatures would reclaim New York City if humans suddenly disappeared. Weisman makes it painfully clear, through careful extrapolation and imaginative descriptions that most of the natural world could get along fine without us, but that we cannot get along without

---

20 Cordova, 152.
21 "Keeping the Original Instructions," 73-84
22 *The World Without Us.*

it. The real question is whether we can get along with and in nature and learn to live sustainably.

One of the most important points Tayac makes is that ritualizing life, especially if in every aspect of life we respond to what is sacred with due respect and care, we see ourselves and each other, as well as the rest of the world, in a very different way. In anthropomorphizing, which is at the heart of much sacred language, we bring all beings into our care while simultaneously giving up control. As we said earlier, personal language is the language of what is holy, as witnessed by the fact that all ethical systems view persons as inviolable (sacred). A major aspect of how these holy beings are to be treated is to not try to control them while treating them with the utmost care. Thus to ritualize all aspects of experience is to approach the world with a special attitude, with a sense of deep responsibility for the well-being of that which is holy. And what references to deities do is to remind us that while we are a part of this holy realm of beings, with special responsibilities, we are not in charge, we are one holy being among a multitude that all deserve care and respect precisely because of our mutual community memberships. To use Cordova's image again, the major role humans have in their niches is to be aware of how this world works and to keep it intact and flowing through proper rituals. I find a similar sentiment and program in the common Buddhist view that we are privileged to be born (this time) as humans who are able to comprehend the workings of the world and help to maintain its harmony. We are the universe aware of itself.

Nature and the Authentic Self

We cannot maintain that the pleasure a man gets from a landscape...would last long if he were convinced a priori

that the forms and colors he sees are just forms and colors, that all structures in which they play a role are purely subjective and have no relation whatsoever to any meaningful order or totality, that they simply and necessarily express nothing....No walk through the landscape is necessary any longer; and thus the very concept of landscape as experienced by a pedestrian becomes meaningless and arbitrary....What mind can resist despair at such a prospect? Who can fail to admit that the homocentric logic of self-interest leads finally not to human satisfaction but to the loss of humanity?
—Laurence Tribe, "Ways Not to Think about Plastic Trees"

We are finally ready to enter into our deepest point about nature and authenticity. When "I" disappeared in that sunrise experience, what was absent was my self-consciousness, not my awareness. In fact, part of why I attained heightened awareness was precisely because my awareness was not split and my energies were fully in the experience rather than also dedicated to ego maintenance. Ironically, part of achieving one's authentic self involves the muting, the transcendence and even sometimes the extirpation, of part of the self, that is self-consciousness. Kathleen Norris notes that narcissism is a handmaid of *acedia*. To focus incessantly on one's self is to lose contact with the realities of life that call for our attention and help make us who we are, and in the process we lose our ability to care, to be involved in the world of which we are a part.

Since ancient times Daoists have understood that the experience of being fully alive, fully in the moment, is to "become one with/in the world." In a small story probably not even written by Zhiangzi himself, this greatest of all ancient Daoist sages (or his protégés) tells of how a woodcarver, commissioned to carve a bell stand for a prince, fasted for seven days and nights until he had rid himself of all "external" motivations.[23] The most obvious and difficult of the motivations the master carver wanted to eradicate was the implied threat of punishment or death if he did not carve a beautiful bell stand. You or I would take at least seven days to reach the point where we were not acting, at least in part, because of a death threat, and most likely we would not even worry about purifying our motives and begin carving immediately because our fear would be so great. So why would Zhiangzi emphasize the need to eliminate such motivations if we are to do whatever we do fully awake and as authentic beings? Is he being obstinate like a child wanting to do things his or her way? Does he believe there is always one and only one right motivation for any action?

He certainly seems to believe that actions done from the wrong kind of motivation will harm the bell stand and the woodcarver. However, I believe that none of our usual ways of thinking about motivation and experience will get at Zhuangzi's insight. For we tend to think of motivation in terms of push and pull, with an implicit model of linear causation. We see ourselves as a physical object that needs to be pushed or pulled to move, to do anything. While there is no doubt that we are physical beings that indeed are caused to move by stimulation, the *experience* the woodcarver seeks—a kind of experience that indicates he is carving properly—is precisely one where he is so fully engaged in and with his craft that his ego concerns for recognition or even his very life disappear. In this state push and pull disappear and one is motivated in a different way.

---

23 For a wonderful discussion of this story see Parker Palmer's essay, "The Woodcarver" (in *The Active Life: Wisdom for Work, Creativity and Caring.*) Palmer uses the version written by Thomas Merton (from *Mystics and Zen Masters*), but a more accurate translation can be found in Victor H. Mair, trans., *Wandering on the Way: Early Taoist Tales and Parables of Chuang Tzu.* Palmer also discusses "The Woodcarver" at length in his book, *A Hidden Wholeness: The Journey Toward An Undivided Life, Welcoming the Soul and Weaving Community in a Wounded World.*

Polish psychologist Mihalyi Csikszentmihalyi[24] calls this state "flow," and his description so successfully fits the experiences of a wide range of people in a great variety of circumstances that phrases such as "going with the flow" have become common usages. Everyone has had experiences, at least as a child, where we are so lost in what we are doing that the passage of hours can seem like a few minutes, where we become "lost" in our activity and are startled when called out of our concentration. The biographies or autobiographies of great artists, who often have large and vulnerable egos, consistently describe the creative act as one where they had to "get out of the way" and "let the muse speak" through them. If anthropologists are to be believed, throughout history people have sought flow in a great variety of ways: through strong physical effort (the Zen of running, etc.), through adrenaline-driven activities such as hang-gliding, in meditation or prayer, or through mind-altering substances. The Daoist seeks to bring flow to our everyday lives—to our work (our "carving"), to our eating or washing, to smelling flowers, to caring for children, and to all our social relationships. To be in flow, as the woodcarver parable helps us see, is to connect what is deepest or most central in our identities with the world at hand. In this chapter I have tried to explain how a major dimension of our identities as natural beings has been eroded by our various strategies to separate ourselves from the non-human world. As a result, a major part of why authenticity is such an issue for contemporary humans is because we have become so distant, so alien, from the natural communities of which we are members.

---

24 Mihalyi Csikszentmihalyi, *Flow: The Psychology of Optimal Experience.*

Becoming "One With Nature" Is Crucial for Becoming Fully Human

In another of his famous scenes, Sartre describes the nausea his protagonist Roquentin experiences as he sits beneath a chestnut tree: "I was there, motionless and icy, plunged in a horrible ecstasy. But something fresh had just appeared in the very heart of this ecstasy; I understood the Nausea, I possessed it....The essential thing is contingency....To exist is simply to be there."[25] Sartre bases his major early work, *Being and Nothingness,* on this supposedly common human experience of feeling *less* than other beings because we, unlike all other creatures we know, do not have a fixed nature—they have a solidity of being, while we are *nothingness* (totally free and thus undefined... and plagued with inauthenticity). Now while Sartre uses this striking literary scene to make some very important points about how we make excuses when we actually have the abilities to be responsible (he says we constantly try to "escape our freedom"), I have usually experienced the "chestnut tree" very differently—with awe or fascination or joy rather than with nausea.

In May of 2007 my family and I, along with a cadre of community college students, had the privilege of spending two nights patrolling for giant leatherback sea turtles. While these ancient creatures can grow to over 2000 pounds and live far longer than 100 years, the three females we encountered weighed a mere (!) 600-800 pounds and were only about six feet in length. For at least 110 million years the leatherbacks have been coming to the beach we were at in Costa Rica for two months each spring to lay their eggs. They are very careful and cautious about when and where to do their duties—there must be a sizeable dry stretch of sand between high tide and the jungle, they

---

25 *Nausea*, 130-31.

prefer dark nights, and any disturbance will chase them away; thus we walked the seven-mile stretch of black, volcanic sand without lights on a dark night, tripping over driftwood and wondering how we were going to find any turtles.

Our guide assured us we would know when one had crawled ashore. When we came to what seemed like tank tracks heading toward the dry sand we knew what she meant. At first these dinosaur-age creatures dig a hole in the sand as large and deep as their massive bodies; then they settle into digging a hole for the 35-100 leathery eggs they will deposit. When they begin digging the egg hole, they are easy to approach as they are in a trance-like state (perhaps they are in flow!). Our task was to identify and measure them, check their health, administer first aid if necessary, and count their eggs as they dropped into the carefully-dug hole. The leatherback sea turtles are endangered and the conservation group we were working with wants to do as much as they can to help protect and preserve them.

In Sartre's sense, these turtles are like oak trees—they are highly programmed from eons of time to methodically, almost mechanically, go through their difficult and exacting routine. One of the turtles we witnessed kept digging for several strokes after the egg hole was too deep for her flippers to reach bottom, and I was brought to tears of awe when, as she was covering the eggs, she would pat the sand after each scoop was carefully laid atop the buried eggs. Once the hole was filled she then covered the cavity she had made for her body and proceeded to rough up a large area to camouflage her eggs from predators.

I did not feel nauseous once during this hour-and-a-half long experience! In fact, tired as we were, having made a difficult trek in the middle of the night along this pristine beach, none of us experienced anything except awe, gratitude, excitement, and wonder. And we had the privilege to repeat such experiences many times as we watched exotic (to us) birds in early morning hours, hiked through a jungle of unfamiliar plants and insects, or perched 120 feet above the ground to witness a wholly different world in the rainforest canopy.

I don't believe that we failed to notice our "nothingness" in contrast to the turtles' "being"; I think, rather, that Sartre has it wrong. We, too, are beings, solid beings with many built-in characteristics, and while we indeed might sometimes (too often) try to escape our physicality, responsibilities, or the implications of our actions, we are identifiable as species beings and as individuals, just as the remarkable sea turtles. We are not a species without an identity. What Sartre has right, though, is that *part* of our identity is our ability to *imagine* our actions or our selves differently, to pick and choose aspects of our being in ways that go far beyond such capacities in other known creatures, and it is this dimension of our being wherein lies our ability to be authentic...or not. Therefore, what Sartre does have correct is that our "nothingness," our abilities to imagine and choose something different, has a dark side as well as the vaunted "freedom" we often thoughtlessly celebrate. In the final chapter of this book we will return to Sartre's analysis of human imagination[26] and explore how it forms the heart of the spiritual dimension of human nature.

To Be Inauthentic is to Be Out of Touch, To Not Care

In her own way, Norris is making a similar point, but she does not fall into Sartre's either/or (instinct or total freedom) trap. *Acedia*, the temptation to inaction, the paradigm of sins of omission, entices us to despair, to escape our calling to engagement with the world (Norris

---

26 The *Imaginary* stands at the center of Sartre's philosophy. In this book he explores the implications for nothingness and freedom that grown from Husserl's insight that consciousness is imbued with the ability to imagine a different world.

says *acedia* is an acid corroding our desire for God); thus for her, our "escape from freedom" is more of a temptation to refuse to be who we are or might become rather than a result of our being no-thing at all. For it is precisely because we are enmeshed in a world not of our own making, but one that greatly makes us, that *acedia* is the heart of inauthenticity. Our fear is not having to make our selves out of nothing, but a desire to escape being the person who beckons from beyond our narcissism.

As I had experienced on a Montana mountainside, I got into flow as I witnessed and worked with the female leatherback bent on fulfilling her biological destiny. The hour-and-a-half we spent with her passed in a flash, and while afterwards I was still reveling in the wonder of what we had observed, I could feel the sacredness of that experiencing waning. My tiredness began to catch up with me, I became aware that several of our students had not returned from their sojourns across the dark sand, my son was complaining—all these realities and a flood of thoughts dissipated my singular focus and lack of self-consciousness.

In their studies of human happiness, positive psychologists such as Jonathan Haidt tell us that much of what makes us happy seems to be hard-wired into us—we all seem to have a "happiness set point" from birth that basically cannot be changed except perhaps by extraordinary people who through deep meditation affect even biological limits to their happiness. Another part of our happiness has to do with our social, cultural, physical and economic conditions, with how rich or poor we are, with how open or oppressive our society is, or with the physical environment in which we live. Happily, many of these conditions are malleable, but whether or not someone rises from dire poverty usually has more to do with large-scale historical and social forces than with what they can do individually. According to Haidt and his colleagues, most of us do have the ability individually to affect our happiness. We can choose to be married, to be a part of a supportive community, to reduce our chronic stress, to be religious, and to maximize our flow experiences. We will return to Haidt's discussion of factors that do or do not lead to happiness in chapter five, but I want to emphasize the convergence of the insights of ancient sages and wisdom traditions with contemporary empirical studies Haidt notes. One reason for seeking flow is that therein lies (an improvement of our) happiness. Another is that flow reveals something important about authenticity: to be authentic is like coming home.

However, as I mentioned in the Introduction and will take up in chapter four, I believe essentialism is one of the mistakes people make in thinking about authenticity—the belief that being authentic is to be in touch with and to act from a deep, core self that is permanent and unchanging. You can see why people would conclude we must have an essential self from our discussion in this chapter; for if we are so wired from eons of evolution that we cannot be fully human without deep connections with nature, and if half of what we are (Haidt calls it our "elephant") is a nearly immutable given, surely we do have an essence that we ignore at the risk of being inauthentic. You can also see why a naturalistic ethics is so attractive and initially makes such sense, because if we have a natural essence then acting consistently with and from that essence proscribes the moral.

No one should ever make the mistake of ignoring our natural characteristics and connections. Human alienation from nature is a major source of harm—from environmental destruction to children developing abnormally to psycho-spiritual maladies including *acedia* and inauthenticity. I believe the natural side of us requires as much close contact with nature as our social side requires community; nevertheless, we (our identities) are no more entirely defined by our biology than we are by our culture, and the interactions between these "sources" (to use Taylor's helpful term) generates selves that are unique and unpredictable and that differ from each other in how they play out their interconnectedness within our human and natural communities.

To Be Authentic is to "Do What I Must"

You will recall that Henry Bugbee believes that to be authentic is to move beyond the feeling of "I should/ought" to "I must." It is to be so much myself in a given situation that I cannot help being that person who does that action in that way. What I do follows organically from who I am. My character, the depths of my very being, would have me act in no other way. But the so-called depths of my being are an ongoing creation, a dialogue among the sources of my self which means that I change over the years, often in fundamental ways. Perhaps this is what Nietzsche means when, in a much misunderstood phrase, he says that above all we need to "develop our style." Not our sense of fashion, but the clarity of our "voice," to speak and act from what is most genuine in our selves. To be grounded. To be at home. To be like a native in our place. But not to be an automaton, or a merely instinctive being. As we will discuss in chapter four, Bugbee believes that we took a wrong turn in the modern world by splitting values from facts and the subjective from the objective rather than to see that in experience (which is where authentic being resides) there is no separation. He is resisting the modern tendency to relegate experience to the merely subjective, thus abstracting or alienating ourselves irrevocably from reality. The "must" he emphasizes is not abstract duty, but a direct sense of obligation to and connection with reality.

Looking back on my sea turtle experience, it now seems a bit odd to think of crawling around on the sand inspecting a dinosaur-age creature and counting each of a hundred eggs as they dropped into the deep hole she had meticulously dug in the sand. That is not something I do on a daily basis, nor had I ever done it before. So why do I claim that the flow I experienced was also being authentic in Bugbee's sense? The "I must" Bugbee emphasizes is not necessarily about habit or routine (although, contrary to what many people think, habitual behavior *can* be authentic); it is instead a matter of acting from one's core identity in a situation. I could have wandered about instead of participating in the turtle's lengthy egg-laying exercise, I could have gone back to my bunk, or I could have stood there and observed at a distance; but given who I am and what I was facing, there was nothing for *me* to do but get down on all fours and participate. It felt perfectly natural, I didn't have to think about it, and I had no hesitation putting my whole being into it. Thus flow happened. I was not pushed or pulled by self-conscious motivations such as "how should I behave as a model for my students?" or "what should I do to make this a good story later?" I was certainly not plagued by doubts about being genuine or following some abstract utility calculus. Thus the "I must" in this instance was in no way a compulsion, and perhaps Bugbee's phrase is not quite reflective of what authentic action feels like. For me it was more like a realization that "there is nothing else I could possibly do here and now that makes more sense." But even this way of putting it makes the decision too conscious, too thought-out. I didn't consciously decide to get on my hands and knees, to help measure that remarkably large creature, or to help tend her wounds. If anything, I found myself doing these things without questioning or wondering or deciding.

You can see why people often say we can best ascertain who someone is, what they are made of, when they meet a dramatic challenge,
and from here it is easy to see why the soldiers we referred to in the
Introduction felt most alive and most human in their horrible war-
time experiences. When an emergency arises we don't have time to
think at any length; such situations call for action, and those actions
can show how determined, courageous, caring, or fair we are when
challenged and cannot hide. Our genuine character, replete with our
weaknesses as well as strengths, usually is revealed when the chips
are down. Dramatic situations such as emergencies or athletic challenges or war call forth our greatest strengths and many (most?) people thereby find such experiences exhilarating even if they would not
choose them again.

You can also see why Aristotle, for instance, emphasizes the importance of training the virtues (the "excellences"), of creating good
habits. For precisely when we most need great strengths of character
we have no time to reflect, to sort out our values or hone our skills.
We must act, and those who tend to be most successful are those who
have developed a "style" that allows them to dive into the activity authentically. While perhaps our true character comes into clarity in
times of great stress, it also develops in everydayness—in our social
lives, in school, and in work. The routine and stagnant activities of
our lives can, of course, stifle our growth and make us mundane, but
they are also the source of much of our identity. As we saw in chapter
one the question is not whether we will work, but why and how? If
we pursue the wrong gods, we risk losing our souls. Or at least we will
be inauthentic.

We have been exploring some of the central characteristics of being authentic by examining how and why nature is a primary context
wherein we can feel most alive and become ourselves. Clearly many

aspects of contemporary life distract us from such experiences as we explored in the previous two chapters. It is time to turn to the difficult task of more carefully defining authenticity so that we might know more clearly how to change our lives to improve our abilities to become real. We will begin with a brief look at the flawed conceptual history of authenticity and work toward a more adequate understanding based on a narrative, communitarian, and in-between perspective.

CHAPTER FOUR

PHILOSOPHICAL REFLECTIONS

We discover what it means to exist in being made to stand forth, in standing forth as we must.—Henry Bugbee

Everything—a horse, a vine—is created for some duty…For what task, then, were you yourself created? A man's true delight is to do the things he was made for.—Marcus Aurelius

We had to learn that it did not really matter what we expected from life, but rather what life expected from us…. Life ultimately means taking responsibility to find the right answers to its problems and to fulfill the tasks which it constantly sets for each individual. These tasks, and therefore the meaning of life, differ from man to man, and from moment to moment.—Victor Frankel

Why Philosophy?

Rather than beginning this book with a definition of authenticity, supported by philosophical and historical analyses, I choose to begin with a discussion of some of the realities that circle around this idea (or better, realities this idea can help to reveal). In one sense, this exercise was unnecessary, as the dictionary meaning of authenticity is pretty straightforward: to be authentic is to be genuine, the real thing, the original. The idea of personal authenticity is borrowed from art where, as we discussed in the Introduction, being able to decide whether or not a work of art, an antique, a text, or another object (for example, money) is authentic can be exceedingly important. By extension, for persons to be authentic is for them to be true to themselves, to be genuine rather than fake. As with most things human, and certainly as with most things philosophical, this seemingly straightforward definition is too simple. Philosophical thinking often begins where dictionary definitions end.

But why, you may ask, should we make the effort to listen to philosophers? They tend to write in technical and often opaque jargon and style, and their ideas seem far away from the kinds of realities we discussed in the first half of this book. Here is where you need to trust me a bit. I believe that without going through some philosophical rigors we will not find a satisfactory understanding of that which we seek—answers to how to lead an authentic life in a world swirling with confusing and alluring distractions that take us from ourselves instead of helping us find and be who we are. So what do philosophers have to offer? A number of very thoughtful philosophers have spent a great deal of time ruminating about authenticity. The so-called Existentialists, from Kierkegaard to Camus, brought the issue of authenticity to the fore of their thinking and a broad cultural awareness n Europe in the first half of the twentieth century and in America after World War II. Subsequent philosophers, especially those in traditions with imposing labels such as structuralism, post-structuralism, deconstructionism, and post-modernism, responded at length to the earlier generation of Existentialists, if in no other way than to show the failings of their predecessors' perspectives. And now a third generation of philosophers concerned with authenticity[1] is emerging which is building on the dialogue between the first two generations and is forging new and very helpful understandings especially of the self (which is the root of authenticity and happiness as well).

How can these often complex and abstract ruminations help with our quest? Properly understood, I believe philosophy involves a kind of therapy. So-called "perennial philosophy" or "wisdom traditions" from around the world have offered advice on the nature of the good life and how to live it. I think in their own ways these contemporary thinkers are following that practice. For example, although it seemed to several early philosophers of authenticity that the path to individual authenticity was to break the many bonds we have with our society and culture—society's ethics, social norms, defined roles and so on—subsequent philosophical dialogue has shown that conceiving authenticity as a matter of forging a totally new and unique identity not indebted to society is impossible even for Existentialist heroes such as Nietzsche's *Übermensch* (overman). In other terms, the atomic individualism that today still remains the ideal of authenticity for many in our culture rests on a false understanding of the self. We need not give up in despair of becoming authentic just because the strategy of eschewing the immeasurable forces of society and culture is impossible and undesirable. I hope to show that through philosophical dialogue—the proverbial give and take of conceptual argumentation and deep examination of underlying assumptions—real progress has

---

1 An excellent survey of the Existentialists is Jacob Golomb's book, *In Search of Authenticity: From Kierkegaard to Camus*. Philosophical critics of this tradition include Marxists and Pragmatists as well as various Postmodernists. The third generation of philosophers concerned with authenticity begins with Taylor (see especially his chapter on authenticity in *A Secular Age* and *The Ethics of Authenticity*), and is strongly represented by writers such as Corey Anton in *Selfhood and Authenticity*, Charles Lindholm, *Culture and Authenticity*, Kwame Anthony Appiah, *The Ethics of Identity* and Charles Guignon, *On Being Authentic*.

been made in comprehending what authenticity *is* as well as what it *is not.* While there may not be, as many philosophers have argued, a substantial metaphysical entity called the self or soul, relinquishing our commitment to its existence can open us to a more satisfying and realistic view of what it means to be a person, which in turn can provide us with a stronger basis for being an authentic person, than the proverbial quest for our "true inner self."

By the end of this chapter I hope to offer you a perspective on the building blocks of, and barriers to, authentic living that will aid your own quest for a coherent identity of integrity, balance, passion, and joy—the stuff of classical views of authenticity that have been lost in the roar of contemporary life that pulls us in so many confusing directions that we are left with wispy identities that follow every fad and cannot find their ways in an ever-changing world. Philosopher Harry Frankfort says[2] that far too many people today are "wanton" selves who are not able to take clear, strong stands on important matters. Frankfort says "wantons" are not full persons with genuine cares and commitments, and a world filled with such people is scary indeed. At the very least they cannot be fulfilled, which means, as we will explore in chapter five, they cannot be happy, there being nothing to fulfill or live up to. Perhaps even more fundamentally, as we will discuss in chapter six, people with such thin identities are not capable of hearing and responding to what is calling for their strong effort, whether it is a religious path, a life of service to a cause, response to a muse, or razor-like focus on a problem. A world without those who can hear and respond to such calls is a world bereft of creativity and of the energy that healthy communities and good lives are made of, and the problem of feckless, meandering, wanton selves I believe is especially serious in late modern societies such as our own.

---

2 *The Importance of What We Care About: Philosophical Essays.*

Most philosophical analyses of authenticity spend a good deal of their time exploring what authenticity is *not*. They proceed *via negativa* and examine *in*-authenticity (or its cognates or near-relatives such as insincerity, lack of integrity, "bad faith" or self-deception). In looking back at the first half of this book, I was surprised to find that I had done the same. Why? Why is it so difficult to discuss straightforwardly what being authentic is and involves, rather than come at it through the back door of what it is not or what keeps us from being authentic?[3] I will try to answer this question, and I believe that doing so will pave the way for greater clarity about what authenticity is. Ultimately I will argue that there are several important definitions of authenticity that not only can reveal a great deal about particular philosophies or philosophical traditions, but that also can inform us about the human condition as we experience it today. I will conclude with a definition that I believe provides a practical and high ideal for human action, development, and being.

Mistakes to Avoid

A first concern about the very idea of human authenticity is that it is a poor analogy with authentic art or dollar bills. My PhD dissertation was on the concept of autonomy which, like the concept of authenticity, is borrowed from another context and applied to individual humans. In places like ancient Athens autonomy was something *states* could have. Much later, by analogy this idea was extended

---

3 In *The Authenticity Hoax* Andrew Potter argues that a huge cottage industry has grown up around trumped-up fears that we are inauthentic and need the cures every variety of self-help elixirs promise. Potter claims that these various "saviors" tell us what authenticity is not but never offer a positive understanding that could be the basis of healing what ails us. I will take up both parts of Potter's strong warning about the authenticity hoax later in this chapter and in the final two chapters of this book where I offer a clear alternative understanding of authenticity and how to achieve it.

to persons: so far as humans are self-governing, they too, could be autonomous. Especially through the influence of Kant, this idea has become a mainstay of liberal thought in morality and in social and political analysis. I argued that because people are very different from states the analogy is imperfect in important ways and has resulted in some serious practical as well as philosophical problems. Perhaps you can see why much confusion about humans as moral and social beings has resulted from accepting this ideal of human morality.[4] Human individuals are not like governing bodies or places with distinct political boundaries, and it is quite a stretch to equate individual thought with legislative deliberation, judicial procedure, or separation of powers. Yet this is what the ideal of individual human autonomy implies as seen in the Kantian tradition which bases morality on the human ability to self-legislate and "legislate for all of humanity."[5] It is small wonder that so many people back full speed away from being moral, for the bar of autonomous moral agency has been set breathtakingly high.

I wonder if authenticity does not suffer from the same problem. If the analogy is apt, you would think that discerning whether or not a person, like a work of art, is authentic would be a matter of checking something like their psychic fingerprints or DNA. But unfortunately, as we will see, where this detective work probably leads is to the discovery that there is no such thing as a sure-fire test for determining whether or not someone is being authentic. Nonetheless, just because we do not find what we expected (such as a test for authenticity) does

---

4 My graduate mentor, Frithjof Bergmann, believes that as a result of similar but many more difficulties with the larger idea of freedom, such concepts are not very fit tools for use. See his *On Being Free.*

5 For readers not familiar with Kantian ethics and metaphysics, Kant believed that all acceptable moral principles are absolute and universal, which means that when I decide what is right or wrong for me I am, in effect, legislating for all of humanity in that I am setting the standard every rational person should follow in similar situations.

not mean that there are no other ways to think about being real than discovering some inner original essence. I believe it is precisely in rethinking the origins, nature, and development of the self that philosophers of authenticity can contribute to our understanding, development, effective action, and happiness.

A second main criticism of the concept of authenticity is that it is dated, a child of a particular era (the 1960s in America, earlier decades in Europe), a movement (the so-called "counter culture," the "hippie generation"), and certain literary and philosophical traditions (Romanticism and Existentialism) that have little coinage outside of specific cultural milieux.[6] On the social and cultural fronts, I hope that the many examples I have given show that the idea of authenticity still has traction and that if anything the desire and need for authenticity is deeper and more widespread today than it was fifty years ago. Philosophically, I believe that Continental writers from Kierkegaard (or even as far back as Rousseau) to Camus have bequeathed us some powerful understandings of authenticity and the self that we would be unwise to ignore or reject. There is no doubt that to analytically-trained philosophers and English-speakers more generally, the words and metaphors of this tradition seem needlessly or even hopelessly opaque or misguided, but I hope to show in this chapter that they have offered a great deal that can help us with the very real problems we are discussing in this book.

A third criticism often made of the quest for authenticity is that it is a solution that is simply another face of the problem.[7] The rebellion against the conformity of mass society or the loneliness of individualism that the youth culture of the 1960s (etc.) so powerfully launched

---

6 See for example, Cf Phillip Vannini and J. Patrick Williams, *Authenticity in Culture, Self and Society.*

7 A classic statement of this criticism is Theodor Adorno in his *The Jargon of Authenticity.* See also Golumb, chapter one, and Potter's entire book (*The Authenticity Hoax*).

results in a narcissistic quest for self-fulfillment that can be even more isolating and bourgeois than the tidy consumerism and mass culture it tries to overcome. Even more challenging is the specter of isolated individuals, however real or self-assured, lacking the social connections and skills necessary to counteract the evils the totalitarianisms of the past two centuries have so amply produced. I believe this criticism, as well, is countered best through a combination of stories and examples along with clear conceptual analysis. While there is much truth to warnings of dangers inherent in attempts to become real, I believe there are versions of authenticity that avoid the pitfalls into which many people searching for personal reality fall. The most serious pitfall of all, I think, is to abandon the quest for authenticity just because many strategies fail, finally, to give a version that is a real improvement to simply living inauthentically. I believe, in fact, that the best versions of authenticity can *help* to create individuals who are both very genuine *and* very tied into communities in such a way that they will be at the forefront of resisting the kinds of mindless conformity that characterizes totalitarian regimes, be they "hard" (Nazism, Communism, Authoritarian Theocracy) or "soft" (consumerism, being a groupie, or being a "company man").

A fourth challenge to any attempt to discuss authenticity is issued by a variety of so-called postmodern critics. Put simply, this critique says that what is at the very heart of authenticity—the self—is a fiction. If the self is a fiction, then how can people find or become their real selves? If true, this is the most profound and damaging criticism of any attempt to define and analyze authenticity, for it attacks the very center of the entire enterprise by claiming that it is totally misguided, based on a false understanding of reality.[8] I hope to show that

---

8 This critique is at the heart of Potter's attack on the quest for authenticity in both *The Authenticity Hoax* and *Nation of Rebels.*

instead of ending our enterprise, this postmodern criticism actually clears the way for a deeper and more accurate understanding of authenticity precisely because it requires a new view of the self that can stand up to philosophical and social scientific scrutiny and is more in line with reality.

Learning From the History of an Idea

Charles Taylor and now others have written extensively about the history of authenticity. They contend that authenticity is a modern concern that did not trouble people in earlier cultures. While I think in one sense they are correct, I also believe it is a misreading of pre-modern cultures to suggest that no one in those societies was concerned with the *kinds* of issues the quest for authenticity is about. Instead, I believe it is more accurate to see hunger for authenticity as a widespread and perhaps automatic *issue* for moderns while pre-moderns typically had no such struggles to become *authentic*. It is even more accurate and revealing to say that pre-modern people did not understand human identity and worth in terms of autonomy; thus they did not conceive of or experience the development of identity as a quest for authenticity. A common form which the process of forming an identity might take, for a pre-modern person, for example, would be to be accepted in a status role in their clan or tribe.

Think of it this way: whether or not, or the extent to which, someone is autonomous has become our yardstick, our criterion, for measuring the extent of his or her authenticity. It is not surprising when you ask someone from our culture what is involved in being authentic he or she often refer first to how *unique* a person is. Because our gauge is autonomy—being as self-governing as possible—our models of authenticity are those who stand out or are non-conformists, whereas we suspect the authenticity of someone whose actions, style, or beliefs are common or typical. So wedded are we Westerners to this way of thinking about authenticity that even astute cultural historians like Taylor cannot see the authenticity, or the struggles to become authentic, that have existed in other cultural traditions.

But if authenticity has to do with *identity*, with becoming (paradoxically) who you are, then people in traditional societies, like people today, were more or less authentic. Identity has always been an accomplishment, the result of development throughout childhood (and beyond) that can be more or less easy, but never automatic or pre-given, for any individual. One significant difference between pre-moderns and us, though, is that probably relatively fewer pre-moderns had difficulty deciding who or how to be because their roles, status, occupations, religion, and fate were mainly set for them by society and circumstances. Medieval peasants, for example, enjoyed little social or economic mobility, and there were few occupations available. Seen from this angle, you can see why Taylor, like most modern historians,[9] views modernism as a great leap forward for humanity. The sources of the dynamism, creativity, and material improvement, as well as the rise of liberal democracies with universal participation, came with the opening up of endless possibilities for human identity and life situations for an ever-greater portion of the population. Seen through the lens of the modern ideology where autonomy is the gold standard, the "problem of authenticity" is a *good* problem to have, for that means we get to choose who and what we will become rather than having it decided mainly by tradition—by family, religion, and social structures.

The problem is, while cultures are ever more fluid as the modern period progresses, people become increasingly unsure of their identi-

---

9 See especially Taylor's *Sources of the Self.* See also Raymond Tallis, *Enemies of Hope: A Critique of Contemporary Pessimism.*

ties and are willing to cling to the best or only sources of the self they can find. Jonathan Friedman puts it this way: "Culture is supremely negotiable for professional culture experts, but for those whose identity depends upon a particular configuration this is not the case. Identity is not negotiable. Otherwise it has no existence."[10] And it is precisely this absolute need for identity that is the source of so many problematic attempts to establish authenticity—such as in-group superiority or even aggression against "inferiors" (racism, fascism, nationalism), surface identifications (clubs, hobbies), or just plain wrong-headed strategies (consumerism, identities gained from hyper-involvement in food purism, or athleticism), and so on.

Sartre and other Existentialists help us see the underside of this vaunted freedom to choose. As we have seen, to make this point vivid, they coined famous phrases such as "being condemned to choose" and of our desire to "escape our freedom." Having to decide nearly everything about our lives can be experienced as a bother or even as painfully undesirable as easily as seeing it as a wonderful gift. As we will discuss below, self-deception seems to increase as life's possibilities expand, reinforcing Dostoevsky's claim in the "Grand Inquisitor" chapter of *The Brothers Karamazov* that what people want is to believe or pretend they are free but simultaneously to escape from the terrible burdens of that freedom.

Most students of the history of the idea of authenticity claim that Rousseau was the founder of the idea that we must eliminate or transcend society in order to find our true selves. Rousseau believed that our *feelings* constituted our genuine self and in order to develop and express this self we need to overcome the influences of society, for society constantly asks us to mute, ignore, sublimate, or deny our feelings. Rousseau would respond to our claim that people in pre-modern soci-

10 Jonathan Friedman, *Cultural Identity and Global Process*, 17.

eties were authentic by saying that they were other- or outer-directed in their identities and thus, while they had clear and strong identities from which they acted, they were unaware of or they had to ignore their true feelings which can only be known and developed by turning inward and away from society.[11] While there have been variations on Rousseau's general perspective, authenticity has almost always been understood as involving deep tension between self and society. For example, in a recent book Parker Palmer epitomizes this tension as a one between "soul and role,"[12] and Taylor has argued that the other-directed virtues of traditional people were about honor and adherence to a *cultural* code, while the virtues of the authentic person had to do with personal dignity, with adherence to a *personal* code.[13]

For Nietzsche and Heidegger—and indeed most other Existentialists and Phenomenologists—authenticity is formulated against a backdrop of mass culture. They emphasize the centrality of uniqueness and individuality. They were writing at a time when the power of religion was giving way to a new force, mass culture shaped by human-centered ideologies—modern collectivisms. I have suggested, in chapter two, that consumerism can be a similar enemy of authenticity. Poets, novelists, editorialists, intellectuals, and many others have warned for two centuries that the "crowd" (Nietzsche calls it the *herd*, Heidegger *Das Man*) can turn people into automata, followers of trends, SS guards, groupies, gang members, "suits," and so on. We have long heard that the great threat to being ourselves is the power of the masses. Yet if Froese's Existential and Daoists philosophers are correct, we are all "carved" by society and culture, by our teachers, parents, television sets, Facebook friends, religion, the internet, and more.

---

11 Sacvan Bercovitch contends that the Puritans were the major source of this turn to individual inwardness in America in *The Puritan Origins of the American Self*.

12 *A Hidden Wilderness: The Journey Toward an Undivided Life*.

13 See *Ethics of Authenticity*.

Thus why single out "the crowd" as somehow contrary to our very being when it/they is/are just one more social/cultural force?

Nietzsche answers this challenge with his immortal response: "God is dead, and we have killed Him." His great fear was that the gaping chasm we moderns find at the core of our being will drive us into the clutches of the herd. For with the absolute gone, not only our surety about our ability to know the truth is gone (as Descartes' *Meditations*, and after him most modern and postmodern philosophers, so amply show), but we also have no secure source of our selves (no soul). Creating a genuine self becomes a challenge for us in a way that it never was for people in the past. The "crowd," as we saw in our discussion of our mediated culture, becomes an overwhelming force (or set of forces) that buoys us about like a cork in the ocean once we are cut loose from the security of a life dominated by religion and traditional culture. It is no accident that religious (or secular!) fundamentalisms are creatures of the modern world, for they act like beacons of light in the dark nights of the soul we experience when the thick cultures[14] of the past disappear.

I believe that the Existentialists, like the Romantics they criticize yet follow (even philosophers as astute and brilliant as Heidegger and Nietzsche), because they are (rightly) so concerned about modern totalitarianisms, have been caught in a conceptual bind of their own making. In juxtaposing autonomy and enslavement, everything given by culture enslaves (because it is not autonomously created), and because our selves are cultural creations we thus have no self when we reject everything about our selves that is not authentic. The terms they have given us in our quest are *rigged*! We cannot be authentic without rejecting the very basis of the self, and thus authenticity becomes impossible (as Sartre starkly says). It is no wonder that in the

---

14 See the next section for a discussion of thick vs. thin cultures.

process of celebrating the human possibilities that are open to us as modern humans, the Existentialists end up painting a most dismal picture of our plight.

As I mentioned in the chapter on technology, followers of Heidegger's philosophy of technology such as David Strong tend to make a similar mistake. Heidegger is a "retro-romantic" in his view that the only technologies that do not unbind us from reality, especially from nature, are simple tools such as hammers or wood fires. The moment a technology becomes complex, such as a furnace with a thermostat (a "device"), it abstracts us from the real world of cutting trees, chopping wood, and so on. By implication, this means the only way to be authentic is to live like Thoreau or perhaps Native Americans before Europeans arrived with their more sophisticated technologies. Our discussion in chapter two shows that while my view is like Strong's in certain ways, I believe this simple rejection of contemporary culture and technology is based on the mistaken ideology of autonomous individualism.

If we return to the basic idea of an autonomous state, how a given polis came into being is not included. Autonomy refers to how a state is governed, not to how it came to be in the first place. Perhaps the key mistake these thinkers and their successors make is to bring *self-making* into the heart of authenticity.[15] For if Nietzsche's metaphor is accurate and the work of art we are is mainly given by nature and culture, to throw out what is not self-made in our quest for authenticity indeed leaves us with no-thing. When Bugbee contends that "I must" is central to our authenticity he is shifting our attention from self-formation to the integrity of our decisions and commitments. He agrees

---

15 Charles Lindholm distinguishes between two senses of authenticity—the origin (genealogical or historical) and content (identity or correspondence) of an entity—and he contends that our failure to separate the two often leads to the kind of confusion we are discussing here.

with Heidegger that we are thrust into situations and that *how* we live our lives determines our authenticity, not the other way around. To a great extent we don't choose a self or to live authentically; instead, we "acquiesce" to reality, we decide to live with integrity, to be the best child of our parents or parent to our child, the best employee, the best Muslim, the best person... we can be. Or not. The hard work is mainly to be in touch with reality and then to be willing to live in accordance with that reality rather than try to escape from it.

This is tricky business, and our linguistic uses reveal how confusing things can become. We sometimes say that someone is a "self-made person," which if literally true means that people can control who they are. A moment's reflection, though, reveals that a person to whom we attribute this accomplishment typically has managed to do more than most people in determining a trend or career or product, not that they began as a blank slate and "customized" a self. Some people, of course, are unusually self-reflective and have greater ability to alter themselves than most people, and thus we sometimes say of such a person that "she re-made herself." But again, no one believes that this creation happened *ex nihilo*, out of nothing. Instead, it is just that some people, whether because of talent or effort or a combination, are able to change themselves more than most people. The refinement of one's self that Nietzsche emphasized with his comments about "self-overcoming" should be seen in the light of his marble-carving metaphor about the self as a work of art: most of who we are is set by nature and nurture, and what we can do is *refine* what we are given. Nietzsche says that to a great extent we do not choose the self we are or will become, but we do get to choose our *style* (to some extent, at least, although that, too, is mainly given).

Thick and Thin Cultures

I believe both perspectives—the celebration of the opportunities to form new kinds of identities, and the paralysis too many choices can bring—can be true for anyone, depending on their circumstances. What the Existentialist critique of modern freedom—to become the person we choose to be—allows us to see is that in the "great transformation"[16] to modernism we left behind some very valuable things. Perhaps the best way to comprehend what we have lost[17] is to use a distinction coined by anthropologist Edward Sapir between *genuine* and *spurious* cultures (or which Clifford Geertz, following Sapir, calls *thick* and *thin* cultures). Genuine cultures are classically represented by hunting and gathering societies that not only offered few life options, but also had universally accepted myths and worldviews, traditional practices, and a rich set of rituals for nearly every occasion. In his classic 1924 paper, Sapir says that

> "The genuine [thick] culture is not of necessity either high or low; it is merely inherently harmonious, balanced and self-satisfactory. It is the expression of a richly varied and yet somehow unified and consistent attitude toward life, an attitude which sees the significance of any one element of civilization in its relations to all others."[18]

In such a culture, Sapir contends, "nothing is spiritually meaningless," and people are not frustrated by any aspect of their lives. From our modern perspective, with our great emphasis on choice, we tend to view such cultures as stultifying places that rob their members of opportunities for individuality and free expression. Sapir begs to dif-

---

16 See Carl Polanyi, *The Great Transformation: The Political and Economic Origins of Our Time.*

17 See Peter Laslett, *The World We Have Lost.*

18 Edward Sapir, "Culture, Genuine and Spurious," reprinted in *Katarxis* No 3, 1-7 (www.katarxis3.com/Sapir.htm), 1

fer: "...a genuine culture refuses to consider the individual as a mere cog....The major activities of the individual must directly satisfy his own creative and emotional impulses, must always be something more than a means to an end."[19] And in a startling reversal, Sapir contends that "The great cultural fallacy of industrialism ... is that in harnessing machines to our uses it has not known how to avoid the harnessing of the majority of mankind to its machines."[20] For Sapir, the genuine culture "works from the individual to ends," which he calls an "internal" culture; in contrast, an "external" culture such as our own, "works from general ends to the individual."

What Sapir is after in his distinction between genuine (thick) and non-genuine (thin) cultures is to get us to use a different yardstick to measure the worth of a culture, and by extension the measurement of authenticity. Efficiency, wealth, or variety of choices doesn't necessarily make for a satisfactory culture, and autonomy doesn't necessarily bring authenticity. Instead, Sapir suggests that we think in terms of meaningfulness and spiritual satisfaction wherein the individual internalizes a culture that provides him/her with strengths, balance, meaning, and integrity. A genuine culture gives the individual the tools necessary for vigorous creativity and spiritual growth. He contends that in our own culture, "part of the time we are dray horses; the rest of the time we are listless consumers of goods....In other words, our spiritual selves go hungry, for the most part, pretty much all of the time."[21]

V.F. Cordova, a contemporary Jicarilla Apache philosopher, whose work we will examine in detail shortly, would agree with Sapir. She contends that many Native American cultures today do a much better

---

19 Ibid,, 2
20 Ibid., 2
21 Ibid., 5

job "feeding the spiritual lives" of their people than does mainstream America even though materially Native Americans are among the poorest people in the country. She also argues that people in her (internal) culture are much more creative and secure in their identities precisely because they have not been cut free from strong cultural/social definitions.

A thick culture provides a context within which people are both guided and equipped to make meaningful choices about what to do and who to be. They help people live a balanced, creative and genuine life in a fashion Daoists call "in between." As we will show, this view of authentic life refuses to choose one pole or another of the basic dichotomies we habitually turn to: 1) between nature and nurture, 2) self and community, 3) freedom and responsibility, or 4) objectivity and subjectivity. A thin culture like our own has the wonderful advantage of freeing people from oppressive versions of traditional cultures, from parochialism and myopic, superstitious or even jingoistic beliefs, or from the kind of uniformity that drives so many contemporary Japanese youths to escape to their rooms rather than face oppressive conformity.[22] Sapir's insight is that such a culture can cut people loose from the very structures (for example, initiation rituals) and meanings (adequate stories, or "myths to live by" as Joseph Campbell puts it) needed for humans to thrive.

My first quibble with Taylor, et al. is not so much that they are wrong to claim that authenticity is a problem for moderns in ways it was not for people in traditional societies, but that they underestimate the importance of traditional sources of meaning in authentic self formation. Taylor is correct in asserting that the kinds of selves available to modern humans are different in many ways from those

---

22 In Japanese this phenomenon is called Hikikomori and is chronicled in painful detail by Michael Zielenziger in *Shutting Out The Sun: How Japan Created Its Own Lost Generation.*

which people could choose in traditional societies. Liberal, democratic, cosmopolitan, and multiculturally-educated people arose during the Age of Enlightenment, and few modern people would want to reverse history and return to more homogeneous cultures. However, as discussed in the Introduction, many people today find the strictures of religion and even of theocracy quite attractive, and I believe their distrust of, or even disgust with, modern cultures comes from more than just the "loose morals" or material over-indulgence of people in modern societies. This rejection of modernism is also linked to a desire for authenticity.

The Existentialists were correct in seeing that many people don't necessarily embrace the openness of modern choice and experience it as oppressive rather than liberating. But a further clue to the rejection of modernism by many people is to note that people in traditional societies were authentic without struggling with most of the kinds of problems moderns face as a result of being "set free" from the dictates of thick cultures. One way to comprehend this seeming contradiction among historians of ideas such as Taylor, Appiah, and Tallis is to note the admiration anthropologists have had for people in many traditional societies. For example, many descriptions of the behavior of Sioux warriors at the Battle of the Little Bighorn indicate that they chose individually whether, when, and how to join the battle against Custer's forces. Even though the Indians won that battle, this individuality probably helped defeat their nations in the larger war against a central-command-following American army. Many accounts go on to admire these "mystic warriors of the plains"[23] as among the strongest, most upright, disciplined…in short, some of the most magnificent humans who ever lived.

---

23 See the massive volume by Thomas E. Mails, *The Mystic Warriors of the Plains.*

The "father of American anthropology," Franz Boas, tells a similar story about his experiences among Canadian Eskimos on Baffin Island. He spent a winter observing their amazing adaptations to life in a land most of us would consider totally inhospitable and he came away with a firm belief that humans are the same everywhere. Boas argued for the "psychic unity of mankind," a belief that all humans have the same intellectual capacity, and that all cultures are based on the same basic mental principles. Variations in custom and belief, he argued, are the products of historical accidents. In a film about Boas's discoveries, *The Shackles of Tradition* (1986), the filmmakers make the crucial point that *if* tradition places "shackles" on people, in the future others will see that our own culture, even with its emphasis on autonomy, also puts "shackles" on us. I believe, however, the point should be put in quite different terms. Much of why we consider social conditioning and structures to be shackles is because we see the world through the lens of autonomy and independence. The obvious general problem with this common but very wrongheaded desire to escape from social conditioning is that if we were to succeed in eliminating all social influences we would not become humans. We would be biologically human animals, but we would not be human beings with our language, religion, sophisticated emotions, reasoning, advanced technology, and science...in other words, our civilization.

What immersion in a thick culture means is that your identity is not greatly in doubt because the values, stories, beliefs, and myths that carry this identity are not in doubt. Being genuine (a true warrior, good Indian mother, spouse) does not involve the doubt, confusion, and choice that greet modern children and youth (and many adults) as today they navigate the tricky shoals toward mature adulthood.[24] No doubt sometimes it was difficult for pre-modern people to remain true to the commitments and values which formed their cultural ideals (they were, after all, as most American anthropologists following Boas assert, fully human); but knowing and affirming those ideals, and internalizing them as one's own, was not. And that, perhaps, is the key to comprehending why authenticity is so problematic for modern humans. We have added a dimension of choosing our identities over and above the inevitable difficulties of being true to who and where we find ourselves. For us the more difficult first step is *deciding* who we are, which, as we will see, turns out to be awfully like the proverbial paradox of pulling yourself up by your bootstraps.

I believe this added layer of difficulty modern humans have becoming authentic accounts for a very important aspect of the philosophizing about authenticity you find among Existentialists and Phenomenologists. Mike Martin, in the introduction to his collection of essays on self-deception, makes the very revealing claim that "…some degree of self-awareness is a prerequisite for being a self at all."[25] Other writers in the Continental tradition make a similar point in a variety ways. Think of Dostoevsky's miserable Underground Man, who is afflicted with hyper-self-consciousness and is proverbially inauthentic, or the incredible journey to become self-aware Nietzsche's Zarathustra makes on his road to becoming an *Übermensch*, or the painful self-awareness of several of Sartre's characters as they attempt, always unsuccessfully, to escape the temptations of bad faith. But surely it is silly to say that an un-self-reflective person is not a self. In fact, it might be easier not only to be a self, but to be an authentic one, precisely if

---

24 A sad but telling irony is that today many American Indians have serious identity problems as a result of the decimation of their traditional cultures and the allures of modern culture to people living in such grinding poverty.

25 Mike W. Martin, ed., *Self-Deception and Self-Understanding*, 5

your situation does *not* require radical self-consciousness, if becoming a genuine self is not made difficult by so many "existential" choices. What this tradition of historians probably has right is that in order to come to a clear, mature, and strong self in a modern pluralistic society you must do a great deal of self-reflection, and that is the heart of why authenticity is an issue for us today in ways it was not in the past.

The Centrality of the Self

Clearly if we are to comprehend authenticity we must comprehend the self. I believe a useful first frame to put on this complex and much-studied phenomenon is to propose a continuum from essentialism to constructivism with a variety of views in between. Essentialists believe that there is a deep, inner core self that, although it may have to be discovered (Plato talks about re-collecting one's knowledge, experiences, self), is there from birth. Thus the process of becoming one's self is to uncover or re-member (Plato again) our true nature and not be distracted or tempted by false identities. Ironically, perhaps, genetic determinism is a variation on this thesis from theories of the soul as it claims our true identity is pre-set—cosmologically for soul theorists, by nature for genetic determinists. You can see why this position is attractive if you consider that some people are born with musical or mathematical talents, some are introverts while others are extroverts, still others are natural athletes, and so on. Everyone seems to be born with a set of predispositions that include character traits, talents, and aptitudes as well as physical features.

At the other pole are perspectives that emphasize the role of culture in identity formation, with deconstructionists perhaps being the most extreme. This tradition emphasizes how differently people turn out based on where and when they live and what they experience in their time and place. Most constructivists do not deny the role of "nature" in determining identity, but given a native ability in mathematics, athletics, piano playing, and so forth, how that orientation plays out depends mainly on how one's culture "constructs" identities. You can see the attractiveness of this kind of position if you think of the differences between people with particular orientations or abilities across cultures and history. One of the things postmodernists seem to be claiming when they say there is no self at all is that insofar as people have identities they are "unreal" in the sense that they are "merely" constructs. In other words, they want to emphasize how mistaken they believe essentialists are.

Before turning to the disputes between these dichotomous positions, it is instructive to see what they have in common. Both poles on this continuum recognize that identities are always in the process of becoming, of turning potentialities into actualities, even as a person ages. The essentialist might believe there is a true, inner core self, but the process of revealing that self has no end (unless perhaps enlightenment is that moment). There is always another illusion or layer to peel away. Constructivists, of course, view the self as a project perpetually under construction. Furthermore, both sides agree that human development unfolds in typical or predictable fashion. Developmental psychologists tell us that the three broad phases of moral development—pre-conventional, conventional, post-conventional—are programmed to occur at age-specific times. This predictability was driven home to me when my son Carl noted, the very day he turned six, that my having driven through a yellow light was against the law. Before then he was learning the conventions of our society, but he was typically pre-conventional in that he often ignored society's boundaries. From that fateful day on, he became rather rigid in his commitment to following the rules, offering living proof that the switch from pre-conventional morality to the conventional stage happens around six years of age and can happen suddenly. (Once he became a teenager, of course, all that changed again![26] But you would expect this as a person naturally morphs into the post-conventional stage where youths are searching for the underpinnings of the rules of society and morality.)

The larger point I am trying to make is that even positions at the poles of this continuum are not as rigid or contrary as it might appear on first examination. Essentialists realize that the particularities of one's experiences have a great deal to do with how someone's self unfolds, and constructivists do not totally deny the role of nature in shaping identity. Often words can seem to draw lines in the sand that are misleading or non-existent. Buddhists, like Daoists and many postmodernists (and also Hume), contend that there is *no self*—the famous Buddhist doctrine of *anatta*. If you study Buddhist writings, however, it turns out that what they are trying to do with this doctrine is weaken people's commitments to the ego, to make people less self-centered, and to open people to identification or union with "all beings." They are not denying that people have unique and lifelong fingerprints or personality characteristics, nor are they denying social identities; instead, they believe they are being objective in denying an inner essence that is unchanging throughout life. For Buddhists, the self is malleable (a construction, or as Existentialists say, a project) and too strong a commitment to a particular self over time can stultify growth and render people out of touch with reality—including their own changing inner or personal realities.

The western philosophical tradition that begins with Hume and extends to deconstructionism, actually assumes that the essentialist definition of the self is true and then denies that humans can be one.

---

26 In *Emile*, Rousseau says that the onslaught of puberty throws you back to "zero" again.

Their goal is to deny, in the strongest terms, the "ghost in the machine," the unverifiable, non-material self—the soul—of the essentialists. In place of reifying (thing-ifying) the soul/self, this contrarian tradition says that we are only a set of characteristics (the Buddhist bundles of perceptions, emotions, desires, sensations, and so forth) that changes continually as new ideas, feelings, and so on pass through our awareness. For these thinkers the problem they want to prevent is not so much egoism as it is the damage done through false belief. Whole metaphysical, religious, and ethical systems, they contend, have been constructed around false beliefs in the transcendental or non-material self, and such beliefs have been at the heart of stultifying systems and practices that have prevented intellectual and scientific progress.

While I disagree with the strong view that says there is no self of any kind, I do believe Buddhists and others are on to a very important re-orientation of our self understanding. Whether we examine people through social scientific lenses or through the lenses of our own or other's experiences, I believe there is no doubt that on a nature/nurture continuum the accurate description is "in-between."[27] We clearly inherit, through our genes, a great deal of what gives us our identity, and we clearly gain much of our identities through culture. Exactly how much of our identity comes from these two general sources is impossible to quantify and probably differs with each person, and thus the most helpful perspectives might be metaphors such as Nietzsche's block of marble. This simple metaphor says that we should view ourselves as a work of art in progress, as if we were a block of marble (nature) that is carved, for the most part, by others (nurture) by the time we are self-aware enough to take over some small part of the carving ourselves (self-development—using inherited tools, of course). The

---

27 "In-between" is Katrin Froese's label for a perspective she believes several Existentialists share with Daoists. See her *Nietzsche, Heidegger and Daoist Thought*.

marble sets serious limits on the work of art (self) that might emerge, and any good sculptor realizes the importance of working with what is given (many sculptors say the object that emerges was "in" the marble, that you cannot create something that isn't already there). Two further crucial insights emerge from this homey metaphor. First, if we are "carved" by the wrong person, or in the wrong way, or at the wrong time, or with the wrong tools we will be less magnificent than we might have been—parents and educators beware! Second, if we take an artist's approach to our children, students or selves, we probably will get very different results than if we use, say, a scientific or technological metaphor. Think of the differences it would make if instead of a person being a work of art you viewed child-rearing and creation of a self as a matter of proper "programming" or of rigorous science-based training. The choice of a basic approach to the project of self creation in itself has profound implications for what selves get created.

Philosopher J. Baird Callicott makes a similar point in comparing and contrasting the atomistic and mechanistic view of nature and humans with an ecological one. He says that the former view paints a picture of a

> natural environment consisting of a collection of bodies composed of molecular aggregates of atoms. A living natural body is in principle a very elaborate machine. That is, its generation, gestation, development, decay, and death can be exhaustively explained reductively and mechanically. Some of these natural machines are mysteriously inhabited by a conscious monad, a "ghost-in-the-machine".[28]

In contrast, Callicott says, ecology, like the new physics, talks of "fields" in which entities are moments in a network and where "...a

---

28 "The Metaphysical Implications of Ecology" (*Environmental Ethics*, vol. 8, 1986, pp. 301-16). Reprinted in David R. Keller, ed., *Environmental Ethics: The Big Questions*, 402.

thing's essence is exhaustively determined by its relationships [and it] cannot be conceived apart from its relationships with other things [in that network]." Seen from this perspective, "...individual organisms are less discrete objects than modes of a continuous, albeit differentiated whole, the distinction between self and others is blurred."[29]

The Self (and Thus Authenticity) as "In Between"

There is always some accident in the best things, whether thoughts or expressions or deeds. The memorable thought, the happy expression, the admirable deed are only partly ours. The thought came to us because we were in a fit mood; also we were unconscious and did not know that we had said or done a good thing. We must walk consciously only part way toward our goal, and then leap in the dark to our success. —Thoreau, Journal entry, March 11, 1858

The in-between perspective, found especially in Daoism, but also in many process philosophies, emphasizes process and change, not permanence or essence. This is true not just with selves, but with all reality. Froese contends that the Daoists, like Nietzsche and Heidegger, believe that all things are fleeting and relational, and that ultimate reality is unknowable. Being itself is unknowable because we are limited and because it is not static. Heidegger uses another metaphor in thinking about the process of knowing things in the world—it is a dialogue (dance) with things themselves that breaks down the subject/object dichotomy (our second dualism denied, the first being nature/nurture). He believes that the fundamental reality we experience is the *world*, in contrast with the *earth*[30]: the former is the lived world that is meaning-

---

29 Ibid., 405

30 See especially Golomb's chapter on Heidegger.

ful as we experience it (Kant's phenomena), while the latter is being itself, as it is in and of itself (Kant's noumena). However, because the world involves our "subjective" meanings does not mean that it is *merely* subjective. The dance with reality is an ongoing process of revelation, of meaningful unfolding of a world which, although always limited, is rich in meaning and ever-changing truth. For him, thinking is a kind of *attunement* brought about by, as well as originating in, a reality that reaches out to us as much as we to it—he says we are "thrown" into a world not of our making, but that calls us to respond.[31] If we do not despair that we cannot know ultimate reality and do not believe that only such knowledge is true knowledge, then life is continually fascinating, enticing, enchanting. Heidegger's perspective can help us learn to be at home again in a world of which we are so small a part.

Heidegger gives us very suggestive metaphors and often uses language in new ways. He has been roundly criticized by more analytic philosophers for his dense writing and heavy use of poetic language, but if he is correct, such usage sometimes not only is the best anyone can do, but it is also exactly what we need to do in order to be liberated from the metaphysical and other conceptual straightjackets in which we are encased. Froese believes that classical Daoists, and especially Zhuangzi (Chuang Tzu), can clarify and add to Heidegger's and Nietzsche's thinking, particularly in relation to the self and its authenticity.

Like Heidegger, Bugbee, Taylor and others, the Daoists emphasize process. Everything in the world, including the human self, is continually changing, in motion. This underlying dimension of reality requires us to recognize that the self is developed and never complete

---

31 The sixth and final chapter of this book is about "calling," an idea which is very much in keeping with Heidegger's emphasis on thrownness and attunement, but one which I will approach more through Kierkegaard's image of choices along life's way.

or final and that various sources contribute to its unfolding. The self happens in motion *in between*. Furthermore, just as Heidegger tries to dissolve the metaphysical dualisms of nature/nurture and subject/object, Zhuangzi contends that freedom and necessity (our third dualism) are not at loggerheads. For him, as for most Daoists, freedom is attained by attuning ourselves to nature. Experientially, we feel unfree when we try to push against the forces of nature. Freedom comes when what we want coincides with what is. This does not mean that a person can only be free if they live apart from society. This Daoist principle agrees with my intuition discussed in chapter three that being at home in nature is part of being human. While we are social beings through and through and would not be a human self without culture, a fundamental source of our inauthenticity is being out of touch with nature in and around us. Our society gives us tools, linguistic and otherwise, to comprehend and deal with the realities into which we are born or are thrust. But as we will explore in chapter five, we are also given "tools" by nature, many of which are non-conscious, and if we are not aware of ourselves as natural beings we cannot truly know ourselves or be at home in the world. As natural beings our world includes nature not as a resource to be exploited but as the place where much of our identities lie.

In a way, Daoism does intersect with essentialism. To be inauthentic is to be out of touch with who we are, and, as I will argue in chapter six, the path to authenticity is a pilgrimage to our roots where the route necessarily takes us through the wilderness of our deep biological past. Remember, though, that for the Daoist (as well as for Nietzsche and Heidegger) who we are is not an eternal essence, an unchanging self that lies like a golden nugget at our core. Rather, who we are is a work of art in process and is often best discovered (glimpsed) by being away from the distractions of the crowd. Here, though, we come to one of the greatest difficulties for this in-between philosophy: if to a significant extent we are forged in, through, and by culture/others, why must we escape them to find and be our true selves? Especially if our "true" selves are fleeting social creations?

A Narrative Theory of the Self

Bugbee[32] emphasizes that what is most important is being authentic, not being original, unique, or fancy (or fanciful). The first crucial step is to be in touch with reality (Heidegger's "world," if not "reality itself"). In a strong sense, this is a matter of "getting our stories straight." The world we can (and do) know comes to us as meaningful, and meaning is carried in *narratives*, stories in a broad sense. Scientists tell us stories about how the world works, how it was created, what will happen if, and so on; "common sense" is a set of generally accepted story lines about a wide variety of things; and certainly religion brings its powerful meanings through stories. One way to put the Buddhist contention that there is no self is the postmodernist contention that the self is a collection of narratives. The self *is* narrative in its basic structure. With Hume, the Buddhist view of the self is an empirical claim: if you examine the content of your experience you will never find a self. Instead, what you will find is an ever-changing set of impressions, beliefs, emotions, etc. Postmodernists add the idea that we constantly and automatically weave this raw material of experience into a set of *stories* about our health, our relationships, our place in the world, our desires and needs, our value and identity, and so on.

Recently I had the great joy of hiking with my family in the Snowy Range in southeast Wyoming. After lunch I stretched out for a nap

---

32 See especially *Inward Morning*, 62. See also Crawford, 208

and awoke to witness a set of clouds morphing above me. My first impression was how simple and beautiful the clouds were. Then I was struck by their constant change. Finally, I began to see "faces in the clouds."[33] This brief but very pleasant experience suggested several things to me about the self, most fundamentally that it is not just the religious who see faces in the clouds, for when it comes to the self, we are very much like the clouds in several ways. First, the stuff we are made of is not unlike the water vapor that constitutes clouds. Instead of measurable substance, our selves are made of vaporous materials such as ideas, values, desires, emotions, memories—the so-called aggregates of the Buddhists. That doesn't make the self *unreal* (unless reality must have weight and extension), but it does make it *ethereal*. Second, like those mountain clouds our selves are constantly in flux as the content of our experience shifts from one idea, emotion, desire, memory, sensation, or value to another. In a very real sense, our self is different at every moment, and one strong implication of this reality is that there is no inner core, real me to find. Except that—and this is my third point—just as I automatically began seeing faces in the clouds, we constantly and automatically are making meaning of all we experience including our selves. Perhaps this constant self-interpretation is what Mike Martin had in mind when he asserted that one cannot be a self unless she is self-conscious, but the curious thing is that just as we have to catch ourselves making meaning of the clouds or other aspects of our experience, the same is true with regard to the

33 Anthropologist Stewart Guthrie bases his theory of religion on this metaphor. See his *Faces in the Clouds: A New Theory of Religion.*

self. For the most part, we make meanings of our selves, we concoct the story of our selves *un*-self consciously.[34]

According to Bugbee, in order to put together the truest stories, we must approach the world with openness and humility, we must strive to be as objective and honest as possible. This is very difficult. Nietzsche said that intellectual honesty is the most difficult action we face. Why? Not only because we can never know reality itself, but precisely because we are storied beings. For if the world comes to us as storied, the allure of any given story line can distract us from seeking the (or a) true (or best or most honest) one. A first temptation is relativism. In Heidegger's *world*—the one in which I believe we all live—we are tempted to say that any story line is as good as any other one. Or at least we contend that there is no way to prove that a given story is false. But surely the lessons of modernism not only warn us about believing we know an absolute or eternal truth—they also teach us that we can sort out stories according to which ones are better or worse or more or less true. Your life might include chronic pain or a difficult decision, but the story line that you are worse off than anyone else alive surely is a self-pitying exaggeration that is not true and will not serve you well.[35]

We have already introduced a second temptation, self-deception. We are tempted to choose a false story line in order to protect ourselves or make life easier *for ourselves*. The trick, of course, is that the

34 Martha Nussbaum, in *The Fragility of Goodness. Luck and Ethics in Greek Tragedy and Philosophy*, contends that we must become like writers creating characters in novels. See also Nussbaum, "Finely Aware and Richly Responsible: Moral Attention and the Moral Task of Literature" (*The Journal of Philosophy*, 1985, 515-29).

35 In his critique of MacIntyre's and Nussbaum's narrative theories of the self, Rudiger Bender ("The Aesthetics of Ethical Reflection and the Ethical Significance of Aesthetic Experience: A Critique of Alasdair MacIntyre and Martha Nussbaum," EESE 1/1998, 1-15) charges these two contemporary philosophers with the inability to provide substantive goods because of the infinite possibilities for imaginative variation in modern works of art, be they novels, paintings or selves. We will return to this challenge shortly.

label, self-deception, makes it sound as if we are lying to ourselves (we are both liar and lyee), which is a logical impossibility. As many of the essays in Martin's book on self-deception contend, the label is not accurate to what occurs in our attempts to avoid being honest about ourselves as a way of guarding against unwanted pain, humiliation, difficulty, or effort. The idea of the narrative self can help reveal how we can do this for it is much easier to ignore reality when we are in the grip of a plausible (but false) story. Remember, in a world where reality comes to us storied, any given narrative can be meaningful even if it is not true (or not accurate in this situation). If I was in excellent physical shape in high school because I was an active athlete and could eat most anything I desired in great quantities without it affecting my health, continuing that story line through my more sedentary freshman year of college probably will result in gaining the infamous "freshman 15" that will remain and grow as long as I continue telling myself the story that I am in top physical shape and that my metabolism remains constant. I am sorely tempted to continue telling myself this increasingly false story because facing the realities of ageing would mean some serious adjustments in my actions; and after all, my narrative isn't entirely false when you examine my physical condition compared to many others and to myself several years down the road should I fail to change my story now.

Stories seem like a flimsy hook on which to hang something as important as our identities. Not only can we be tempted by "self-deception" or the siren call of relativism, but our stories can be misread, stolen/borrowed/copied, revised endlessly, or hidden in a drawer. Surely this way of thinking about our selves is fraught with as many difficulties as essentialism or the no-self! Happily, sometimes seeming weaknesses can also be strengths. If you think about it, we are continually modifying our life stories, we do indeed copy others (children need role models, we all need mentors, etc.), many people's stories are poorly written or they have poor scripts ("grade-B lives"), and so on. The narrative view, therefore, is attractive because it lends itself to comprehending important features of becoming and being a self that essentialism and its denial overlook. If what we said earlier about the ubiquity of self-consciousness in today's world is true, Nussbaum's likening self formation to writing a novel seems especially relevant. To write the stories of our lives well we must examine carefully the many interpretations of the narratives we might choose.

Interpreting Stories of Our Selves

Optimism is not about whistling happy tunes to ourselves when life gets challenging. It is about disciplining our minds to create more empowering explanations of what's going on.
—*Martin Seligman*

Nietzsche offers a second simple but powerful metaphor for the process of becoming authentic in his famous image of development, in *Thus Spoke Zarathustra*: we must first be a camel, then a lion, and finally a child. The camel is the quintessential beast of burden that is willing to take up the task of checking the stories. Nietzsche challenges us, though, not only to learn our own stories, but to study stories from across cultures and history. He challenges us to become very well educated indeed! Thus, while the first and most difficult step in becoming authentic is to check our stories for accuracy, honesty, and meaning, Nietzsche realizes that part of getting to the truest stories is to know them all so that we have the capacity to choose ones that are most meaningful and inspiring as well as most true. This is the second step. It involves judgment and above all, courage. That's where the lion comes in. We must have the courage of the lion to sort through the acquired stories to determine which ones ring true and which do not because in the process we might have to abandon our favorite or most comforting stories.

But abandonment often is not permanent. The proverbial adolescent rejection of religion often turns out to be rejection of a child-ish version of religion and is a prerequisite for becoming faithful as an adult with a deeper and more mature understanding of the less true *version* of religion we held as a child. An old proverb says that in order to learn something important we must first *un*learn a less sophisticated version of the same story. Harvard social psychologist Howard Gardner[36] contends that much of formal education involves such unlearning. He and others give many examples of how difficult prying our children (or ourselves) from our favorite but less true stories can be. For example, most Americans want to believe that we live in a nation that is exceptional in many ways, especially regarding features such as our commitment to human rights. It was very disconcerting when we learned that our soldiers and special agents were systematically torturing prisoners in Abu Ghraib and Guantanamo, and our initial impulse was denial. Much of climate change denial follows the same arc: upon hearing that our entire way of life is implicated in global warming, we are loathe to change that story and we try various forms of rationalization to deny the necessity to change it.

Besides better stories about reality, according to such learning theorists, what everyone should be learning is the art and science of *hermeneutics*, of interpretation. When you gain a sophisticated ability to interpret stories you gain the ability to sort varied stories into kinds and to see where and when they have their greatest and best

---

36 Howard Gardner makes this point in much of his writing. See especially *The Unschooled Mind: How Children Think and How Schools Should Teach.*

use. Much of our ability to judge reality is tied up with our ability to decipher story types as well as to interpret particular stories, and in the process we gain the ability to sort out truth and deepen meaning. We will return to this point in more depth in chapter six.

Unfortunately, many people today are caught in a second trap I call "absolute relativism." As we become adept at sorting stories and realize that all stories contain some truth, we conclude that there is no way to discern if any stories are any better than others. This is a version of the two temptations we just discussed. It results from a too-simplistic, or perhaps too pessimistic, view of our abilities to sort out relative truths. While all experience is a function of the complex interplay (dance) of our stories and reality, some stories are *more* satisfactory than others in a given context. Philosophers and others have the difficult task not only of sorting out kinds of stories and hermeneutic strategies for interpreting them, but they also have to determine scales of satisfactoriness. It is easy to overestimate the difficulty of this task and to give people a dark view of our prospects for finding truth, however fleeting (Heidegger coins the term "truthing" to make the point that we can come to momentary truths). This is why we must pay attention to Nietzsche's third phase, the child. This is no ordinary child. It is the *wise* child, one who has gone through the rigors of disciplined, far-ranging, difficult long-term education and has discerned which stories, and which aspects of stories, ring true and has discarded the remainder (or at least shelved them to be used later, as Merleau-Ponty suggests). The wise child continues to bear the burdens of history, both personal and more broadly, but she does so with equanimity, balance, and joy. This, of course, is where Nietzsche introduces his famous doctrine of eternal recurrence. Nietzsche says that to truly accept reality is to be willing to welcome an endless repeat of the history of the world. While I believe Nietzsche's impulse is the correct one—we must become like a child—I think that eternal recurrence is the wrong kind of doctrine. Yes, we should embrace the world, celebrate it, take joy in it, and accept it. But no, I do not believe this means we have to be willing to say that we must embrace everything that happened exactly as it happened. I am not saying we should deny reality or only love the good things the world offers up. Rather, it is the *tone* of Nietzsche's metaphor that is problematic. Eternal recurrence is too ponderous and, ironically coming from the arch enemy of metaphysics, too metaphysical. What is needed is something more like the playfulness of the Daoist version of the wise child, the sage.

IX. The Wise Child

Where there is no vision, the people perish.
—Proverbs 29:18

It is a great art to saunter.—Thoreau

Nietzsche's Zarathustra and Heidegger's authentic man strive; Zhuangzi's sage wanders aimlessly.[37] The sage "self-overcomes" by being open, not through struggle, and he tries to foster harmonious relationships. Zarathustra wanders because he is not at home anywhere. The sage is at home everywhere. The sage is joyful because he lives in the moment and is interconnected to everything. The authentic person of the Existentialists is always dissatisfied, longing for home. The sage, unlike the Western ideal of authenticity through autonomy, does not establish his particularity *against* others but in harmony with them. The sage is open, mirrors reality, is filled with know-how. The sage delights in the realities of the moment, in the small but substan-

---

37 See Froese's discussion of these contrasts, 97-110.

tive meanings of everyday life rather than having to find great meaning in doctrines such as the eternal recurrence.

Nietzsche, by insisting that we must embrace this doctrine, is railing against the night. He is shouting his rebellion against the nihilism with which we are left at the death of God[38]—a metaphysical response to the death of (religious) metaphysics. The sage seeks intensity and meaning in the everyday world while Nietzsche pushes heroism, striving, and nobility as the only antidote to bourgeois mediocrity. It is no wonder that Nietzsche decries the quiet virtues of Christianity such as humility, faithfulness, and meekness! And it is no wonder that the history of the search for authenticity in the West focuses on self-discovery, self-development, and self-expression—the quest for authenticity has taken on a nearly narcissistic cast in contrast to the quiet, joyful, interconnected wandering of the Daoist sage. Zarathustra seeks authenticity through autonomy, while the Daoist sage seeks it through equanimity wherever she is.

I believe Tenzin Gyasto, the current Dalai Lama,[39] is a living example of the Daoist sage. Here is a man who has seen great tragedy and suffering. During his rein as the 14th Dalai Lama of Tibet he has seen his people killed, tortured, and exiled, his nation dissolved, and his civilization decimated. He resides over a small group of his diaspora in exile in Dharamsala in northern India. Yet he has not lost his faith or his joy of life. He continues to work not only for reconciliation with the Chinese people and government, but his work for world peace won him a Nobel Prize in 1989. How does he continue

---

38 Albert Camus follows Nietzsche in his rebellion against the absurdity of life (lack or death of the grand narrative around which we can organize our lives). Camus' works are focused on this theme: *Resistance, Rebellion and Death; The Plague; The Stranger; The Myth of Sisyphus.* See Golomb's chapter on Camus.

39 For details of his life, beliefs and current activities, see his official website: www. dalailama.com/

his efforts, given the tragic history of his people since 1949, with such equanimity? Clearly his advanced Buddhist abilities and knowledge (his enlightenment) make him a poster child for this tradition, but for our purposes I want to focus on how he is a wise child.

From all indications, the Dalai Lama is joyful while remaining fully aware of the tragedies of his tradition and of the rest of the world. He would love to help his people and culture return to Tibet and works tirelessly and creatively to that end. But many people who have met him comment that he seems fully at home in Dharamsala or wherever he travels. He seems to find great joy in everyday experiences and is notorious for his hearty laugh and playfulness. This Dalai Lama is also noted for his great learning and especially for his scientific curiosity and his willingness to change his perspective when he finds his previous beliefs to be false. *If* he has metaphysical beliefs parallel to Nietzsche's eternal recurrence, two standard Buddhist ideas stand out. The first is his belief in reincarnation. The second is the idea of dependent origination, our interconnectedness with everything that is. I have not found these standard Buddhist doctrines to play the same kind of heavy role as Nietzsche's crushing burden of eternal recurrence. Instead, the Dalai Lama uses the idea of reincarnation to emphasize how fortunate we are to be born human with our incredible abilities to know and to appreciate the world. Dependent origination is at the center of his embracing all people and nature as integrally interrelated.

The Role of Community and Place

In contrast, for the Germans, including Nietzsche and Heidegger, the key to authenticity is autonomous self development, and as we have seen, this path can lead to egoism and even narcissism. Many commentators have remarked how the Existentialists, and modern humanists more generally, replaced the Medieval quest for union with God with the quest for full humanity. Much good has come of this epic transformation. We should not deny or bewail the great art, medicine, or political and material improvements from which we all benefit. Nevertheless, something seems to have gone awry as the noble ideals of Nietzsche's *Übermensch* or Heidegger's authentic man morphed into characters such as Camus' stranger, Mersault. Mersault seeks to be his own person (authenticity as autonomy) and rejects the guidelines, rules, laws, institutions, and restrictions of his society. Perhaps he achieves his goals too well in that he is put to death (symbolically and literally) for not crying at his mother's funeral because he did not feel like it. While Mersault is not Dostoevsky's Underground Man, Camus shows his connections to Dostoevsky in that his (anti-) hero is almost totally self-absorbed in seeking to be a self-made man and as a result his life is meaningless except for this dubious accomplishment. As well, unlike the Dalai Lama, Camus' Sisyphus is intentionally disconnected and tries to find whatever meaning life has to offer through his heroic struggles against the system.[40]

While Camus' characters are very admirable in their Stoic struggles, it is not difficult to see that their self-absorption can easily lead to the many self-development strategies or other unattractive forms of self-absorption spilling from our culture today. In the introduction to this book and again in chapter two we discussed some of the ways in which the so-called self-help movement has been less than helpful to people. While the success of self-help gurus and products highlight the great desire for authenticity in our culture, the amazing amount of money and time spent on following a self-help expert or regimen mainly lines the pockets of people like Oprah and Dr. Phil, but does

---

40 Phil Cousineau, in chapter one of his book, *Once and Future Myths*, has a wonderful discussion of Camus' *Myth of Sisyphus* as a story we can learn from and live by.

not address the underlying causes of inauthenticity. We are now in a position to see more clearly why self-help is, as I suggested earlier, like pulling yourself up by your proverbial bootstraps.

If becoming and being real is a function of developing and acting from a relatively coherent and integrated self (or perhaps said in a clearer way, making and sticking with important commitments), then people should be working to establish strong and lasting webs of relationships and building communities rather than turning inward to "find themselves." While the advice of self-help counselors to find, pamper, and celebrate yourself is not bad in itself, if I am correct in claiming that people living in *thick* cultures were pretty much automatically authentic while those of us in *thin* cultures are plagued with inauthenticity, then turning inward is a textbook case of looking in the wrong place for the wrong thing. Perhaps examples such as the Dalai Lama are misleading because they make it seem like what is needed is heroic devotion to meditation, regular therapy, or visits with a spiritual director, or some other self-help method. What people often fail to comprehend is that strong people emerge from strong communities and that those who attain great heights typically are born with extraordinary talents into strong families and communities and they receive guidance from others who are steeped in a strong cultural tradition.

Bernard Williams[41] warns us not to make too strong a distinction between the modern and pre-modern worlds in terms of the problem of authenticity. Insofar as this problem results from the loss of thick cultures due to the breakdown of tradition from plagues, wars, trade, or the growing cosmopolitanism we have witnessed since the sixteenth century, you can also find plenty of pre-modern locales where cultures

41 *Truth and Truthfulness: An Essay in Genealogy.*

were thinned by the same forces. If Williams is correct, we might well gain significant insight about authenticity by examining what is involved in the authentic being of people in pre-modern societies. Rather than pursue examples from anthropology, I propose to use the descriptions by a contemporary Apache philosopher, V.F. Cordova, which beautifully compare and contrast her Native American culture with modern western ones.

Cordova asserts boldly that humans are made and do not have essences. She is a communalist who believes "there are no individual realities, only communal ones."[42] Like Daoists, she contends that change is the fundamental reality and that everything is interrelated which means that in the life of an individual human "we" is more fundamental than "I." Put differently, Cordova claims that for the Apache personal identity is totally bound up with group identity, and thus the more you can describe a culture (thick description) the more you will learn about an individual. She says that children must be taught to be human, and being human is specific to a group and context:

> "The child must be socialized into a particular pattern of behavior that is understood to be specific to the group of which he is a member. The pattern consists of showing what is involved in living within a community of others. Paramount in this involvement is how one's actions affect the others [including the non-human world of which we are an integral part]....A fundamental assumption is that humans are not fully human when they come into this world....Thus with the assistance of the entire group, the child learns to become a human being according to how the group defines a human being."[43]

---

42 Cordova, 49
43 Ibid., 81

She later puts it this way:

> *"What makes humans human is the recognition that the individual is a part of a greater whole."*[44]

A second major source of identity for the Apache, (and for all Native American groups according to Cordova) is *place*. Just as the individual is defined by his culture, a group or culture is defined by context, by where they originate and live. She asserts that Native American groups had/have a kind of ecological niche view of cultural diversity wherein each group derives its identity, health, and continued existence by living well (*sustainably*, which requires proper humility, ritual observance, and careful attention to detail) in their place (niche).

If we combine these two sources of the (Apache) self, Cordova believes that her people grow up with a strong sense of belonging within a bounded space, and this combination both gives them a deep and intimate knowledge of and respect for the limits and consequences of their actions and provides the necessary sources of very strong and authentic selves. Cordova clearly would agree with Bugbee that how we live our commitments is more fundamental to authenticity than is how we come to be the persons we are (etiology). She would add to his perspective the contention that the abilities to be true to our selves require intimate and complex interrelationships with others (both human and broader nature) into which we are "thrown."

---

44 Ibid., 168

Cordova summarizes her view of being human in a brief Credo.[45] I believe her final two assertions help to make a major point in her theory of authenticity: that authenticity and inauthenticity are *community* responsibilities. In her words,

Becoming a human is a responsibility of the group that teaches the new being [child] what it is to be human in this group of beings....He is taught to be human by showing him that he is one human among others. Because he shares the world with other beings, there is an emphasis on cooperation rather than competition; sharing rather than accumulating.[46]

For Cordova, in contrast to our individualistic culture, "...an individual, set apart from his group, can be more easily manipulated by others. He has no value except 'self-interest,'" and to create individualists, "autonomous beings," is to spawn beings who "... seem to

---

45 Cordova, 151-53. Here is an edited version. 1) Human beings are part of a whole that is greater than the individual. A human being is not something *apart* from the earth...he is a natural *part of* the Earth. 2) A human is first and foremost a 'herd being.' ... The individual has value because of his uniqueness...and because of the potential gifts he brings to the group. But the group is preeminent. The sense of "we" dominates the sense of the "I." 3) Human beings are not alone in having "intelligence." ... Wisdom, or intelligence, consists of being able to see how our actions and their consequences affect the greater whole. 4) Human beings...do not act only from instinct. 5) Humans are not "fallen" creatures; they are what the Earth intended. ... A sense of alienation from the world and its many beings...is not the common malady of individuals but a psychotic disruption, an illness. 6) A human is both spirit and nonspirit, mind and body, matter and energy at the same time.... 7) Humans are not superior to other life forms. They are simply different. .. All of the diversity, together, forms a complete whole that is what the Earth is. She is what she is "meant" to be; humans are what they are "meant" to be. 8) Humans are not "meaningless bits of cosmic dust floating about in an infinite universe." They are an integral part of the whole. 9) Humans are born "humanoid," that is, with the capacity to become "fully human" through the exercise of all their faculties. ... Humans have many qualities that must be fostered for one to become fully human ... . Becoming a human is a responsibility of the group that teaches the new being what it is to be human in this group of beings. 10) Humans, as part of a greater whole, become part of an ever-changing and ongoing process that is the universe in process of being. We have the capacity to change the course of that whole—for good or evil—through our actions.

46 Ibid., 153

spend an inordinate amount of their lifetimes trying to find out 'who they really are.'"[47] In response to a typical criticism by individualists, she argues that "A sense of oneself as a part of a greater whole does not lead to a loss of a sense of self. There is no such thing as a "herd mentality"; instead, there is a greater sense of oneself as a responsible human being."[48] For Cordova, in other words, to be most fully human is to be *interconnected* and *responsible*, to be full-fledged community members.

We have reached what is perhaps the most dramatic difference between our view of authenticity and that of most of the philosophers in Western tradition. While one's community can be the source of abstracting or distancing from reality that requires great effort to overcome, it can (must?) also be the major source of one's authenticity. For whomever we are—authentic or inauthentic—is greatly a result of the communities in which we are raised and live. Thus if we wish to enhance authentic being in our selves, children, or fellow citizens, we should give strong effort toward creating *the right kinds* of communities and narratives. The Amish, for example, have taken the hard road of selecting carefully which technologies to invite into their lives with the goal of enhancing the best social and spiritual lives possible throughout their communities. However successful they are (by many indications they are doing quite well on both counts), as we discussed in chapter three, they are much more likely to generate authentic humans than the larger society with its helter-skelter and laissez faire approaches to technology adoption and use. The same holds true for work. We have so accepted the goal of "unburdening" ourselves that we have a difficult time seeing that we are paying dearly for our comforts and conveniences in the distancing from reality, including clear

47 Ibid., 156
48 Ibid., 157

and direct responsibilities, that is common in our work and leisure. If the major sources of the self, and thus of authenticity or inauthenticity, are social, it is small wonder that at best serious individualism results in the heroic frustrations of characters like Mersault.

One of the terms people often use interchangeably with autonomy or independence is self-reliance. Matthew Crawford makes an important distinction between two senses of self-reliance. The one we are most used to hearing about is exemplified by people who try to escape society and become as independent of others as possible. Crawford's second sense of self-reliance is, as we discussed in chapter two, about "being masters of our stuff," being capable of doing many things for ourselves based on deep knowledge (especially know-how) and skills, but gaining and practicing that self-reliance in and through a supportive community. In Crawford's community, self-reliant people are interdependent with equals, with people who are also capable of skillfully taking care of most details of their lives with the support and friendships of others. A healthy community of interdependent "agents" is one filled with interlocking sets of "masters and apprentices," where people learn from others with more experience and personal knowledge how to cook and take care of children and repair broken appliances and care for a wounded dog, for example.

Crawford's descriptions of United States communities on the margins of bourgeois society are not unlike those Cordova gives of her Native American communities. His emphasis, too, is that strong, self-reliant people come from and require supportive communities. It is very important to realize that while autonomous individualism has become the trope of choice in much of our political rhetoric, we also have serious strains in our culture of the kinds of strong individuals growing from strong communities that Crawford celebrates. For even though we might admire Cordova's Apache communities or

Zhuangzi's sage, importing ways of being authentically human from other traditions is very difficult. The good news is that once you begin looking you can find countless examples to add to Crawford's motorcycle-repair communities. Think of Jefferson's ideal communities of yeoman farmers, the countless religious communities that continue to dot our land, the numerous versions of co-ops in America, or the many institutions such as churches, schools, or even some corporations where you have a clear, complex and strong mix of self-reliance and community.

One of my favorite examples is *Lars and the Real Girl*, a 2007 film set in a small Minnesota town. Often such locales are viewed as backwards and culturally vacuous, but the makers of this quiet little film understand that communities make and can remake humans. Lars is a wounded man who was raised by an incompetent father after his mother died when he was young, and he has become a painful introvert as an adult. In his attempt to break out of his isolated shell Lars buys a blow-up doll that he fantasizes to be real—he talks to her, takes her on dates, gives her baths, and generally takes care of her as if she was alive. After their initial disbelief and no small amount of making fun of Lars's fantasy world, the townspeople show their love by playing along with Lars's illusion with the result that eventually Lars is able to "kill" the doll and fully enter the world of real people. Through small acts of kindness the community helps Lars become the person he inchoately imagined. Good communities are the spawning grounds of authentic humans.

In-Between…Once More

One of the central features of Crawford's attempt to re-valorize manual labor and craftsmanship is his distinction between conceptual and personal knowledge, or between knowing *that* and knowing *how*. He contends that for most people much of the time personal knowledge is more important than theoretical knowledge, and that much of society runs on the creating, building, repairing, care-taking, and healing of people's know-how. Especially in this age of high-powered science and technology. Crawford contends that we tend to devalue the concrete but sophisticated knowledge of the craftsman and lionize the abstract knowledge of the scientist or intellectual.

Because every day I encounter the victims of the devaluing of manual labor, I tend to agree with Crawford. Nevertheless, I believe his epistemological either/or is mistaken. While there are significant ways that these two kinds of knowledge are different, at the very least they are complexly interrelated in everyday life, whether it is among working scientists or repairmen. Much has been written about how much scientific progress has depended on technological innovation, and any visitor to a research laboratory cannot help but notice how the ability to discover new conceptual knowledge is borne on the backs of lab technicians and engineers. In like manner, while the master repairman needs to know in his fingertips how to lay a carpet, or hang a door, or repair a combine or a computer, the materials they work with/on depend on similar technicians and ultimately on sophisticated conceptual knowledge of chemistry or physics. In a sense, they meet in the middle. Neither the theoretical scientists nor the master craftsman need to have each other's knowledge to a full extent, but each depends on the other in many ways.

One way to characterize these two kinds of knowledge is to talk about third- and first-person knowing. Ken Wilber[49] has long championed a simple but very helpful matrix to categorize kinds of knowledge. Think of a grid with third-person knowledge and perspectives on the left and first-person on the right, and add to that a singular and a plural column (singular on top and plural on the bottom). Wilber claims that everything can be comprehended from these four quadrants, but let us focus on a less controversial claim—that at least humans and other higher animals can be. Furthermore, we can learn a great deal about ourselves by looking through lenses from each quadrant. We can, of course, learn a great deal about ourselves and our worlds through first-person singular (I) perspectives, but the same is true if we take on first-person plural (we) frameworks and reports as well. Many of the founding stories of our selves are narratives of our families or groups. Anyone who has read social or natural scientific studies of humans, whether seen as individuals or as members of a group, realizes how much we can learn from those (you) stories as well.

Wilber's point isn't simply the obvious but crucial observation that we can learn a great deal through narratives from each of these quarters, but the deeper idea that we consist of stories from each. They are *constitutive.* The truths from each perspective can come in many forms (for example, fictional accounts can carry great first-person insights, and photographs can likewise add to our third-person perspectives),

---

49 Ken Wilber is a prolific independent scholar who attempts to integrate knowledge from across time, cultures and disciplines, and many of his titles indicate the range of his scholarship and what he integrates. Do not be put off by his pretentious titles as he is one of the most suggestive, interdisciplinary and brilliant thinkers alive today. The matrix of knowledge I am using to talk about the self as in-between can be found in many of his works, but I suggest the following in particular: *A Brief History of Everything, Integral Psychology: Consciousness, Spirit, Psychology, Therapy,* and *A Theory of Everything: An Integral Vision for Business, Politics, Science and Spirituality.*

and we *integrate* these frames in complex ways as we weave our selves. Wilber, in short, is giving us another way to see the in-between nature of the self that can be particularly helpful in understanding Cordova and Crawford's contention that we are *both* individual and collective, a unique self and a member of a group. Everyone always is involved in this integrative process of being formed by and choosing or adapting narratives from each quadrant, and the amazing thing is how seamlessly and mainly unconsciously we do so.

If Wilber is correct, then people raised in the strongest version of collectivism also integrate first-person stories into their selves, and the most ardent individualist, in like measure, integrates third-person and first-person "we" features into her/his self narrative. The question is not whether this happens, but rather what the emphasis or mix of elements is in a given individual's story. For example, the Native American youth Dorothy Lee[50] interviews spends the first 29 minutes of a 30-minute interview telling about her tribe and family and the last minute talking about herself as a unique individual, while the reverse might be true if we interviewed an American teenager. Nevertheless, you don't have to scratch either of them very deeply to find the kind of complex mixture of elements from each quadrant Wilber proposes.

Exactly what the mix will be, of course, depends on many complex factors including what a person's society and culture emphasize or require. As we suggested earlier, the rugged individualists found on the prairies or in the mountains in 18th and 19th century American frontier were needed by society, just as the collectivist selves of Mao Tse Dung's China in the 1980s were called forth by the times. Our question is what combination of narrative elements calls forth authentic existence? While I do not believe that a formula can be found, and that actually to try to find one would be contrary to the enterprise

---

50 *Valuing the Self* and *Freedom and Culture.*

of becoming one's authentic self, I do think that we can see not only what tends *not* to be constitutive of such being but some of what *is*. In a moment we will offer a definition that hopefully captures the contours we have carved out before we turn to a more detailed inquiry into what constitutes an authentic self (chapter five) and the path to becoming one (chapter six).

One Final Myth Dispelled

Similar to the myth of self-help is the so-called self-made man (usually it is men, not women—more on this in a moment). American political culture is full of legends of great entrepreneurs who bucked all odds and created great fortunes and empires all by themselves. Contemporary libertarianism and other quasi-anarchist groups build their ideologies and practices on the basis of myths such as those found in Ayn Rand's novels. These lionizations of people who achieve great power and wealth ignore the variety of factors such as luck, community (and government!) support, and the efforts and the inventions of thousands or millions of others which created the conditions necessary for one money-making scheme to succeed while others failed.

One response, by some philosophers, to such willful ignoring of reality is to focus on what they call "moral luck." An objective reckoning of the role of luck in a given person's plight, whether they are rich or poor, healthy or ill, well or poorly educated, brilliant or slow, should at the least render the lucky grateful, for as Nietzsche's block of marble metaphor suggests, most of what and who we are is a function of fate, and is not of our doing. To make a long story short, philosophers of moral luck such as Bernard Williams[51] argue that because so much of our well-being depends on luck, the luckier someone is the greater are their responsibilities for the less fortunate. To use Rand's metaphor, instead of shrugging off the world, the lucky Atlases of the world should feel strongly obliged to take on more.

A second lesson we can learn about authenticity, from the libertarian parallels to self-help, is to note the tremendous irony of poor and marginal working class people vociferously advocating for this philosophy of privilege. An older version of this irony was a large working class contingent supporting the likes of Andrew Carnegie's Social Darwinism. Many of the people least likely to benefit from a doctrine of economic survival of the fittest were among the strongest proponents of allowing the rich (the strong) to "eat" the weak.

In my class on work I have long found it incredible that so many working class students, who predictably will never transcend the limits of their working class origins and most of whom probably will be worn down young by this life, nevertheless support laissez faire libertarianism. Why? Part of the answer lies in their very desire for something more and better and it is the hope that they, like the elite, will win the lottery of life that has them struggling, often against impossible odds. Yet, the game is rigged. While there are enough people who break through class barriers to keep the myth of mobility alive, the occasional success story is much a part of what helps to perpetuate America's class system.[52] Perhaps, because it is so often repeated that it drowns out the many other possible stories of life in America

---

51 A short list might include Bernard Williams, *Moral Luck*; John Rawls, *A Theory of Justice*; S.L. Hurley, *Justice, Luck and Knowledge*; Peter Singer *How Are We to Live*, *Practical Ethics* and *Writings on an Ethical Life*; Peter Unger, *Living High and Letting Die*; and T.M. Scanlon, *What We Owe Each Other*.

52 See the 2005 *New York Times* collection of stories about class in America (*Class Matters*) for powerful stories about how class affects and ensnares people from all levels of society.

they might listen to, the libertarian narrative of the rewards of luck and effort has captured their imaginations. If you add our capacity for self-deception (or our natural hypocrisy as we will discuss in the next chapter) to this desire for a better life and the paucity of alternative narratives in their lexicon of tropes (Nietzsche's point about the importance of an education that includes such stories now becomes clearer), you can begin to understand why the very people who are condemned to failure support a set of social and political conditions that nearly guarantee that result.

While I believe class is an even more important factor in shaping most Americans than either race or gender, my point here is to use a common hypocrisy about class to underscore how a false narrative can undermine authenticity. It's not just that supporting Social Darwinian or libertarian ideologies helps to perpetuate a system that keeps people from the very goals they seek, but that such narratives guarantee that people will have what Marxists have long called "false consciousness." In the second chapter of this book we described how consumerism fails to satisfy our deep desires for being real, and consumerism is a specific example of a more general point we are now prepared to understand. If the narratives provided by our culture fail to comprehend the realities of our situation *and* help us link our lives in deeply meaningful ways to others, we will be lost, often so dramatically that we do not even recognize the emptiness that is the main symptom of our inauthenticity.

Before taking stock of where we have come in this lengthy and complex chapter, I want to make good on a promise by discussing briefly a third lesson we can learn from the images of heroic entrepreneurs that lure us into the grips of dangerous narratives. I believe women are less susceptible to such narratives than men because the focus of women in America, whether because of nature or nurture (or both, as I suspect), has been on relationships rather than on individual struggle and achievement. Perhaps this is changing because of cultural movements such as feminism, but those with childhoods that emphasizes attention to family and community relationships are less likely to be mesmerized by false stories of stoic heroism and individualistic struggle for success than those who have been raised on narratives about individual triumph against great odds.

Taking Stock

> To be a philosopher is not merely to have subtle thoughts nor even to found a school but so to love wisdom as to live according to its dictates, a life of simplicity, independence, magnanimity, and trust. It is to solve some of the problems of life, not only theoretically but practically.
> —Thoreau, Walden, "Economy"

In keeping with our narrative view of the self, Charles Guignon suggests that what philosophers and other thinkers can contribute to our quest for authenticity is to help us find the best metaphors. Given what we have discussed in this chapter by now I suspect you should see the relevance of Guignon's recommendation. Unless we get our stories straight we will continue to be frustrated because we will be looking for the wrong thing in the wrong places. Guignon argues, e.g., that the proverbial search for a deep, inner core me that is pre- or asocial not only is fatally flawed but is very dangerous and the alternative to essentialism proposed by many postmodernists—to "de-center" the self—simply adds to people's vertigo. People need coherent, integrated identities, and as Nietzsche saw so insightfully, if a solid foundation is taken away (we have "killed" it/him) they will seek equal or even more problematic hard absolutes such as modern totalitarianisms, or fundamentalisms, or softer herd mentalities such as consumerism.

So precisely what is the alternative definition of the self, and therefore of authenticity, we are proposing? A narrative self is a *telling* rather than a substantive thing, and this narrative telling is a creative process in which we are embedded and participate. Nietzsche is a narrativist when he tells us to "become what you are," to own and own up to what you are and develop your self with *style*. At its best, this metaphor encourages us to view our lives as an ongoing aesthetic process of becoming authentic in which we (playfully) attempt to create cohesiveness and unity. Notably, though, Nietzsche's overman, while steeped especially in the historical sweep of metaphors of self is alone in his quest, cut off from the nurturing waters of others that give our souls shape and sustenance.[53] Alasdair MacIntyre[54] contends that Nietzsche's focus on self formation as essentially an aesthetic process indicates how he has separated the individual from community and thus in the end offers one more version of the liberal individualism he so profoundly critiques.

Heidegger is also a narrativist and a constructivist who believes that a decisive action can steer us from becoming a mere member of some "herd," and for him this action is to confront death. He adds to our understanding of authenticity by emphasizing the importance of *gravity*, a seriousness we achieve by taking ownership of our life and developing a constancy and steadfastness through commitment to our core values and their implications and applications. Note again

---

53 We will pursue the ways others shape and nurture us in the next chapter on happiness. See especially John O'Donohue, *Anam Cara: A Book of Celtic Wisdom*. Nietzsche has long been criticized for ignoring social and political life in his discussions of human nature.

54 See chapter 18, "After Virtue: Nietzsche or Aristotle, Trotsky and St. Benedict," in *After Virtue: A Study in Moral Theory*.

that the emphasis in Heidegger is on how we live rather than on either how we came to be who we are or an inner essence.

Guignon also discusses MacIntyre's emphasis on *actionable narratives*, stories we adopt that guide our actions, and on *tradition*, which allows us to dovetail our individual stories with larger narratives. Like Heidegger and Nietzsche, MacIntyre believes that to become authentic requires finding and shaping adequate stories, ones that help make sense of our lives as we live our parts of the broader stories in which we participate. MacIntyre believes that such narratives make us and tie us to reality in ways that allow us to be agents, which for him means to act virtuously; thus he is against various forms of individualism and views the self as a social entity that takes shape as it plays its roles in larger narratives.

MacIntyre's critique of liberal individualism and case for communities that provide narratives and realities for people to be virtuous reminds me of both Cordova's discussion of how Apaches become strong people capable of full and exemplary participation in community life, through the thoroughgoing guidance of intact communities and Crawford's vision of self-reliant agents who become responsible actors through immersion in good work guided by mentors. In both cases there is no pretense of self-made humans or of autonomous individualism; instead, what it takes to become a master mechanic in Crawford's example or a fully capable adult for Cordova, are a set of stories that are "actionable" in that the physical conditions for living those stories are also made available by one's community.

Finally, Guignon discusses how Taylor's idea of *moral space* provides needed detail to our emerging definition of authenticity as living good stories. We need a sense of direction, an orientation in our horizons of action that provides a sense of meaning. Through such stories we develop an identity, a shape to our selves (style) that becomes ever-more clear and coherent as we strive to bring forth the world envisioned in our story.

Now, perhaps we can proffer a definition of authenticity based on this very different perspective of human nature. To this point we have been preparing the way by showing both the need for and barriers to authenticity and by analyzing the many conceptual landmines that people have set or stepped on in bringing us to a crisis of identity. Here is a working definition of the narrative view of human authenticity: **people are authentic to the extent to which they live actionable narratives that provide gravity and meaning and tie them into meaningful stories of their communities.** Most of the remainder of this book is an attempt to flesh out this definition and to show how achieving a durable authenticity might be achieved in a world of growing distractions that dis-integrate us.

In chapter five I hope to show that authenticity and happiness are not only compatible, but that they are conceptually and practically intertwined. European Existentialists not only misunderstood authenticity in various ways, but they also gave it a bad name by counter posing it to happiness. They believe you can be "happy," perhaps, by being inauthentic, but authentic people seem condemned to unhappiness. The American counter-culture movement of the 1960s, on the other hand, believed that true happiness requires authenticity, but their impulse was to set people adrift from tradition which, I believe, undermined both authenticity and happiness by turning people to another form of individualism and even to narcissism.

Finally, in chapter six we will turn to the most difficult and most important dimension of becoming authentic, the spiritual—notoriously one of the most confusing aspects of human experience. Claims to truth about spirituality have been the source of much mischief and evil, and certainly of much misunderstanding. I enter this realm with trepidation through the idea of *calling* in the hope of showing that because spiritual matters impinge on us in deep and mainly mysterious ways, we ignore this dimension of life at our peril. The idea of calling helps to emphasize and clarify what it means to say we discover our stories and thus our selves. Rather than set us apart from society, living stories that constitute an authentic life immerse us deeply in our worlds.

CHAPTER FIVE
HAPPINESS

There is only one thing that is truly insufferable, and that is a life without meaning....There is nothing wrong with the search for happiness. But there is something greater—meaning—which transfigures all. When you have meaning you are content, you belong.—Laurens van der Post

If you deliberately plan on being less than you are capable of being, then I warn you that you'll be unhappy for the rest of your life.—Abraham Maslow

Emptiness

A quarter century ago I experienced a profound emptiness. During the most dreadful season of my life I lost my job, my farm, my family, my life. Given the common list of "stressors" or causes of situational depression therapists look for, I hit a grand slam. Throughout that dark period of my life I experienced many emotions—profound sadness, self doubt, grief, fear, anger, contrition—the full array of feelings that overwhelm people when they go through divorce, job loss, or separation from a beloved place. Underneath all of these terrible emotions, though, a seemingly bottomless chasm, a void at the heart of my being, stared at me with increasing unavoidability. No doubt this devil-ish (remember the "noontime demon" we discussed in the chapter on work?) emptiness was in part caused by the dramatic upheaval in my life, but in part it precipitated the array of negative emotions I was experiencing. It was as if I was an alien in my life, a mis-fit no longer "home" at home. I no longer was right for the part of main character in the story of my very own life.

I believe I experienced something, perhaps more clearly and resoundingly than is usual, that drives people to seek some way of becoming more authentic, more real. Fundamentally what such emptiness calls out for is something to fill it, something to give weight to a being that is too light, too unattached to anything with real gravity. What had connected me solidly to the earth were family, work, connection to the land, roles in the community, and a conviction that who I was and what I was doing was a story worth enacting, a life worth living. When those were eroded and ripped away, almost simultaneously, it took years for me to re-weave another life. Philosopher Martha Nussbaum used a similar metaphor when talking about how the death of her mother felt like something tearing a gouge in the fabric of her being that took years to repair. Others use the metaphor of a physical wound to emphasize that a scar inevitably remains from such a trauma. Happily for me, the great emptiness is gone, but the memories of it persist and I still sometimes relive some of those painful emotions from a quarter century ago.

Existentialists, especially Sartre, contend that we all have (or are) this deep emptiness at the heart of our being, and that it is so dread-ful that we go to great lengths to avoid facing it. In the process we practice the falsehoods Sartre rehearsed so powerfully—self-deception, escape from freedom, social pretense (role playing), and following the crowd.

I agree with Sartre and others that the metaphysical pit at the core of my being I faced that unforgettable summer filled me with dread, and I sought to escape its vortex in conventional ways—new relationships, drink, work, therapy—but as I have argued in the previous chapter, this emptiness is *always* there *only* if you pine for a deep inner core self or soul that is permanent. If, instead, you follow the narrative and communitarian view of self I have described, metaphors such as re-weaving or physical healing or learning to live another story make more sense, and you realize that traumas or even everyday disruptions are inevitable and that while we can be wounded or have the ecological balance of our lives upset, usually we can return to "normal" even if the "new normal" is different in many or even profound ways.

To put this point in different language, and to follow Aristotle rather than Sartre, humans naturally tend toward happiness and we are possessed with amazing abilities and resilience to help us achieve and maintain this state. In my despair and unfathomable emptiness I was profoundly unhappy. Now that I have re-created myself (or better, that I have been re-created, a critical distinction we will return to shortly), I am happy again, happier than I was in the first half of my life. While I am much more aware of the fragility of my life, my relationships, my health, and other aspects of my good fortune than I would have been without my crisis, the emptiness is gone. Gone not because I am escaping my freedom in Bad Faith or perpetually practicing self-deception, but rather gone because the story I am living fits who I am. I feel real.

The Happiness Hypothesis

Philosophers, poets, mystics, and theologians have been writing about happiness for millennia, and often the conclusion they have reached is that happiness, perhaps like authenticity, is at bottom an incomprehensible mystery. This insight is expressed in a poem by Jane Kenyon:

Happiness

There's just no accounting for happiness,
or the way it turns up like a prodigal
who comes back to the dust at your feet
having squandered a fortune far away.

And how can you not forgive?
You make a feast in honor of what
was lost, and take from its place the finest
garment, which you saved for an occasion
you could not imagine, and you weep night and day
to know that you were not abandoned,
that happiness saved its most extreme form
for you alone.

No, happiness is the uncle you never
knew about, who flies a single-engine plane
onto the grassy landing strip, hitchhikes
into town, and inquires at every door
until he finds you asleep midafternoon
as you so often are during the unmerciful
hours of your despair.

It comes to the monk in his cell.
It comes to the woman sweeping the street
with a birch broom, to the child
whose mother has passed out from drink.
It comes to the lover, to the dog chewing

a sock, to the pusher, to the basketmaker,
and to the clerk stacking cans of carrots
in the night.

It even comes to the boulder
in the perpetual shade of pine barrens,
to rain falling on the open sea,
to the wineglass, weary of holding wine.[1]

For half a century now, psychologists, practicing what Martin Seligman[2] calls Positive Psychology, have been investigating the art and science of happiness. While they would probably admit that there are aspects of happiness that are difficult to describe or account for, we now know scientifically much of what is involved in happiness or its lack. Happiness is complex, and as we will see getting the many ingredients of happiness to form a becoming ecology can be difficult, but happiness may be much less a mystery than Kenyon's poem would suggest.

Social psychologist Jonathan Haidt has written a clear, comprehensive, and thought-provoking account of happiness, one that calls on wisdom traditions from around the globe. It also describes what Positive Psychologists have learned through their longitudinal cross-cultural studies.[3] I will use Haidt's summary as a baseline for

---

1 Jane Kenyon, "Happiness," first appeared in *Poetry*, February, 1995

2 See especially Seligman's website called Authentic Happiness www.authentichappiness.sas.upenn.edu/Default.aspx and his book by the same title (*Authentic Happiness*). On his website you will find a number of free happiness questionnaires that will help you discern your own level of happiness.

3 Jonathan Haidt, *The Happiness Hypothesis: Finding Modern Truth in Ancient Wisdom.* As expressed in footnote xii in the introduction to this book, also see work by Ricard, Seligman, McKibben, Layard, Lyubomirsky, and Csikszentmihalyi.

our discussion of the relations between happiness and authenticity.[4] My central goal in this chapter is to further our comprehension of authenticity by relating it to a similarly complex and misunderstood phenomenon, happiness, in order to underscore the importance of conceptual clarity when dealing with such important social and personal realities. Whether or not you are happy or feel real depends, in large measure, on what you believe they are about. And the promise is that, contrary to the long-standing view that authenticity involves profound unhappiness (despair), becoming more authentic could actually increase your happiness. I believe that getting clear about how happiness and authenticity are related is central to understanding how both of these phenomena are crucial for living a good life.

Self Understanding

Haidt begins with what is by now the standard social scientific understanding of human beings—that much of what we are about as psycho-social entities is sub-conscious and mainly beyond our control. Our "lower" brain controls most of what goes on in our bodies and in our reactions to the world around us. And that is a good thing! Would you want to consciously monitor your heart, metabolism, digestion, hormone levels, and the range of other functions your brain and body take care of while "you" are doing other things? Or, would you want to have to think whether or not to flee if you run into a beehive or are faced with some other imminent threat? This "half"

---

4 You can read a similar account of the concrete ways to achieve happiness in Lyubomirsky's *The How of Happiness*. She gives about a dozen practices that tend to mark the lives of happy people: expressing gratitude, cultivating optimism, avoiding overthinking and social comparisons, practicing acts of kindness, nurturing social relationships, developing coping strategies, learning to forgive, increasing flow experiences, savoring life's joys, committing to your goals, practicing religion and spirituality, and taking care of your body through meditation, physical activity and acting like a happy person.

(at least) of who we are goes even beyond body functions or primal responses to affect fundamental aspects of our selves. According to psychologists, much of our emotionality, sociality, and basic personality are hard-wired. Some aspects of this "given" part of our selves are modifiable, but much is effectively beyond our control. To emphasize the proportion of our selves that is set by evolution, Haidt refers to this complex of pre- and sub-conscious aspects as an *elephant*, while our consciousness is the *rider*. To a great extent the elephant is in charge of what this "divided self" is and does, but with discipline and effort the rider can learn to be at home with and even have some control over what occurs.

Haidt gives two caveats about riding our elephant as he prepares us to understand happiness. First, we must be aware of our natural tendency to "confabulate," to take credit for making objective rational decisions about what we do when in fact we are rationalizing. While it is especially difficult for hyper-rational people like philosophers to accept, Haidt argues that our "gut minds" (elephants) decide and then "we" (conscious minds) create a rationale for the decision rather than our conscious, rational minds deciding and then our bodies obediently following "our" directions. Sometimes our conscious, rational minds greatly shape our actions, but not nearly as often as we tend to believe. This tendency is in line with a more general feature of human nature that Haidt gives the uncomfortable label of "hypocrisy." He says that "we are all hypocrites" in that we are much better at and more prone to judge others objectively than we are at seeing our selves clearly. In a fascinating *New York Times* article[5] Errol Morris gives an account of our self-blindness as described by another social psychologist, David Dunning. Dunning raises a set of interesting questions

---

5 Errol Morris, "The Anosognosic's Dilemma: Something is Wrong But You'll Never Know What It Is" (Part 1), June 20, 2010.

about our inabilities to recognize and understand ourselves and our worlds because we are not bright enough, in one way or another, to realize what it is we do not know or even that we don't know. The causes, and thus likely the cures, for our hypocrisy may be beyond our purview.

Haidt's second caveat is that we are best off viewing the rider role as that of an advisor rather than a general. Put differently, we must work *with* our elephant and not pretend that we (conscious mind) are in charge, for that kind of effort usually ends in frustration and self-deception. I would add my own caveat to Haidt's description: we must not take his two minds language too literally. He is not a psychological dualist who believes that our sub-consciousness is unknowable or inaccessible, nor is he a metaphysical dualist who holds that we have separable souls that inhabit the body temporarily. Rather, these dual (and sometimes dueling) aspects are part of a whole self that is a complex ecosystem with different aspects. Just as in natural ecosystems different beings can wax or wane in influence at different times, these human *elephants* and *riders* vary in how much influence they have in a given situation.

Humans Are Hyper-Social Animals

The language is Haidt's—*hyper* social. He and a host of other social scientists believe that humans rank near the top of any list of species that are highly social. Their contention is not that we are hive animals like termites, ants, or bees wherein our social organization is set by nature. Instead, they're telling us that any understanding of humans must begin with our social nature because we are extra-ordinarily capable social creatures who have amazing "radar" that tunes us in to our "herd" and that virtually everything we do and are is linked to society and culture.

It is not accidental that Haidt spends two of the four chapters leading up to his definition of happiness discussing our hyper-sociality, for our happiness (and, I believe, our authenticity) is inextricably bound up with our relationships. All life forms, of course, are genetic offspring of their predecessors. Many can get along well without social relations. We cannot be humans, however, except in a merely biological sense, without socialization. To be human is to be social, as the basic facts of linguistic communication show. Without language we would not be human, and to be linguistic is to be social.

Our interdependencies with others go even farther. *Materially*, no one manages alone. Even the proverbial rugged individualist, the mountain man of the old west, had gear that was made by someone else and he gained much of his knowledge from others—horses and guns and traps and hardtack and coffee and...well, you get the point. Clearly most of us today are linked to countless others across the globe and across time through thousands of times as many material ties as those proverbial loners of the past.

Our interdependencies with others run yet deeper and more personally, for our very *identities* are social constructions, to a great extent gifts from society—our families, friends, actors and the characters they portray, religious leaders, teachers, politicians, historical or fictional characters...the list of those who help form us is nearly endless. What makes us unique is the cast of characters that has carved us and in what ways, not whether or not or the extent to which we are independent of such influences. For (and this, finally, is my main point) even the persona or identity of being independent is one social type, one trope among many.

Think of it this way: society creates the kinds of characters it needs (thinks it needs) at a given time. Having grown up in rural South Dakota during a hard era (the 1950s and 60s), people had to be independent (or perhaps self-reliant in Crawford's sense is more precise) to be successful—whether they were poor farmers living far apart in a semi-arid land having to fix their own machinery, or tend to their own wounds, or veterinarians like my father who, with no back-ups, had to be very inventive to figure out how to save an animal or deliver a calf. They managed to get along without many of the complex systems most of us have become a part of but, contrary to our language and mythology of being self-made, *who* they were was not primarily of their own doing.

Perhaps this point can be illustrated best by reflecting on the church my family attended throughout my growing-up years in small town South Dakota. Virtually everyone in town belonged to one or another of our community's churches and most people were regulars, for it was there, once or several times a week, that these hard-working people got much of their social nourishment. A great deal of the time and energy of church life revolved around the social groups and their activities. No one doubted the value of most of these groups as it was obvious that people who spent so much time working and living alone, often under very hard conditions, wanted and needed social time. On the other hand, the selections from and slant on the Bible, and also the music I recall, emphasized being both self-reliant and relying on God or Jesus. It was a major Christian virtue, in my Methodist Church, to seek your individual salvation, to "walk that lonesome valley by yourself," and if you did so with perseverance and courage you could be assured that God was walking it with you. You were taught to be independent, and in a sense that lesson had to be reinforced regularly to keep people, who naturally are so thoroughly social, sane and healthy while living in such isolation.

I also learned to be tough, to keep my own counsel, and to get through difficult times by working hard. I had a paper route beginning in the fourth grade and I recall many times when I had to deliver papers on cold and windy days, and my first full-time job (five and a half days per week, with 14-hour days) was working on a farm throughout the summer between seventh and eighth grades. Today such a regimen would be considered too harsh by most people or even child abuse by some, but in the context of my childhood it was common if not simply normal. You can be assured that I learned quite young a major cornerstone of the independence trope—that no one will hand you anything you didn't earn through hard work. But I also learned how much I craved and needed social relations. Anyone who has been schooled in being independent can tell you of the central tension, or perhaps even paradox, of learning to go it alone while simultaneously realizing the importance of social connections for your material, emotional, and spiritual survival and health.

I am not defending or criticizing the particular practices I experienced as a youth, nor am I claiming these are the only ways people are socialized to be independent or self-reliant. Rather, my point is that *all* human ways of being in the world are socially constructed *including* being independent. In a recent article[6] philosopher J.M. Bernstein puzzles over why many of those who have formed the so-called Tea Party cannot see (or chose to ignore) the myriad ways their lives are intertwined with and dependent on others. If you point out to these often well-heeled middle and upper-middle class people that they depend on others for building their homes or roads, making their clothes, eye glasses, or furniture, growing their food or educating their

---

6 J.M. Bernstein, "The Very Angry Tea Party," *The New York Times*, June 14, 2010.

children they probably would admit the layered and complex inter-dependencies we have been discussing. But there is something about similar interdependencies with government that trigger the "independence" response in many people with such political leanings: get government out of my life (except for roads, food protection, education, defense, fire fighters, social security...). What?

I agree with Bernstein's analysis of what is just a recent example of this strong, and often very materially productive, strain in American social and political ideology. As I explained in the previous chapter, a strong strain of Stoicism (including Puritanism) runs throughout the history of the quest for authenticity in the modern world. Bernstein takes us back to Hegel's critique of Rousseau. Remember that Rousseau believed that our true selves are pre- or a-social and consist mainly of our "deepest" feelings, many of which are anti-social. He thought that only if we could be independent of society could we discover and develop our true selves, and only if we were able to do so would we be happy. Hegel's critique of Rousseau's radical individualism is that this, like all other identities, is a product of society. To understand Rousseau's ideas about ideal human nature and living you must understand who he was in his context and what social factors brought him to his appealing but inadequate social philosophy.

Rousseau himself saw that something was missing in his individualism when he proposed his inchoate doctrine of the general will. Much of psychology and especially social psychology today is aimed at comprehending the complex interplay of individual and society that Rousseau pointed to with this doctrine, and at the very least social scientists agree that to be human, to have a human personality and identity, is to have the building blocks and nutrients of society coursing through our psycho-social veins.

It is best to comprehend the calls for independence by libertarians, such as Tea Party members, not as a general desire to live in isolation (who would grow my coffee or bananas, where is that garbage collector, who should I call to get that neighbor's dog to quit barking...?), nor as an individual desire to secede from government, but rather as more specific complaints and concerns about particular governmental actions, agencies, or regulations. I believe it is most unfortunate that people with specific concerns (all of us at one time or another!) tend to commit the fallacy philosophers call "hasty generalization"— where we quickly go from noting that a few people have a certain view to generalizing that "everyone" does, or where we see that government does something poorly and then conclude that we should get rid of government. You can also detect no small amount of magical thinking in calls for getting governments (or corporations!) "off our backs," as if simply wishing them away would solve all our problems. Unfortunately usually what is needed is hard, cooperative, long-term effort to build and maintain the kinds of institutions we need to solve our collective problems and serve our collective interests. Unfortunately, such effort is pretty unattractive.

When I use the term "collectivism" to refer to my neo-Hegelian perspective on authenticity, I am calling attention to our fundamental sociality and not to any particular social or political system such as socialism or communism. I believe this is a crucial point because if we believe humans can be human, or can best or only be fully human, if they are not dependent on (or interdependent with) others, we are bound to blunder because we begin with a most basic falsehood. If we seek to be independent in some kind of Rousseau-like sense we will be pursuing fundamental goals such as happiness and authenticity in the wrong ways and in the wrong places, and we will be most frustrated in the process. As we will explore shortly, such deep frustration tends to lead to ramped up efforts (the failure of consumerism to satisfy our needs for authenticity and happiness often leads to more consumerism), acting out (our frustrations can lead to anger and violence), or cynicism (a self-imposed paralysis), all of which plague our social and political landscape today. Conceptual confusion can have far-reaching consequences. If happiness for the hyper-social beings we are is not to be found by pretending to be radically independent, then, where does it lie?

Our Happiness Set Point

Have you ever noticed that some people seem naturally more (or less) happy than others? I have a colleague whom I sometimes want to shake because she is always so bubbly, effusive, positive...so happy. Sometimes, of course, such people are acting, covering insecurities or masking serious problems. This woman seems to be genuinely, extraordinarily happy. I also have a friend who reminds me of Eyore in Winnie the Pooh—there seems to be a perpetual gray cloud hanging over his head. He's not a bad person, he isn't someone who has a practiced cynicism like many cultured people, and he doesn't have other characteristics of a depressed person; he simply can't seem to help being pretty unhappy even though his life conditions (health, relationships, wealth, etc.) are not particularly problematic. According to Haidt, my colleague, my friend, myself, and each of you are tuned to a given frequency level of happiness.

Haidt gives us a simple formula for *Happiness*: $H = S + C + V$. *Happiness* is a combination of our *Set* point, the (mainly social) *Conditions* of our lives, and personal *Variables* over which we have control. If he and other social scientists are correct in their claims about the dominant influence our *elephants* play in who we are and what we do, it is not surprising that they contend that the extent to which we are happy is set by our genetic inheritance (Haidt says the range is from 50-80%). Some people can, through extraordinary effort and techniques, vary this Set point some, but the kind of evidence scientists have for this claim seems very strong. You would think, for example, that winning the lottery or losing a limb would alter your level of happiness permanently. What studies show, however, is that although the initial effects on a person's happiness are as you would expect—lottery winners are happier and amputees sadder—within a year people return to the levels of happiness they had before their dramatic life changes. Haidt calls this phenomenon the "adaptation principle." Speaking of lotteries, one of the implications of this point is that some people fare better than others in the happiness lottery just as some are better looking, brighter, richer, stronger, and so on.

While most of us can do little to affect our set point, there is much to do in relation to this elephant if we wish to maximize our happiness. Mainly, we need to become self aware in ways that will allow us to ride our elephant skillfully. You need not look far to find a range of books, courses of study, institutes, or gurus to help with this process, which in yet one more way reveals our hyper-sociality. We need teachers or mentors to help us navigate the difficult shoals of self-discovery and development both because so many wise people have preceded us and because others, especially wise people, can know us better than we know our selves. Even in the process of refining our selves once we are mainly "carved," we are usually most successful if we have proper guidance.

I believe the difficulty of excavating and learning to work with our mainly hidden elephant is the major reason why doctrines such as Rousseau's deep feelings or Plato's soul are so attractive. If psychologists are correct that this submerged elephant is remarkably powerful in our lives, it is difficult to know and even more difficult to control. No wonder so many people come to view it as a foreign entity!

However, I believe we should resist this temptation most strongly, for to buy a metaphysically dualistic interpretation is to buy no end of philosophical and practical problems. For example, one result of hypostatizing (thing-izing metaphors) our dual nature is that we will never comprehend our selves. The so-called rider and elephant are two aspects of a single being, you or me, and to separate them in principle is to deny our integral self (as Ken Wilber calls it[7]). Just as we can experience or metaphorically characterize "mixed emotions" as dueling entities, perhaps even going so far as ascribing one to the devil and another to God, in similar fashion we can turn one aspect of our selves into a separate entity as a way to describe our experience of being divided. Any therapist can give you examples of our tendencies to "other-ize" psychological (or social) aspects with which we don't identify, and they can also tell you how important it is that we take ownership of these "foreign" objects if we are to become whole and healthy.

There is no shortage of philosophical literature on metaphysical dualism, whether on a grand scale (physical vs. spiritual reality) or within our selves (mind-body or soul-body dualism). I think the preponderance of philosophical thinking today agrees with psychology in denying the ultimate reality of the metaphysically divided self, but for our purposes the most important thing is to realize that *if* happiness (or becoming real) is your goal, integrating rather than dividing the self is essential. You may not like the fact that you tend to become angry easily and you may wish to end that tendency, but with regard to happiness or authenticity no good will come of denying that you tend toward anger in various circumstances. You also may not like

---

7 See especially *Integral Psychology: Consciousness, Spirit, Psychology, Therapy.*

your happiness set point, but denying it as a part of yourself can serve no purpose if you wish to improve your happiness.

The Conditions of Life

Even though much of our level of happiness seems predetermined, the good news is that from 20-50% of our happiness depends on more than our genetic code. We are not fated to a fixed level or quality of happiness. Also, as Haidt emphasizes, our happiness is a journey in which we can progress based on how well we learn to ride our elephants and, to extend the metaphor, build lives that provide proper care and feeding. Just as far too many people around the world are discovering that not every food regimen is good for our bodies, so too if we do not take care of our psycho-social selves they can be similarly malnourished.

To pursue this last point first, it is important to note that in the year 2000 we crossed a nutritional Rubicon where worldwide we had more people who had too much nutrition rather than too little. I believe that in the contemporary United States something similar is happening, where a growing percentage of people have too much social stimulation and are experiencing a kind of psychic obesity (another way of describing the busyness side of *acedia*, perhaps) with overflowing in-boxes, schedules, and social networks. Just as physically obese people become increasingly unable to engage fully in active, healthy, physical lives and thus spend inordinate amounts of time and resources on doctors and medicine, psychically obese people can become obsessed with their networking with the result that their stresses increase[8] while their quality of life decreases. Technologies that promise improved sociality can, if we imbibe in the wrong things or too much, bloat us to where we are overwhelmed and incapable of quality social activities.

Haidt reinforces this metaphor of dysfunction in his discussion of a fascinating set of examples of conditions ('C' in his formula) that can diminish or prevent our happiness: commuting, noise, lack of control, shame, and relationships. His emphasis on *bad* relationships (a crummy boss or colleagues, an incompatible friend or spouse, a poor teacher or mentor) I would add *too many*, for if we are overwhelmed by maintaining our Facebook "friendships" we have too little time for the kinds of quality relationships that are critical for happiness.

I believe a lack of control is a major ingredient in the dissatisfaction and anger that we are seeing in the emerging Tea Party phenomenon. Although many Tea Party members may be confused about independence, a recurring theme of this movement, which appears to be as much social as political, is that social and political forces beyond our control are dictating more and more aspects of our lives. Whether or not that is true, ironically these activists are responding in classic *communitarian* fashion—they are joining together to affect change in our institutional practices. Individualists unite!

The same could be said for nearly all examples of the conditions Haidt discusses. If we wish to increase our happiness by commuting less, suffering less noise or changing our working conditions or relationships, we need *collective* effort to affect *systemic* problems. Most

---

8 A great deal of recent research indicates that stress is a major factor in many forms of ill health, from obesity to depression to diabetes to migraines to heart disease and a shorter lifespan. A recent video from National Geographic, *Stress: Portrait of a Killer*, nicely summarizes this research. Much of what the scientists in this documentary recommend we do to change this growing pandemic agrees with Haidt's recommendations for improving happiness—work less, socialize more, volunteer, give to others, laugh, get married, slow down....

people suffer long commutes because we, collectively, have built our lives so that we live in one place (more than half of Americans live in suburbs), work in another, shop, recreate, or worship at yet another distance, and the only way to get from one place to another is to commute. In our workplaces many people are locked into inflexible schedules or stuck in cubicles because of how the workplace is organized. And while these conditions contribute substantially to many people's unhappiness are mutable, they cannot be transformed without collective systemic changes.

While much of our happiness lies beyond our individual control, the news about the conditions of our life is doubly good. First, if we join with others we can often ameliorate such conditions. Many employee groups have negotiated flexible scheduling or "tele-commuting" as ways of dealing with poor working conditions such as having no say over their schedules or long commutes. Second, the process of cooperating with others to solve mutual problems can, in itself, add to our happiness because it brings increased sociality. When we work together for common goals often we form deep friendships that are based on mutuality and trust as well as on common interests.

The Variables of Life

A person can make himself [sic] happy, or miserable, regardless of what is actually happening 'outside,' just by changing the contents of consciousness. We all know individuals who can transform hopeless situations into challenges to be overcome, just through the force of their personalities. This ability to persevere despite obstacles and setbacks is the quality people most admire in others, and justly so; it is probably the most important trait not only for succeeding in life, but for

enjoying it as well. To develop this trait, one must find ways
to order consciousness so as to be in control of feelings and
thoughts. It is best not to expect shortcuts will do the trick.
—Mihaly Csikszentmihalyi

Haidt calls the other kind of mutable factors in happiness variables. These are the more individually malleable aspects of one's life and personality that are so often highlighted in pop cultural practices labeled self help. Conditions and variables often are complexly related. We might work with our employers through our union to make telecommuting possible, but working from home, as many people are discovering, can require great personal effort and change in one's discipline, sense of home in relation to work, self understanding of what it means to be a professional, and so on.

Perhaps the clearest and quickest way to show the link between conditions and variables is to examine the phenomenon of *flow*. Polish psychologist Mihaly Csikszentmihalyi labeled this crucial psychological concept in his attempt to describe what our "optimal experience" is like and how to attain it. You likely have experienced flow. Perhaps it was playing basketball, making love, singing in a choir, reading a good book or, if you were lucky, while working. Being in flow usually involves losing track of time and being so involved in what you are doing that your self-consciousness disappears. People often describe flow as the experience of oneness, or being totally absorbed in the experience. Accounts by or about great artists or spiritual heroes are testimonies to flow, but the good news is almost everyone has experienced flow, at least as a child.

If you have experienced flow you know what I am talking about; if not, no amount of description can capture such peak experiences. But why is flow a pivotal idea? First, to be in flow is to be happy, or at least to be in a state where there are no major irritations or conflicts, whether internal or external. Second, flow can teach a great deal about meshing our activities with who we are so that authenticity and happiness occur together. Learning the art of balancing both the many aspects of our lives and especially our so-called inner and outer aspects is much of what the art of living is about. Third, whether or not we are in flow depends on both conditions and variables. If the conditions of our life are optimal, our opportunities for flow are maximized, for to have the stressors and interruptions of noise, busy-ness, commuting, or poor working conditions limits flow experiences. On the other hand, people who have learned to control their variables in the right ways experience flow more often and more readily even when conditions are not optimal. What, according to Positive Psychologists, are these variables?

Some are fairly obvious, such as the ability to concentrate, the absence of internal conflicts and stress, a positive outlook. Clearly how we approach the world is crucial and is summed up by the phrase "seeing the glass as half empty or half full." To me the most telling variable Haidt discusses is *gratitude*. People who are more grateful tend to be happier than those who feel less gratitude.[9] Why? Why would gratitude be an important ingredient of happiness?

Part of the answer, undoubtedly, is that grateful people are viewed and treated better by others than those who are not grateful (who wants to be around an "ingrate"?). But besides the relational payoffs of being grateful, it is important to see how variables like gratitude work. Gratitude is more than a feeling or attitude. It is a basic orientation or relationship to the world. Gratitude is a choice to be thankful for good health or employment rather than to emphasize the ways

---

9 I highly recommend you take the gratitude inventory on Seligman's website, *Authentic Happiness*.

in which your body malfunctions or your job is not ideal. Grateful people can be "Panglosses" and refuse to face hard realities, but as we discussed earlier, they can be like the Dalai Lama and embrace the world knowing full well the suffering that abounds. Most people acquire their "attitude of gratitude" growing up around grateful role models, but Haidt includes it as a variable precisely because the ways and extents to which we are grateful are malleable.

It is no mere coincidence that all religions preach gratitude and most supply a deity to whom we can be grateful, for gratitude is a deeply spiritual issue and phenomenon as we will explore in chapter six. In fact, some theologians contend that gratitude is *the* fundamental human impulse that generates religion.[10] The psycho-logic of our natural gratitude seems to require a being to whom we can be grateful. After all, our everyday model of gratitude is that we are grateful to someone who does something kind for us, and if we are feeling grateful for important things no human gave us (our lives, natural beauty, the moral luck of being born into a good family) we are prone to feel a need for a deity to whom we can give thanks.

I am not concerned here with theology, though; instead, I want you to see how complex such basic attitudes are, how powerful a role they can play in our happiness, and that we can become more grateful (and thus happier) through our efforts. Whether, for what, and how we are grateful depends on a number of factors including our metaphysical beliefs, our attentiveness to details and our sense of history as well as our current situation, our reference groups, the religion we grew up with (or not), our ecological sense of interconnectedness, and so on. Each of these factors itself is a variable that lends itself to learning and change. We have discussed the importance of a thick *culture* for

---

10 Confucius thought gratitude is a basic vitrue.

becoming authentic; here we can see the importance of a thick *description* of each person if we are to begin truly to comprehend them.

A remarkable statistic is that among academics, scientists tend to be *more* religious than humanists.[11] While science does not pursue ultimate metaphysical questions about the existence of God, what apparently happens to many scientists is that as they learn more about the intricacies of nature, whether the details of evolution, astronomical realities, or the mutability of viruses, the more in awe and the more grateful they feel. Humanists look at the world through the lenses of history where they study the details of wars, intrigue, and plagues, and they tend to become more cynical about the world. This is a broad generalization, of course, and the extent to which it is accurate is not the point. Instead, note that *what* you study and *how* you study it affects your sense of gratitude. If you find a world that is ever more complex and perhaps even mysterious, your appreciation for every aspect of the world increases. If you discover a world that emphasizes how humans do terrible and dumb things and never seem to learn from their mistakes, it is difficult to be in awe or grateful.

The link between gratitude and happiness is itself complex. However, a core idea is similar to what we saw with flow: the extent to which you get into flow or are happy depends on whether or not *you* (your self consciousness and self concern) *disappear*. In a very real sense, your happiness is not all about you! This insight is central to the ancient Greek story of Narcissus. Narcissus cannot quit admiring himself in the mirror (lake) and he reaches the point where the mirror no longer works at all. To focus too much on yourself is to undermine

---

11 While academics tend to be less religious than the general population in America, American academics are much more religious than their counterparts in countries where religious belief and attendance are lower than in this country. Among academics, though, both natural and social scientists are more religious than humanists. See, e.g., Dean R. Hoge and Larry G Keetor, *Determinants of College Teachers' Religious Beliefs and Participation.*

the very self-satisfaction you seek. We have already discussed how this confusion plays itself out in the current self-esteem movement in our schools where children are rewarded simply for showing up rather than for actually accomplishing something.

Scottish philosopher Thomas Reid, writing in the 18th century, reached a similar conclusion about happiness: you cannot attain happiness by seeking it. The direct approach to happiness does not work any better than obsession with yourself makes you an admirable and attractive person. In both cases, what you seek is an "epiphenomenon,"— as a result of doing something else you become a "beautiful person" (whatever that might mean to you) by reading great literature or volunteering in the community or playing beautiful music or exercising and eating well or by accomplishing something important. Then you become happy. Happiness is not a destination but rather is something that happens as we wander through our lives and have experiences filled with things like flow, accomplishments, meaning, and gratitude. Happiness is a function of gratitude precisely because being grateful puts our focus on something/someone besides our selves.

Relationships!

Given that Haidt spends half of his walk-up to his happiness formula discussing our hyper-sociality, it is not surprising that much of the second half of *The Happiness Hypothesis* focuses on how our happiness is inextricably intertwined with others. We have already seen that being grateful can add to our happiness because it links us to a larger world and beckons us to look at the gifts life offers. Being grateful also enhances our happiness because humans are drawn to grateful and happy people. Clearly this is one more way in which "the rich get richer," but remember that gratitude is a variable that, while depending somewhat on our birthright, can also be developed.

What other connections are there between our personal happiness and our relationships with others? If you think about it, the list is quite extensive, and you can see the appeal of being independent (non-dependent or non-interdependent) simply based on how much of our personal well-being, including our happiness, seems to depend on others. It's rather scary, as any parent of a teenager can testify, the extent to which others can influence our attitudes, character, behavior, and ideals, as well as the quality of our experiences (including how happy we are).

Let us begin with other-directed actions, in particular with *altruism*. Philosophers and economists often fuss about whether or not altruism is even possible,[12] given how much emphasis in our culture is placed on how selfish people are. Thomas Nagel, for example, wrote an entire book carefully arguing against the common view that we are all egoists at heart. Positive Psychologists have no such reservations. They do not deny that sometimes we are selfish, but according to Haidt the stronger reality of humans is our orientation to others—to fit in, to be accepted, for reciprocity and recognition—not to being selfish or isolates. In fact, I believe these psychologists would agree with Hegel and Nietzsche's contention that if anything, a truly selfish act is a rare accomplishment, that what we call selfish is actually behavior in the service of others. If you hearken back to our discussion of consumerism you will recall that a strong case can be made for the proposition that consumers have internalized the values and motives the advertisers wish them to have and thus their "selfish" behavior ("it's all about me") is actually in the service of the sellers ("it's all about them").

---

12 A short list might include Thomas Nagel's classic case for altruism, *The Possibility of Altruism*; T.M. Scanlon, *What We Owe Each Other*; Stephen J. Pope, *The Evolution of Altruism and the Ordering of Love*; and Elliott Sober, *Unto Others: The Evolution and Psychology of Unselfish Behavior*.

Even if you take a more moderate position, as Nagel does in his book, and argue that usually we have mixed motives (I am doing this for myself *and* to please my mother), there seems to be little doubt that our actions are often other-directed, and that's all we need to make the connection between how we relate to others and our own happiness. In a classic study of human development, The Harvard Study of Adult Development, which began in 1937 and ran for 70 years, Harvard psychologist George Vaillant tells us that about 15% of the men in his long-term study were full-fledged altruists, while most fit Nagel's mixed pattern. Vaillant's study[13] also reinforces Haidt's description of us as hyper-social. Although he adds many subtleties and depth to a field with much data but little complex analysis (for example, why do countries with the highest self-reports of subjective well-being also have the most suicides?), Vaillant concludes that the central factor in human happiness is relationships. I am happier, in most circumstances, when you recognize me, preferably in a positive way.

Ironically, people are so hungry for recognition that far too many people seek negative recognition rather than go unrecognized! Think of the proverbial abused spouse who stays with her tormentor in part, undoubtedly, out of fear, but who also prefers to be given attention, however painful and degrading, than not to be recognized by the one she loves. When I worked with emotionally disturbed teenagers in Alaska, many of these troubled youths had difficulty being good because they were so used to gaining recognition through negative behaviors. I remember vividly a young man who was beginning to make real progress in leaving behind his destructive patterns and who was receiving strong encouragement from the staff for doing so, but

---

13 See a recent summary discussion of Vaillant's work in the June, 2009, *Atlantic* by Joshua Wolf Shank, "What Makes Us Happy." Vaillant's website is www.adultdev.bwh.harvard.edu

one night he went on a bender, breaking every window in sight. I was shocked that he seemed pleased being reprimanded and punished until more experienced staff members told me that his self-identification was of a criminal and thus the recognition he felt he needed was the sort consistent with being an outlaw. Turning around this complex relationship between identity, behavior, and recognition, and keeping him from a life of criminality and punishment, was very difficult indeed. The good news, though, is that although someone could gain your acclaim by being selfish, and some people have turned this strategy into an art form, just as most people are not attracted to ingrates, the same is true of selfish people. Thus genuine and satisfying recognition tends to follow altruistic acts, and the upshot is that typically my happiness increases when I do something good for you. Thus as Hegel contended two centuries ago, we are interdependent with others for our deepest well-being and identity.

Haidt goes on to make an even more contentious case—that being virtuous enhances our happiness. This, too, is an ancient philosophical debate (remember, the subtitle of his book is *Finding Modern Truth in Ancient Wisdom*) dating back at least to Socrates and Plato in Greece and Confucius and Zhuangzi in China. Plato's Socrates asks if "virtue is its own reward," and many a skeptic has answered "no." If the skeptics are correct, those who curry virtue are fools who are wasting their time being honest, learning to be courageous, just, temperate or wise. Again, Haidt sides with the conservatives who believe developing a virtuous character pays off, at least in terms of happiness. Why? Becoming and being virtuous is hard work. This variable can be accomplished, but for most of us it can be a difficult lifelong pursuit.

The answer again lies with our hyper-sociality. Most everyone responds positively to virtuous people. We want people of high character to be our bankers, child care workers, teachers, leaders, friends, spouses, and so on because we believe they are more likely to be trust-worthy, wise, judicious, fair and courageous—in short, to be the kind of people who will play their roles in predictably beneficial ways. Thus if you want to get that most desirable job, or mate, or into the best college you will be more likely to succeed if you are virtuous than if you are known as a liar, a cad, or lazy. And finally, to complete the circle, if you have others' approval you are more likely to be happy.

The Skeptics

All this seems so obvious. Why, then, do so many people question the connection between virtue and happiness? The skeptic's position seems almost cliché because it seems so true—"in the real world, good guys finish last." Part of the answer is that first we are ambivalent about others. In lovers we want someone who pushes the envelope of the risqué, while we prefer a spouse who is solid and conventional; in finance we admire risk takers but we want bankers who are conservative with our money; or we seek teachers who have a reputation for being outspoken iconoclasts but we want an education that will give us the most solid background. Second, as we have seen, becoming and being virtuous is long hard work. Third, it is not always clear that the costs are worth it. In fact, too often being virtuous can get you killed, thrown in jail, or ostracized. Yet we look for peers and teachers and coaches and mentors for our children who not only are virtuous but who will help them become virtuous.

There is a second kind of skepticism about happiness and virtue based on doubts about how genuine happiness is.[14] Their concerns are not exactly that people are pretending to be happy when they are not ("act happy and you'll be happy"), but more that the happiness most commonly delivered in our thin culture is not worth having, either because it keeps us from genuine happiness or because it keeps us from the important things that can flow from despair, conflict, struggle, or even boredom.

Surely this is a very important set of concerns that at the very least question the validity of studies based on subjective self reporting. I attempted to address the first concern (we are pursuing false happiness) in my chapter on technology, especially in relation to the "gospel of consumption" that has people running treadmills of spend-and-consume with no end or real joy in sight because this gospel is based on a faulty understanding of human happiness. Once people examine the underlying logic and psycho-logic of consumerism they tend to realize the hollowness of this strategy for gaining happiness. Furthermore, this example helps to show that great harm such as environmental destruction, wars, and great injustices can follow from pursuing the wrong dreams (or ideologies).

The second objection to linking authenticity with happiness raised by these skeptics, takes us into new territory. Even if happiness and authenticity can be linked, do we lose something essential when we

---

14 The list could be quite extensive, of course. Certainly the Existentialists are the most famous thinkers who doubted the connection between happiness and authenticity. See Jacob Golomb's book on Existentialism for a detailed discussion of this important challenge to my view. I will use Kierkegaard, who connects authenticity with despair, as our prime example of this profound skepticism when we take up the inner dimension of authenticity in chapter six. Recent skeptics include Jean M. Twenge and W. Keith Campbell, *The Narcissism Epidemic: Living in the Age of Entitlement*; Jacqueline Olds and Richard S. Schwartz, *The Lonely American: Drifting Apart in the 21st Century*; Eric G. Wilson, *Against Happiness: In Praise of Melancholy*; and Jean-Paul Pecqueur's poetry in *The Case Against Happiness*.

do so? Is there something crucial in the experience of *despair* that accompanies many people's quest for authenticity that we miss if we strive to become happy as well as authentic? This question is central to the final chapter of this book and takes us into the interior dimensions of authenticity we have mainly ignored thus far. Before we turn to this most difficult challenge, I must make good on my promise that an extended study of happiness will pay handsomely in our quest to comprehend and experience authenticity.

Happiness and Authenticity

> *You have to practice happiness.*—Phil Cousineau

> *Deciding what to say and how we say it is made less complex by those who follow the sufi tradition. Their teachings on this are fiercely unambiguous: Whenever they speak, their words must first pass through three gates. The first gate—Is it True? The second gate—is it necessary? The third gate—Is it kind?*
> —Wayne Muller, A Life of Being, Having, and Doing Enough

Failings of Individualism

A dear friend (let's call him 'Frank') was as serious a seeker of authenticity as you will find. He spent his too-short life searching for a way of life and being that would set him apart as a genuine, unique character. Frank decided young to seek his spiritual fortune, his authentic identity, not in wealth as had his father, but in experiences, especially artistic ones. He lived simply, subsisting on about $5,000 per year, residing for free in a small cabin behind a Victorian mansion (he called it the "big house") provided by a friend. He ate simply, fixing his food in the combined bathroom/kitchen of his tiny dwelling, and he got most of his books, films, and music from the public library. To earn money, several times each year Frank would set sail to some exotic port or sea journey aboard a U.S. Naval vessel on which he would teach math to sailors for six weeks at a time. Often he would have the Navy leave him in Italy, or Singapore, or India when his tour of duty was up and he would spend a month or two wending his way home.

Besides being a math genius, Frank was a gifted pianist and a lover of classic literature. In his efforts to forge a life he invented a "recitation method" for, as he put it, "filling his head with strong language" by reciting his beloved Shakespeare, Dante, or Milton each morning. So central was this method to his quest for authenticity that nearly every time Frank "happened" to stop by at dinner time to be invited to a home-cooked meal (about once each week) we heard details about the particulars of the day's recitation.

For most of his adult life Frank lived and travelled alone, but he learned to seek out friends, and a wonderful variety of people attended his funeral. After a brief ceremony and comments by his sister, a line of people gave testimony to his bright and playful spirit. Each praised Frank as a genuine character who would be missed. He would have been pleased! However, his suicide gave testimony to a deep unhappiness and despair that belied the gaiety and laughter he tried to show the world.

Like me, Frank had been raised in South Dakota and Iowa. His father was a banker and millionaire several times over. He was also a miser who was legendary for his tight-fisted ways such as his refusal to use the wiper blades on his car when it rained lest they wear out, or for his use of the same toothbrush until the bristles disappeared. Not surprisingly, Frank's father had a miserable social life, quarrelling nearly constantly with his wife throughout Frank's childhood and until his death after more than 50 years of marriage, the last ten of which he spent as an isolate in his bedroom. While Frank was able to study the piano growing up, his home life and schools in small Midwestern towns were not supportive of someone in love with high culture, and his efforts to create an authentic life built around the classics drew little understanding or support from his family. To his lasting credit, Frank remained a faithful son while attempting to construct a life which was very different from the one in which he was raised.

In many ways Frank's story fits the classic description of authenticity as a kind of Bohemian life. He was in rebellion against the unhappy limitations and problems of Bourgeois society, but in seeking a more authentic life he was deeply unhappy. It is interesting that he had no "roadmap" for his spiritual journey. Although he read some of the Bohemian classics such as Rousseau, Thoreau, Kerouac, and Ginsberg, he did not develop a systematic critique of the bourgeois life he was rejecting or a coherent philosophy by which to live. Perhaps Frank was the proverbial misfit who was destined to despair and self destruction because of the chasm between who he really was and the life and identity afforded him by a superficial culture (or between his interior and exterior lives). Perhaps. In no way do I want to discount the seriousness of Frank's depression or diminish the difficulties of his struggles to create an identity. However, I believe he was, unfortunately, also a classic example of what can happen if you are confused about authenticity and happiness.

When Frank's parents died he inherited a great deal of money, and that money was the catalyst that drove him to suicide. Although he had the money for a year before his death, Frank was unable spend any of it. He tried. We helped him find a more attractive place to live, but he quickly sold it and retreated into his (womb-like) cabin like a child returning to the comfort of his mother's arms when the world becomes too much. Although he had long befriended lonely and sometimes homeless people, Frank was unable to give away any of his wealth even though he had some understanding that generosity is a well-known path to happiness. Instead, the money was a terrible burden precisely because it threatened to give him gravity, to tie him to the institutions and practices he had long struggled against—banks, governments, taxes, and property ownership—the bourgeois life. Frank had, to an extent far greater than he realized, defined himself like the proverbial teenager in rebellion, as *not*. This *via negativa* freed him from the burdens of community life to be an outsider,[15] and it was precisely the appearance of lightness that was so attractive (and deceptive) about Frank.

This lightness came at great cost. In his suicide of course, but while he was alive Frank bore the yoke of hyper-consciousness. Most people are relatively at home in the identities they have grown up with and into, and while outsiders like Frank are often correct in their criticisms of the superficialities of identity provided by our culture, for most people there is relatively little pain and effort involved in being the person they have become. As much Existentialist literature attests, to attempt to be free from social conventions and given identities is painful and difficult especially because of the effort of constant vigilance to avoid the cultural pitfalls you're rebelling against.

Two Cautionary Notes

All of this is well-trodden ground. Yet Frank's tragic story can add two important cautionary notes, and help us clarify the complex connections between happiness and authenticity. His example not only shows the sad paradox that to define one's self *via negativa* is tantamount to admitting that what you are rejecting has all the power, but in the end he also resembled his father in strong ways. Certainly

---

15 For an insightful look at the Existentialist or Bohemian strategy of defining one's self *via negativa* see Colin Wilson's book, *The Outsider*. Wilson has written extensively on this concept, and his subsequent books include *Beyond the Outsider* and *The Outsider and Beyond*.

Frank's frugality was not a duplicate of his father's, but his was equally pathological and I believe his inability to spend money helped trigger his suicide. While Frank worked hard to overcome the anti-sociality that plagued his family, he was a loner through and through, a rugged individualist who was neither rugged (my wife affectionately—but accurately—called Frank a hothouse flower) nor an individualist, as his need for an audience and for friendship was palpable. Unfortunately, he was largely incapable of the mutuality and intimacy the friendships he so desired required. When all is said and done, like every other human, Frank's "sources" (including his father's influence) ran through his veins, and the impossible effort to try to build himself from the ground up was a burden he could neither comprehend nor carry. As Cordova and so many others I have referred to have said, like it or not we are greatly our culture, language, family, peers, teachers and so on. To be human is to be shaped continually throughout our lives by contemporary factors and forces and also by ones that are far beyond this moment, place, our bodies and our abilities to fathom or greatly change.

The second cautionary note is good news. To seek authenticity in an attempt to reject one's society and culture is doomed to failure and surely will bring unhappiness, but to become real may neither require dramatic rebellion nor acquiescence to superficiality. If we can navigate *in-between* the various factors that divide us to become who we really are, we can be very happy indeed. How is this possible?

Frank, like me and many members of our generation of Americans, came of age in the 1960s. It was the golden era, if you will, of the counter-cultural movement, and at the heart of this movement was a desire to forge a better and more authentic way of life. Unlike many commentators such as Potter and Heath, I do not disparage the idealism and efforts of beatniks, peaceniks, hippies, and other bohemian attempts to change the course of American society away from the growing materialism and accompanying drive toward world power that has wrought so many unfortunate results. I believe these efforts to alter our policies and practices were mainly correct in connecting them to our images of the good life and human nature. But like Frank, I believe the so-called 1960s radicals were sorely disappointed insofar as they attempted to impose an entirely new regime without taking seriously how they individually, and their movements collectively, were beholden to as well as enmeshed in the very culture and society they wished to change. You need not look far today to see aged hippies, still sporting beards, pony tails and tie-dye shirts, working as lawyers, actors, bankers, or even politicians and living bourgeois lives. As we discussed earlier, individualists have hamstrung their abilities to change themselves, let alone their societies and cultures.

The Compatibility of Authenticity and Happiness

Tracing the trajectories of 1950s and '60s Bohemians[16] is a different project from mine, however. The point of my examples is to emphasize not only the impossibility of remaking themselves and American society and culture as envisioned by America's "existentialists," but also to show why failure was inevitable and how the attempts often revealed a profound misunderstanding of self and society.[17] Our first conclusion about the relations between happiness and authenticity, thus, is that while they are not the same, they are not necessarily op-

---

16 A good place to begin this study is David Brook's popular book, *Bobos in Paradise: The New Upper Class and How They Got There.*

17 Many social engineering efforts, especially modern secular ones in the 20th century, but also theocratic ones today, should give pause to anyone considering radical social reconstruction. Perhaps the most dramatic example is Pol Pot's Cambodia, but certainly Hitler's entire career can be seen as such an attempt, as can Mao's China or Stalin's Soviet Union. For theocratic examples contemplate Afghanistan's Taliban or Iran's current theocratic polity.

posites or in conflict. You need not be unhappy if you choose to be authentic, and you may be authentic in pursuing happiness. Only if you choose strategies such as many of those in the counter-cultural movements of the 1960s, in which the goal is to delete the past and begin afresh, is it nearly inevitable that authenticity and happiness will be in conflict if not incompatible.

A second link is that a crucial ingredient in happiness, community, is also central to authenticity. You can almost map the increase in the desire for authenticity onto the social changes and growth of multi-cultural diversity in the modern world. Cordova's impassioned defense of authenticity *through* culture highlights how important living in a thick culture is to people's connectedness and integrity in traditional societies where being real is not much of an issue, and we have seen that as our culture has thinned, authenticity increasingly becomes a challenge. Frank sensed this and spent his time in Iowa City, the place in Iowa most friendly to divergent views and practices of the sort he pursued. If communities form around new or counter-cultural ways of being then they have a chance of becoming viable, and by joining the group a person has a chance of being authentic in that new mode of being. Still, in seeking uniqueness and non-conformity individu-alists run a great risk of failing both at happiness and authenticity. Frank steadfastly refused, at a great cost, to join any group or even join with others in a mutual project out of fear of having the purity of his authenticity corrupted—at the cost of rendering unattainable that which he sought so desperately. Perhaps a helpful way of putting this point is to speak of our hyper-sociality as our "essence," and if positive psychologists and most social scientists are correct in this assessment then you can see why individualist strategies for authenticity fail—in seeking themselves, their "real selves," in isolation they guarantee they won't find them.

Two caveats are crucial at this point. What Frank and most other seekers of authenticity realize is how important the "interior," first-person life is. Any reader of cultural critiques such as Kafka's "Metamorphosis" comprehends that the dogged pursuit of exteriority alone can leave a person with no interior life and the critical dimensions of full humanity it brings. In a culture like ours, with its many distractions and centrifugal forces that pull us away from healthy interiority, it is far too easy to leave our interior lives undeveloped. Most people, working the standard work year of 2000 hours (40 hours per week, 50 weeks per year) along with the shadow work required to support such a full work schedule, have little time for such "luxuries." But because an interior life that fits with one's exterior life is crucial for becoming authentic, any life pattern, including ones that involve a rich social life, must have time for a rich interior life as well. Authenticity, remember, lies in-between many dualities including what is external and internal to us, and it is about *integrating* the many dimensions and sources of the self.

A second critical caveat is that the external/internal dichotomy is far too stark. In her study of Hellenistic philosophy,[18] Martha Nussbaum makes a strong case that Greek philosophers after Plato were much closer to the truth than Plato in arguing that a strong opposition between reason and emotions is mistaken because emotions have their logic and because our rationality often (usually?) is also passionate. In a similar vein I have been arguing that our interior lives are brimming with things from our external lives—images, ideas, faces, music, places, work, and so on; and our external lives, of course, always necessarily involve our subjectivity.

---

18 See Martha Nussbaum, *The Therapy of Desire: Theory and Practice in Hellenistic Ethics* and also *Upheavals of Thought: The Intelligence of Emotions*.

I hope that by beginning with a solid grounding in a social scientific understanding of human nature and its implications for happiness we have avoided becoming lost in the individualist's no-man's land of unhappiness, bad faith, escape from freedom and despair, and that instead we can enter the interior dimensions of our selves with clearer heads, realizing that to focus inward does not require denouncing our communities and other external ties. Our next and final chapter is about *calling*, about the longing for deeper reality than the common everyday spectacles and surfaces our culture offers in such profusion, but it is about doing so through communion with others, about deepening our selves through learning from guides and fellow travelers while becoming ever clearer about who we are and what we desire. To our definition of authenticity as **living actionable narratives that provide gravity and meaning and tie us into meaningful stories of our communities**, we can add process and the future: **becoming authentic is an ongoing quest through which we can ripen as human beings.** Before turning to this quest, let us conclude briefly with several further important things we can learn about authenticity from the study of happiness.

The Role of Virtue

Happiness and authenticity are both descriptive *and* normative concepts. Empirically we can discover whether and how happy or authentic people are feeling and any variety of forms of life can bring either or both. We can also inquire into which experiences of happiness or authenticity are most worth having. Put differently, much of the literature on happiness and authenticity is concerned with the nature and etiology of the self. Everyone has a self and the happiness and authenticity that flow (or not) from it. However, not every identity is desirable or optimal.

This is perhaps the central place where I part company with Potter. He is convinced that because of the serious confusions about authenticity that abound in the history of this concept, and because of the resulting harms that have occurred, we should abandon the concept and the quest. To a great extent, I agree with his diagnosis and analysis of this problematic "religion of modernism." In contrast, though, I believe that if we properly understand the self and what being an authentic self is about, this concept can be a very useful guide to being fully human.

Our earlier discussion of virtue and happiness highlights how normative questions of quality and worth have entered this discussion historically. Socrates' question of whether virtue can and does bring happiness goes deep into the territory we want to explore with regard to authenticity as well as happiness. Is virtue inherently valuable, good in and of itself rather than for the social benefits it might bring us? You will have to read Plato's *Republic* to see what Socrates (Plato) thought the answer is (a clue...they thought it was), but it is Aristotle's answer that I think is most instructive for our purposes.

In a sense, Aristotle's serious answer is like the glib, one-line summary I just gave to Plato's book-length reflection: of course one should be virtuous if happiness is what you seek. (Remember, Aristotle thought that the definition of happiness *is* what humans seek.) Why does Aristotle not find this to be a difficult question? In short, the answer lies with his theory of human nature. Think of it this way: for Aristotle our natural tendencies are not only hyper-social, but that means we naturally tend to want to be just, temperate, courageous, prudent, and so on. To strive to become fully human is to strive to be virtuous. The real punch line of Aristotle's definition that "man is a political animal" is that a virtuous person is the most fully human, and that in developing our most excellent qualities we will be most happy. Virtue is its own reward because naturally we will be most happy when we act, for example, with the greatest generosity. Perhaps this is the central point of the parable Jesus tells of "the widow's mite," and it certainly seems to be the gospel Bill Gates and Warren Buffet are preaching when they recommend that all billionaires give away at least half of their holdings (Buffet has given away 99% of his!).

If Aristotle is right about our hyper-sociality containing a natural orientation to the virtues, parents are triply correct in wanting their children to be influenced by virtuous people. Not only will they be more successful and more excellent and therefore happier, but they will, to use our term, be more authentic and won't have to struggle to do the right thing when the time comes because they have been practicing virtue from an early age. Had Frank grown up in a family and culture that prized the kinds of sensibilities he came to love, I seriously doubt he would have had to struggle so hard to become authentic.

"Losing One's Self" to Become Real

This brings us to our final two connections between happiness and authenticity. Just as both are about integrating the dimensions of our life and being—about the right fit between our desires, talents and work, for example—experientially they are both about flow and *losing oneself* in the moment. To have the experience of being totally at home in the moment is to feel real *and* to be happy. Positive psychology tells us, remember, that this occurs when all the "stars" are in alignment— our natural set point, the conditions of our lives that are mainly determined by society and culture, and the variables over which we have significant control. As we will explore in the next chapter, the experience of flow is the first-person counterpart to the integration of the factors that constitute the self as seen from a third person perspective.

Finally, if our society is supportive of the right kinds of conditions, including an education that involves self-knowledge, then we will have the opportunity to *develop* a clear and solid identity which we can live out. In one sense, of course, children can be and are happy and authentic; and as Nietzsche and Zhuangzi show us, at least metaphorically the ideal is to become child-like. But remember the caveat they gave. The goal is to be a *wise* child. Cordova makes the same point when she emphasizes that in her tradition children are not considered full-fledged persons. Lest this sounds harsh, bear in mind that mainstream American culture and society do not heap adult expectations, rewards, or responsibilities on children precisely because they are "adults in training."

From this perspective, happiness is not about momentary pleasures but is a word used to summarize the tenor of a person's life: "she was a happy woman even though she suffered many challenges." And as we have seen whether or not people have happy lives is, in significant measure, a matter of how the society *and* the individual shape the factors that affect their lives. We know that conditions as diverse as commuting, noise, social relations (especially marriage and friendships), inequality, personal time, good work, and distractions, all of which are malleable, can be "engineered." We also know that individuals can change their attitudes, patterns of thought, use of resources, leisure time activities, group memberships, and friendships and thus profoundly affect their personal happiness.

It is curious that Haidt recommends three strategies for dealing with depression—meditation, Prozac and/or cognitive therapy—but does not mention relationships. At the very least a lot of "talk" therapy is, as my former sister-in-law once said about her counseling practice, purchased friendship. In the final chapter I want to turn attention to the development of personal practices that can enhance our authenticity by taking seriously the third-person understandings we have gleaned from the study of happiness. At every stage of life we can grow and develop, and this is as true of our spiritual selves as of our physical selves. Often the kind of emptiness or despair we have discussed in this chapter can call us to a more authentic life, an important insight most beautifully expressed by Rumi:

The Guest House

This being human is a guest house.
Every morning a new arrival.
A joy, a depression, a meanness,
some momentary awareness comes
as an unexpected visitor.
Welcome and entertain them all!
Even if they are a crowd of sorrows,
who violently sweep your house
empty of its furniture,
still, treat each guest honorably.
He may be clearing you out
for some new delight.
The dark thought, the shame, the malice,
meet them at the door laughing and invite them in.
Be grateful for whatever comes.
because each has been sent
as a guide from beyond.

    — Jelaluddin Rumi, translation by Coleman Barks

CHAPTER SIX
CALLING

There are moments of silent depth in which you look upon the world-order fully present. Then in its very flight the note will be heard...These moments are immortal, and most transitory....No content may be secured from them, but their power invades creation and the knowledge of humanity, beaming of their power stream into the ordered world and dissolves it again and again. —Martin Buber

Writing this Book

In other cases, one may commend the work apart from the workman; not so here; he who touches the one touches the other. —Montaigne, "Of Repentance"

A man receives only what he is ready to receive, whether physically or intellectually or morally, as animals conceive at certain seasons their kind only. We hear and apprehend only what we already half know.—Thoreau, Journal entry, 1860

I work at a community college where there is no incentive to take on writing projects, especially not a full-length book. Nearing the end of my teaching career, I had no plans for any major projects…of which I was aware. Then one fine evening in April of 2008 a woman asked me why I wasn't writing the book I was meant to write and instantly I knew that she was right and even what the topic was. I felt *called* to write this book. The experience was not the same as I described earlier where I felt pulled out of myself when I was working with turtles or basking in a sunrise. In this instance, I was there, fully in my everyday conscious and social mode. It was more like a light being shined into a corner where suddenly, finally, you can see something you've been overlooking. Something important you didn't know you were missing, although you might have had a vague sense you were missing something. Later I realized two things had to come together for this calling to emerge: I had to be ready for it, and the call had to be issued. In my case the call came in the form of a question from an insightful person I had just met. With fresh eyes she read me like a book and somehow knew of a deep desire that was unconscious to me. My readiness is only now becoming clear.

Calling ordinarily is a religious theme—after all, calling implies a caller. I believe it is a mistake, though, to grant religion sole owner-ship of this rather mysterious but vital concept and reality. Calling is about some very deep but common and crucial perceptual realities, and it doesn't necessarily have theological implications, although it may well have metaphysical ones. To hear a call involves making what later seems like an obvious connection, but which had eluded you; what you came to realize was lost in plain sight. Usually we reserve the word *call* for profound and major spiritual insights, but I believe such profound moments are paradigms of what often happens on a much less grandiose canvas. I have never felt that God or some super-natural agent called to me from beyond the veil to write this book, yet I definitely felt (and continue to feel) called to write it, and doing so has added a significant dimension to my life that would have gnawed at me yet consciously would have gone unnoticed.

Callings are moments of realization that seem to come from beyond that can lead us in unanticipated directions. Given our discussion of the narrative self, one way of framing calling is to say that a call comes when a new narrative enters our lives, when a different interpretation of the meanings of our lives snaps into place without our conscious effort. Calling is connected to the proverbial existential issue of the meanings or purposes of our lives. Henry Bugbee believed that all of our genuine connections to reality (he talks of "touching") are calls because when we are in this mode we are open to the mysterious, the unknown.

I was delighted to realize I "had this book in me" and working on it has been edifying, if sometimes difficult. But for many people their calls have remained submerged and unattended because they did not want to live the lives they were called to begin. Moses resisted God's call to return to Egypt and take up the cause of the enslaved Jews, and he had profound conversations with this voice from beyond about the implications of what he was being asked to do. Similarly Jonah resisted the voice pounding on the door of his awareness, but his mythical fish adventure reminds us that once such inspiration surfaces it is both difficult and dangerous to ignore. Callings are powerful phenomena. And they are tremendously varied in content. One person might be called to help the poor of Haiti, another to write music, a third to adopt a child, and so on. Yet they do seem to have some characteristics in common:

> 1. As we have suggested, callings often require significant life changes to new projects or activities that change the narrative arc of one's life. But if Daoists like Bugbee are correct, everyday perceptions can contain calls when we

are "invited" to open ourselves to hidden dimensions in everyday realities.

2. Often people's initial reaction to a call is to ignore, deny, or rebel against the challenge, especially those that might add significant responsibility or alter dramatically their lives. Most calls seem to come from beyond and are unbidden; however, when people *seek* their calling they often come up empty handed.

3. Finally, for what is central to the themes of this book, calls are usually to increased authenticity, to a life lived more fully and more in touch with realities both internal and external.

The Turn Inward

What lies behind us and what lies ahead of us are tiny matters compared to what lives within us.—Thoreau

Henry Bugbee's book, *Inward Morning*, like much writing on authenticity, urges us to look inward, to our first-person experiences to comprehend this elusive phenomenon. Until now I have urged that we spend our time looking at ourselves from a third-person perspective to avoid reducing the self and authenticity to "mere subjectivity." Yet I have also espoused an "in-between" perspective, realizing the mistakes that have occurred when we ignore personal experience as we try to understand identity and authenticity and view them strictly from third-person perspectives. I believe the key is to move beyond dualisms such as objectivity/subjectivity and fact/value that have, as we discussed briefly in our philosophy chapter, relegated the self (and thus authenticity) either to "mere subjectivity" or to total social construction.

Let us review briefly what we have garnered from the various "objective" viewpoints we have considered:

1. Authenticity is about achieving a genuine identity, and identity is, in great measure, a social creation in which we participate but over which we have limited control.

2. Much of our identity is set by our genetics (for example, our happiness set point) and by the conditions of our lives.

3. To achieve an authentic identity in modern societies requires time and effort, and it is an accomplishment that must be continually re-gained.

4. Authenticity is such an issue today because we live in societies that often distract us (for example, by the demands of work, the habits of consumerism, or the allures of technologies) from developing and living our genuine character.

5. Finally, while achieving authenticity can require jettisoning aspects of our given identities, to a great extent what authenticity requires is settling into and living one's identity with excellence. In large measure, to be authentic is *to identify with one's identity*.

This final chapter is about what is involved in this identification process.

It is no coincidence that the major writings on authenticity, even today, come from Europe and in particular from philosophical traditions that are related to Existentialism and Phenomenology, for more than any other modern traditions they take personal experience seriously. The great Danish philosopher Søren Kierkegaard, for example, insists that in our scientific, third-person quests for truth we should not ignore subjective truth. He, like Bugbee, insists that while acting and living authentically have their social dimensions, fundamentally being authentic is about our *interiority*.

It would be a great mistake to write off Kierkegaard as being a "mere" subjectivist. He never denies the reality and importance of objective, third-person truth. Instead, he is concerned that another source of truth, subjective experience, can easily be ignored in our strident pursuit of empirical, third-person knowledge. Also, for Kierkegaard, authenticity has nothing to do with a deep inner or essential self—for him authentic selves of this sort don't exist. Authenticity is about acts or ways of life, not about finding and living out some pre-ordained identity. But it is also not about blind conformity to a socially constructed identity. For Kierkegaard, and as we have seen for Nietzsche, Heidegger and classical Daoism, authentic identity is in-between. In an important sense, Kierkegaard, like many philosophers in this broad phenomenological tradition, is warning us about *reducing* humans to descriptions and definitions of whom we are that are too simple and one-dimensional. Their strategies are not unlike anthropologists in the Geertzian tradition insisting that thick descriptions are necessary for even beginning to understand someone (including ourselves) or a group, and Kierkegaard's emphasis on first-person singular experience resonates with Wilber's quadrants.

For Kierkegaard, to be authentic is to be passionate and sincere.[1] You can see why he is considered an Existentialist with this focus on the quality of our acts and thus our choices, and yet Kierkegaard simultaneously affirms a crucial aspect of my view that to a great extent much of what it means to be and act authentically is *unbidden* or a gift. In his most famous work, *Either/Or*,[2] Kierkegaard describes in detail the three kinds of lives we might choose—aesthetic, ethical, or religious life—and he contends that no rational arguments can be given to convince us to choose one over the other. He argues that each of these ways of being human is self-contained, and the only way to enter into them is to take a great "leap of faith." Such a leap is less about knowledge or dogma than about commitment (passion) to something we believe but cannot prove (sincerity). Perhaps the association with religious leaps of faith is too strong, but I believe Kierkegaard's emphasis that authentic selves are "performatives," realities that take shape in action, is very true. At the same time, it would be a great mistake to ignore the other side of callings—we must listen and respond, but reality must call.

Remember Nietzsche's metaphor of treating yourself like a work of art? Let us say you are a proverbial 18-year old college freshman forging a new identity. As you take classes that inform you about the lives of other people, be they historical or contemporary, actual or

---

1 There is a resurgence of interest in Kierkegaard in part because scholars are realizing that the traditional label of "Christian Existentialist" applied to him can lead us away from most of his important insights that are not confined to Christianity. Jacob Golomb's fine book, *In Search of Authenticity*, is but one example of this renewed interest in Kierkegaard. It is interesting to note again that the precursor in English-speaking philosophy to the renewed interest in authenticity is Lionel Trilling, who offers an analysis of authenticity in terms of sincerity. Nietzsche, of course, focuses (rightly, I think) on integrity, but he also emphasizes intensity. Clearly Kierkegaard is tapping into an important vein: while authenticity may not have to do with an inner core self, it does have something to do with intense personal choices.

2 *Either/Or*, Howard and Edna Hong, trans.

fictional, from your own culture or another, you are acquiring some perspective necessary to comprehend your own, mostly given, identity. You come to realize that much of what you value or believe is what people like you value or believe, that your parents have been not just the rudder of your ship, but also the mainsail, that despite your desires that it be otherwise the messages from the media have shaped you in powerful and subtle ways, that biology is, to a significant extent, destiny, and so on. Unfortunately many teachers today, as well as far too many students, do not pay enough attention to this self-discovery dimension of college or of education more broadly, and even fewer people capitalize on post-college opportunities for discovery and growth. Think of how much we learn about our parents, and thus ourselves, as we face the daunting routines and tasks of a new job, or how we get an inkling of what it was like to parent us as we parent our own children.

If so much of who we are can become clear to us only partially, late, or inchoately, we can begin to see why Bugbee emphasizes the *unbidden* or *grace* or the *gift*. So very much of what influences us and who we are is not chosen. Why, then, does Kierkegaard emphasize *choosing*? His person in the throes of the crucial existential decision of how to live and who to be does not choose in some simple, uncharged way. Rather, in all sincerity and with great passion he takes a leap of faith even though he is not at all certain about the "whisper" he has been hearing—whether it is real or what it is. With regard to authentic being, to take seriously and respond to this gift from beyond, to this new perspective or narrative possibility, is to leap, without a net, into a new way of being who you are.

It is small wonder that most people who seek their calling come up empty. First, when faced with the vast unknowns that callings can bring, most of us shy away from Kierkegaard's existentialist leap.

Second, the dynamic of calling is much like that of happiness in this regard: if you seek it, it will elude you, for the essence of a calling is being unbidden. When the Amana Colonists came to eastern Iowa in the late 1800s they had a beloved leader, called a *Werkzueg*, who led them. When he died, the story goes, a man who clearly was next in line was inspired to become the next *Werkzeug*, but he refused the call. As a result, the Amanans had to change their mode of governance. Years later, in the 1950s and 1960s, a man who wanted to be a traditional leader sat on a hill waiting for inspiration that never came. This man was true to his tradition in that he refused to pretend he was called when he was not. You have to wonder how many self-proclaimed religious leaders have been as honest.

While I believe Kierkegaard is right in insisting that the paradigm of such a dramatic response to life's possibilities is religious conversion, the pattern he describes fits many "lesser" callings. When I decided to become a college teacher rather than a minister or social worker, what I knew was that I found great meaning in learning and especially in philosophy, and I admired the lives of a number of my teachers. I really did not know myself well enough to realize how my personality fit philosophizing and teaching better than other career possibilities—clarity about that came only after suffering (mainly unconsciously) four years of social work and finally realizing (again, not very consciously until years later) that I was not particularly gifted or interested in dealing with people's personal and social woes. Furthermore, I gave no consideration to the fact that teachers get a lot of days of the year out of the classroom (when you total it up, the typical college teacher meets students about seven months of the year), how much more or less money I could have made in other endeavors, nor what tenure tracking would mean for my sense of security and the meaning of my work. Perhaps I was more naïve than many people in choosing my career, but my point applies to most everyone in a variety of circumstances. A friend recently told me that if she had known what being a parent entails, she probably would have postponed having or never would have chosen to have children. Quite possibly her perspective will change as the hardships of the past few months become more ancient history, but choosing something as major as a mate, to be a parent, to invite your ailing parent to move in, or to move to a new location usually involves a fairly substantial "leap."

Why Leap? Choosing a New Narrative

Heidegger agrees with Kierkegaard and Nietzsche about many aspects of our human situation in a world where we are adrift without strong guidance systems. He contends that whether or not we choose a "God path" we are stuck selecting the major contours of our lives without the assurances people in the past received from their thick cultures. He differs from his predecessors in his insistence that, like it or not, a primary feature of our being is that we are *thrown* into a social world largely not of our own making. Thus for Heidegger, whichever life story we choose to live, not choosing is not an option, for the inauthentic life is as much a choice as the authentic. In this sense, the answer to the question, "why leap?" is straightforward—because we cannot avoid doing so.

But Heidegger's insistence that we are social through and through (thrown into history, irrevocably) can take us to a less obvious and more interesting answer to Kierkegaard's question. Remember that Kierkegaard believed that because choosing a life narrative is a leap of faith, there is nothing you can say to someone to convince them to choose an aesthetic, ethical, or religious life. If we begin with the perspective that we are social beings, the curious thing is how we became *in*authentic, alienated from our homes, for after all we are native to the worlds we inhabit. Heidegger's analysis of this curious modern phenomenon is much like my own—I lose myself in the (common) world by succumbing to distractions.[3] Heidegger puts it in terms of ownership—I become an entity in this world owned by others, and everyone becomes an "other," no one is him/herself. The reason Heidegger gives for why we succumb to these distractions is the central Existentialist insight that we fear freedom. We experience deep anxiety at having to choose and we are tempted to give to others our freedom to choose, all the while pretending we are free. Although Heidegger says we should not blame society for our tendency to escape from our freedom because such freedom is a great burden, we should note that this analysis makes it clear why consumerism has become such a dominant replacement for community. In a mass-market society sellers are more than willing (often more willing than friends and family) to carry our "burden" of choosing whom we should be and how we should live.

Rehearsal of this classic Existentialist analysis brings us to a very interesting result of Heidegger's analysis: he claims that *I owe it to myself to be myself.*[4] Whether we are religious or secular, in an age where we have so many distractions from the natural process of forging an identity and where we are so tempted to give over this difficult process to someone else, we tend to ignore or not hear the call to become a person with a solid character. In one sense, this is a call from within, as it wells up from our natural desire to be an individual; but as we

---

3 For a fascinating look at what we are missing living distracted lives, see George Prochnik, *In Pursuit of Silence: Listening for Meaning in a World of Noise.* Prochnik brings contemporary scientific studies, as well as everyday examples, to the very Daoist perspective that silence is fundamental to perception, to experience. Perhaps this is what several western religious mystics have meant when they say things like "God is in silence," or even "God is silence."

4 Golomb, 112.

have seen, the call also comes from outside of us. Experientially, it does not matter if the "voice" we hear is from our deep psyche or from something/someone external to our body. In either case, we experience it as mysterious, hidden, unbidden, from "beyond," and it feels like a gift, an act of grace.[5]

Given his more social orientation, Heidegger then makes a crucial point that individualists like Nietzsche and Kierkegaard overlook: my call to authentic being is also a call to others. Because we are hypersocial and learn how to be by mimicking others, if others witness me on the path to authenticity my response to the call I hear will affect them as well. This is a version of the well-worn insight that people's characters and actions are not only valuable in themselves, but also have centrifugal influences on others. This is why, for example, we want our children to spend time with peers, teachers, scout leaders, and others who are of good character. Heidegger's point also borders on an important idea that proponents of "open societies"[6] value highly: we are *all* better off, everything else being equal, if our society values people being enabled to listen to and respond to calls, for only in such societies will large numbers of people be able to exercise their creativity in exploring what it means to be fully human. There are strong social as well as individual reasons for listening and responding to our calls.[7]

---

5 Ken Wilber contends that our interpretation of our callings depends on where we are in our spiritual development. If we are, for example, in the mythic stage we will attribute the calling to an external figure such as Jesus or a Bodhisattva, whereas if we are in a more advanced, integral stage, we would attribute it to the spirituality within us. See his *Integral Spirituality*.

6 Isaiah Berlin, in his famous books on liberty and its enemies, and Carl Popper in his writings on the open society and its enemies, following after people like Mill in *On Liberty*, are very adamant that it is in open societies where human flourishing, including people being free to explore their identities and become authentic, can occur best.

7 Crawford's perspicuous phrase is "excellence ramifies outward!"

The Great Paradox: Only the Authentic Can Hear the Call

One of the important truisms of life is that we see what we are ready to see and hear what we are ready to hear. I recently broke my femur (the large leg bone connecting the knee to the hip) in a bicycle accident and was on crutches for several weeks. As a result of being forced to pay attention to everyday activities such as walking, bending, dressing, personal hygiene, and sitting/standing, I now notice and appreciate similar details in the lives of other handicapped people, and I am greatly impressed by how several people I know with long-term disabilities cope successfully without complaint. While laid up I appreciated more than usual how interdependent my life is with my wonderful wife and friends, and I am humbled by the realization that I actually do little that doesn't depend on gifts from people near and far, now and in the past. You can see why so many people emphasize that *gratitude* is a fundamental attitude in being able to touch reality as well as providing the backbone of religion and ethics. As a result of my new limitations I learned a bit more why the idea of "dependent origination" is at the heart of Buddhist teachings—everything affects and is affected by everything else; all is intertwined. However, one need not suffer a serious injury for this principle to be in play. Everyone always experiences the world based on their orientation, on their experiences, concepts, beliefs, and prejudices. You will experience supermarket meat differently if you visit a slaughterhouse or a CAFO (confinement feeding operation), you will pay more attention to hand washing if you suffer the flu, you will appreciate the small things along your way more if you walk with a child, and so on.

If this is true, then who is most likely to listen for and hear calls? An authentic person, or at least someone who is on the path toward authenticity. Who most needs to hear a call? *Inauthentic* people, of course, people who probably have many barriers to any suggestion that they follow a different drummer or adopt a different life story. Furthermore, most likely someone who has not heard the call to authenticity (remember, Heidegger and others are saying that being called to authenticity is natural, it is built into human development) is surrounded by inauthenticity and has little likelihood of encountering authentic things or people. It is no wonder that Kierkegaard believed so strongly that you cannot rationally convince someone to leap in response to the call, for the psycho-logic of calling is like the psycho-logic of food, or yards, or music. What you eat, especially as a child, will be what "food" tastes like to you; the music you are used to, especially as a child, is what "music" sounds like; if the neighborhood of your childhood is filled with acres of mowed grass you will not be impressed with or accepting of the proposal that everyone in your current neighborhood grow "unsightly" prairie instead. I have a friend in her late 50s who most young people would see as an "old lady" (she has become frail and moves slowly) who still most prefers heavy metal music because that is what she loved as a teenager. This reality about us is why producers/sellers are so anxious to convince children to consume their products, as they have found that if someone is "branded" as a child they will tend to remain brand loyal throughout life.

These everyday and ubiquitous examples help uncover two further revelations about the "paradox of authenticity." First, the same kind of psycho-social difficulty (paradox) that authenticity represents is as common as cell phones, and perhaps is summed up best in the cliché that "the rich just get richer." Second, this first paradox of authenticity can help us understand the critical paradox of recognition and motivation: we have what Hegel called a "poverty of desire" by which he meant that we do not really know what we truly desire. Helping someone, including ourselves, recognize what we need and desire, and then making the changes necessary to meet or satisfy those needs or desires can be exceedingly difficult. But not impossible.

As a first step toward understanding and dealing with this pair of paradoxes, consider the so-called self-help movement. Like Andrew Potter, Charles Guignon[8] is highly critical of our culture's infatuation with self-help strategies to deal with any variety of issues. He contends that self-help gurus such as Dr. Phil or Oprah (or thousands of others) typically are guilty of the following transgressions:

1. They tend to give primary valorization to feelings. Whatever you feel is the most important aspect of any situation, and any feeling is legitimate.

2. Usually there is a strong dichotomy between the inward and the outward, with the former always being good and the latter tending to bad. Thus what is inward tends to be authentic, the real you, and what is outward is inauthentic, an imposed reality. A closely related fallacy of the self-help ideology is that what is social is second-rate, it is the realm of make-believe and masks (inauthenticity).

3. Self-help valorizes self absorption. The basic message is that a lack of self absorption is what ails you rather than realizing that often if what you want is to become more fully human or to discover who you are, turning inward in a narrow sense might be entirely misguided.

4. The self-help movement tends to worship childhood. It fails to include a full understanding of the life-long development of a mature person. This failure typically involves a misunderstanding of the long maturation process that is the journey to authentic character.

8 Charles Guignon, *On Being Authentic (Thinking in Action)*.

5. Of course, a key belief of this movement is that the real self is deep inside, and often an onion metaphor is used to prescribe a "peeling away the layers of falsehood" to get at your deep, inner core self (essence).

I believe Guignon and Potter are basically correct in their critiques of much self-help materials and activities, although I am not as familiar with this very widespread (and lucrative) movement as they are. Clearly they believe these attempts to help people deal with a variety of personal problems, especially including a sense of unreality or inauthenticity, suffer from the failings of individualism I have been discussing. I share their judgment that much self-help not only seems to be ineffective, but also that it can be dangerous. It is ineffective because, as we saw with happiness, only a small fraction of our happiness or unhappiness is responsive to individual efforts, and a great deal depends on our communities. As part of an overall strategy certain kinds of individual efforts are critical for improving our well-being, but in isolation they tend to be self-defeating and frustrating.[9]

Perhaps a helpful way to illustrate the limits and dangers of self-help is to think about the identity shifting that apparently is on the rise among pop music stars. A host of female singers, for example, not only enact persona that their followers find attractive, but they have taken to enacting a variety of persona depending on the occasion and their artistic judgment. The kind of shape shifting that Madonna and Lady Gaga are using to enhance their careers can be fun and instructive for their young audiences. However, while such playfulness underscores the theory of the social construction of identity, it also illustrates some of the limits of self-help. The meanings and effects

---

9 For the kind of self-help/community-help guides that offer real help precisely because it includes both, see Joe Robinson, *Don't Miss Your Life: Find More Joy and Fulfillment Now.*

of a given persona depend on a complex array of public meanings without which no communication would occur. This Wittgensteinian point about the impossibility of a private language underscores the limits of dealing with complex social-psychological phenomena alone or in such uncontrolled circumstances. Especially for impressionable young people, developing an identity in a world of possibilities without strong guidance can clearly bring sad or even tragic results. Put differently, what is lucrative for shape-shifting stars, like advertising, is playing with the same kinds of explosive material that religions are warned to treat with the utmost care—the identities, psyches, and lives of vulnerable human beings. The dangers that concern Guignon go beyond the wasted dollars and opportunities for charlatans because if people try to fix by themselves, what is a social or deep psychological problem, they could do more harm than good. Self-help can be less than helpful.

Is Authenticity Always Desirable?

A specter has haunted us throughout our attempts to comprehend authenticity, a specter with two heads: first, that authenticity is not attractive to many people, and second that whether or not authenticity is a good thing depends on the self that is seeking it. As our examples from popular culture show—be they of pop singers projecting multiple persona or consumers seeking to be cool—many people enjoy wearing masks and are more interested in trying out multiple identities than seeking the gravity and solidity of character we have argued authenticity is about.

There is little doubt that the first critical point is correct—many people are at least momentarily more interested in playing with identity than seeking to solidify or give it gravity. Such playfulness clearly can be fun, but it can also indicate a serious undertone. As more than a decade of watching our local alternative high school students "play Goth" has revealed to me, a major reason many young people try on unconventional persona is to send a message of rebellion, and rejection to the conventional identities they are offered. Taking on various identities can also indicate a serious search for authenticity, for an identity with which one can identify. Playing multiple identity games in no way undermines my analysis of authenticity, but instead helps to show what a complex, varied, and widespread quest it has become in a culture of rapidly shifting identities. Also, there is nothing necessary or sacred about people always being on a quest for authenticity, nor is it a contradiction for someone seriously forging an authentic identity to try on various masks.

The contention that not all authenticity is worth seeking is more difficult to deal with because it challenges an unspoken normative dimension of my theory. Diane Rothbard Margolis,[10] a feminist sociologist who believes that selves are socially constructed,[11] claims that societies create the selves they need at particular moments in time, and thus the shelf life of a given self (ideal type) depends on its usefulness. Particular selves come and go. Her main examples are what she calls the *exchanger* and the *obligated* selves. The former is the male persona that has come to dominate in market economies in the last two hundred years—the rational, self-interested, utility maximizing business person who minimizes emotions and tends to treat himself, as well as others, as property available for exchange. The obligated self is the female role in such economies, the helpmate who does the shadow work, is focused on relationships and plays a supporting role

---

10 *The Fabric of Self: A Theory of Ethics and Emotions.*

11 To which I would assent, but the crucial questions have to do with out of what and by whom?

for the exchanger. These ideal types are minimally descriptive, but her analysis helps make the case that ways of being a self, the narratives of identity we have available, are mainly created by societies at particular times for particular reasons, however aware or intentional we are in choosing these pre-cast identities. Furthermore, as both of these types are being criticized strongly today, we can see the force of the contention that not all identities or their authentic manifestations are desirable. History shows us that an exchanger personality could be authentic in his role as an entrepreneur, researcher, or political leader; likewise, a woman playing the role assigned her as helpmate could identify with that narrative arc as well. Margolis, like most of you, I would suspect, would find neither of these characters attractive, however authentic they might be.

To put it baldly, even if someone is authentic the further question is whether or not that version of authentic being is a *good* thing. Authenticity does not seem to be an absolute value any more than freedom is. We might agree that a person would be free in choosing to act a certain way, but the fact of freedom does not answer the prior question of whether or not what they choose to do is a good thing. We can say the same thing about laws—a particular law might improve our freedom, but is that a good thing? The answer, of course, seems to be that it depends on what the freedom portends or whether or not that identity is worth living. In contrast to this challenge, I have been operating with a normative notion of authenticity that presupposes it is both a *natural* inclination and that it is a *good* thing as a person becomes increasingly authentic *if* they are developing in a certain way. How can we meet this challenge?

The answer, I believe, is to acknowledge the legitimacy and importance of the challenge but to carve out a clear version of the normative view of authenticity we have been developing. Because authenticity is a function of our selves, and selves are malleable, most certainly someone could opt to become a genuine jerk, a person of stunted development, or even someone who is genuinely evil. This is the challenge de Sade raised in his pursuit of evil. Part of being human is to have the ability to do evil, and his characters developed this capacity to an art form. They became authentically evil.[12] I believe that part of why Kierkegaard refuses to try to convince people rationally that they should enter in one or another of his three stages on life's way is his recognition that any of life's narratives we might choose is a major existential choice, the choice of who and how to be, and that no one can decide for us.

On the other hand, while trying to avoid essentialism, Kierkegaard, Heidegger and other modern thinkers do have a kind of naturalism in that they believe we naturally tend toward this fundamental existential decision. To be human is to wonder why we are here, to want to have purpose and meaning in and for our lives, and it is to want to be an individual. I believe that we also have a natural desire to be a person of character, and this desire is the basis of my normative theory of authenticity.

Our Desire for Character

The authority of the lived life is a mysterious power which everyone senses and no philosopher explains. – Goethe

In one sense Hegel's odd proposition—that we do not know what we really desire[13]—is easy for us to understand. After all, we have been hearing about the subconscious for more than a century, and the idea

---

12 Albert Camus has a terrific discussion of Sade in *The Rebel*, as does Susan Neiman in her more recent *Evil in Modern Thought: An Alternative History of Modern Philosophy*.

13 The so-called "poverty of desire" is a major idea in Hegel's influential *Phenomenology of Spirit*, published in 1807.

that much of what we are about is unknown to us is the basis of a great deal of contemporary theory and practice in the social sciences and education. But a *poverty* of desire? Virtually all critics of contemporary life in so-called developed countries decry our unquenchable desires. The problem doesn't seem to be a *poverty* of desire, but the impoverishment of our world as a result of the fecundity of our expanding desires. These critics are right of course—we desire far too much stuff and as a result we are ruining the planet. But there are deeper insights in Hegel's concern. For one thing, as we explored in the chapter on happiness, what so many of us desire not only is infused in our psyches through advertising, but the satisfaction of these desires has little positive connection to our happiness or flourishing as humans.

The further dimension of Hegel's fecund idea, for our purposes, is his belief that something deep within us that takes years of tender care to grow gets twisted or buried in the avalanche of desires heaped upon us. Hegel's way of stating our hyper-sociality, as we have seen, is to say that our fundamental desire is for recognition, but as one of his major critics and followers, Nietzsche, so strongly argues, we also desire *to be moral*. It may sound even more odd than talking about "the poverty of desire" to say that Nietzsche, who announced the death of God and espoused transcending our inherited herd moralities, believed our fundamental desire is to be moral, but our discussion of Aristotle at the end of the previous chapter should help makes sense of what he means. Nietzsche, like Aristotle, was a virtue ethicist, which is an ethical perspective that has been returning to respectability in recent years. A virtue ethicist believes that who we are is more fundamental than what we do (consequentialism) or what we intend (deontologism). If we are of moral character then we will intend and tend to do the right thing. Nietzsche believed that we have a powerful natural desire (the "will to power" in its best interpretation) to discover, develop, and express (camel, lion, child) our character, and the positive side of Nietzsche's writing focused on revealing this process. The critical side of his writing, of course, was aimed at exposing and eradicating the influential and difficult ways our societies and cultures quash this nascent desire, including enmeshing us in herd moralities. His point, therefore, is not that we don't desire to be moral, but rather that because that desire is so fundamental to our identities (recall that Taylor claims, in *Sources of the Self*, that our moral values are fundamental pillars of our selves), it is ripe for hijacking, just as our desire for recognition is hijacked by advertisers. Nietzsche believed we have a deep desire for integrity, which includes much of what we have said authenticity includes: to discover, develop and express one's talents, to feel a deep connection between who we are and what we do, to have an integration of our many aspects and to be a person of gravity. How is this galaxy of characteristics connected to morality? A crucial feature of his *Übermenschen* (overmen), the humans who accept and yet transcends their histories (inherited stories), Nietzsche tells us, is that each overman will be as different from other overmen as we are from the apes. Thus while the *content* of our morality might differ from person to person, the *desire* to be moral does not, insofar as morality is about being a person of character.

If I am correct in my understanding of Nietzsche, then a deep meaning of Hegel's poverty of desire can help us articulate the normative feature of our theory of authenticity. For Nietzsche goes to great pains to explain how the invasion by others' desires (including values, stories, images, etc.) can impoverish our own, with the result that our natural desire for becoming a person of character gets colonized by someone else's stories just as our desire for water gets transformed into a desire for products from Starbucks or Pepsi. It would be a great mistake, however, to be too individualistic about this point. While people of all ages need time and space to wonder and imagine in this process of forming character, we must not forget that we are mainly made of biological, cultural, and social material not of our own construction. Thus not only is it impractical to suggest that most people follow Rousseau's *Emile* and become isolates to escape untoward influences, but such a scenario would not particularly improve the process of authentic character formation. What would?

The Centrality of Edifying Stories

Don't be satisfied with the myths that came before you. Unfold your own myths. –Rumi

Out of the struggle with ourselves, from the fire in our souls, comes the thing that never existed before—the music, the art, the words that make life endurable, and more, creative and sublime. –Phil Cousineau

To answer the question of how to satisfy our desire for strong character in terms we established in our philosophical chapter, of what would help people most in satisfying their deep desire for gravity, for being real, for authenticity, would be to learn to live the right kinds of narratives. People want stories that have them playing the roles of strong characters, if not of heroes, and they want stories that tie them to communities where they can contribute something important. They also want stories that will not only ring true to their deepest desires and emotions, but that will also help them explore and develop this interiority. People want and need *edifying* stories, stories that build or instruct our moral and spiritual character.[14] What are these stories?

---

14 The dictionary also links 'edify' with 'edifice,' with building or establishing.

The short answer is *myths*. Not just myths in the sense of ancient stories of legendary beings, but myths in a broader sense coined by the old Roman writer Salutius who said that myths "are things that never happened but always are."[15] In mythic imagination time, space, and emotion are compressed, revealing meanings and possibilities for our lives. Such stories help us see in new ways, they call us to change the trajectory of our lives, and they connect us to eternal truths.

Phil Cousineau contends that what is needed is greater familiarity with strong myths and the ability to imagine ourselves living those myths. Cousineau is a disciple of Jung and several second-generation Jungians (Hillman, Campbell, and May) who shares their belief that the emptiness or nothingness rife in modern societies is a lack of meaning, and that what people desire are the kinds of stories (the paradigm being myths) that provide such meaning. Rollo May told Cousineau that "Our powerful hunger for myth is a hunger for community," and that even more than meaning people are "really looking for…a deep, [numinous] experience of life."[16] A numinous story or experience, Cousineau explains using the words of psychologist Edwin Edinger, is one which "carries an excess of meaning or energy, transcending the capacity of the conscious personality to encompass or understand it. The individual is awed, overwhelmed, yet fascinated."[17]

Cousineau's book is an attempt, not unlike Campbell's best selling *Myths to Live By*, to reveal the many ways we experience myths, and how these myths (or their absence) affect us. He shows beautifully the variety of contexts and stories that he would suggest are involved in myth making, from various novels and movies, to children's stories and even television series. Cousineau joins a chorus of contem-

---

15 See Phil Cousineau, *Once and Future Myths: The Power of Ancient Stories in our Lives*, 3.
16 Cousineau, 14.
17 Ibid, 15.

porary educators who encourage parents and teachers to expose their children and students to the best possible stories to help build their imaginations and their characters; and like latter-day Nietzscheans, they decry the paucity of the stories children (and adults) hear from our popular story tellers, especially those who create movies and television stories. As one anthropologist who studies traditional societies with thick cultures put this concern, "when television, rather than grandmothers and grandfathers, tell the stories, the culture withers." I would add that this change of stories and story tellers is another reason why authenticity is so difficult for us.

It is interesting to note how central imagination is in this process of building character. To a great extent, if we cannot or do not imagine ourselves doing certain things or being a certain way they will not happen. Imagination is not only crucial for artistic, technological or scientific creation, but it is also vital for self-development. If you recall, Sartre's book, *The Imaginary*, is central to his entire perspective. He contends that imagination is the basis of our freedom and identity (nothingness) because no matter what we do or are, we can always imagine something different. Thus whatever I do or am is based on what I imagine. While I believe Sartre at this point commits a major fallacy by turning our abilities to imagine not doing something into a kind of negative essence[18] (nothingness), and like so many post modernists he moves in exactly the wrong direction by abstracting us from direct contact with reality, he is spot on in locating our ability to alter ourselves and our futures in the imagination. Given the centrality of imagination in human affairs, you can see why hearing edifying stories, especially as a child, is critical for our development as a human.

---

18 Philosophers call this the fallacy of misplaced concreteness. Nothingness is not a thing or essence, it is simply our ability to imagine a different outcome from the one that seems most likely.

If authenticity is a coming together of our interiority and exteriority, and of our individuality with cultural and social givens, we can easily settle for less than we need or desire if the narratives from which we choose are inadequate. In my teaching I like to borrow a phrase from the singer/songwriter John Prine, "my baby done done me wrong songs," when referring to impoverishing narratives that negatively affect how many people live. A related trope is "grade-B movies" (books, television shows, and so on) that do little to edify. If, for example, what seems normal or possible is to settle for whatever mate you can find, to take on a pattern of spending every evening in front of the television, to view educated people as "pointy-headed" or oneself as incapable or not in need of learning or growing or changing, or to believe that anyone who works with their hands is ignorant or incapable of intelligent conversation, you probably have adopted seriously self-limiting narratives because of the stories you have (and have not) heard.

Think back to our discussion of consumerism, the most pervasive narrative in our lives. Most people who try to live this narrative of material progress and success have not heard serious alternatives or cannot imagine following a different story in a land where most everyone else believes this myth. Yet as Haidt and many others contend, following this story is not the yellow brick road to happiness or personal fulfillment. In fact, it appears that *even if* you are among the lucky and are successful in living this powerful myth it will not bring you what you really need and desire. This is not to say there is one best story, for there are many edifying myths. Rather, what the mounting evidence that consumerism is a "false god" (untrue myth) tells us is that for a narrative to usher in authentic living it must resonate with some deep, inborn human characteristics such as our hyper-sociality and need for community, our need for time and play, and our strong desire for moral character.

The power of imagination plays out in another way in what we learn from the stories we hear. Cousineau makes it clear that whether or not a myth truly edifies depends on the ways and extents to which we are able to discern the deep truths of the story and apply them to ourselves, especially to our inner lives. An English-teacher friend complains that most students can tell the plot or story line of most novels she assigns, but few are able to relate to the psychological or deep personal dimensions of most stories. Of course various things happen in a novel or in real life, but usually what shapes the physical events are people's desires, intentions, and choices—their interior lives. Thus what many people fail to acquire along the way are the interpretive tools necessary to understand myths. It is no accident that college teachers in the humanities, like their counterparts in the sciences, spend much of their time teaching methods. Science teachers want their students to graduate steeped and adept in the scientific method. Humanities teachers desire that their students be equally accomplished in the arts and sciences of interpretation, of hermeneutics.[19] While some of the tools and skills necessary to interpret narratives of all sorts simply come from long and rich familiarity with a variety of quality stories, the ability to look at them using the many sophisticated perspectives that have been developed has a kind of multiplier effect. You can now see that the Luke Skywalker stories are both hero and coming of age stories with parallels in many great

---

19 Hermes, from whose name 'hermeneutics' derives, was the winged messenger in Greek mythology (Mercury in the Roman pantheon) who carried communication between the gods and between the gods and humans. One of the powerful points of this myth is that when we learn some truth about the world we are learning the secrets previously only known to the gods and revealed to us through their messenger—a gift, often surprising and unbidden.

historical myths (and these other stories resonate in this new telling, old wine in new wineskins), you realize that Star Wars is a retelling of epic struggles between good and evil and that the violence needed to defeat the empire contains the seeds of future, unending cycles of violence, and so on. You also realize that the important insights and truths of Star Wars do not depend on its historical literalness. In fact, if you read it as literally true, the mythical powers of the story die. No, there is not, was not, will not be a Yoda. Yes, Yoda embodies the kindly mentor and sage who has to trick and challenge his apprentice into seeing and doing things in different ways if he is to mature.

Unfortunately, we live in a time when we are paying a great price for literalness about religious myths. We live in an age of *fundamentalisms*. In America we still have a significant minority that fails to comprehend dependent origination or the truths of evolutionary science because they read the Biblical creation myths literally, and this lack of hermeneutic sophistication plays out in some unfortunate ways in our political and educational systems, and in our inability to respond adequately, for example, to very real environmental problems. Reza Aslan[20] describes similar hermeneutic ignorance among perpetrators of the 9/11 bombing and other Islamic extremists who believe that the war between the forces of good and evil should be taken literally (another example of misplaced concreteness) and justify them (on the side of good, of course) doing whatever harm they can to us (on the other side, obviously).[21] A more nuanced and informed reading of the Koran shows, for example, that *jihad* is about the struggle we all face

---

20 *Beyond Fundamentalism*

21 Haidt devotes a chapter of his book to this tendency we have to reduce matters to simple categories such as good vs. evil. In chapter four, titled "The Faults of Others," he calls this tendency "naïve realism" and contends that much of the conflict and violence in the world can be attributed to this temptation to demonize our opponents and ignore our own foibles.

as we try to develop our moral characters given our strong temptations to give in to a wide variety of lesser ways of being, but it takes a better hermeneutic approach than literalness if people are to attain such an understanding.

To enter into the complex territory of competing modes of interpretation would be fascinating, but it would take us far astray from our concerns. From what little we have said about hermeneutics, however, it is clear that a great deal hangs in the balance between interpretive strategies—for example, whether people from different religions get along or are at war with each other, whether or not religion and science are seen as compatible, and how we interpret and enact the myths we live by. Conflicts between hermeneutic perspectives also play major roles in our efforts to become authentic. A paradox of authenticity is that in our development to be our own selves we need strong guidance. All religious traditions emphasize the importance of teachers (gurus, guides, mentors, spiritual directors). Perhaps the need for a wise mentor is imperative because spiritual development and experience are so profound and challenging. But this imperative is really no different from the need for ever-stronger guidance by teachers as we move from common sense learning as children to more sophisticated learning as we mature. One might think that graduate or post-graduate students would be ready for total independence, for they are far more knowledgeable about their subjects than undergraduates or secondary students, but what and how they are learning requires special attention and the most disciplined "submission" to another's directions in their development.

We have argued that the path to authenticity should be covered with stories, especially potentially edifying ones. The irony of our situation should not be ignored: the best road to becoming our selves, to discovering, developing, and expressing our genuine voice is to hear the best old stories plus the best tools of interpretation others have developed. Given the challenges of living in modern societies, providing this nourishment appears to be a monumental task. Yet as our examples of Native American cultures indicate, human societies have been performing this task quite well for millennia. We have explored some of the kinds of distractions that take us off the scent of becoming authentic, but in some ways our task of helping our children and ourselves become authentic is easier than we might think. For some of the sources of distraction also can be sources of assistance. Television has replaced grandparents as story tellers, and this is a sad loss because that was a crucial link between generations that is difficult to replace. However, television (movies, videos, etc.) *can* tell edifying stories, often in ways that stir the imagination better than most grandmothers could. Children's books, like other forms of entertainment and education for children, have multiplied exponentially in number, and thus it is difficult to sort through to the good ones; but it is wonderful to discover that there are now many more good ones than existed even a generation ago. How can we find the good ones?

What we and our children need is Nietzsche's tuning fork. You will recall that his "lion" has the heavy burden of taking all the stories and "truths" that abound and sort them through as if taking each scale from the dragon of culture to see which rings true and which doesn't. Nietzsche makes it sound as if we are entirely on our own in this arduous process, but that is far from the truth. We get a tremendous amount of help from others, not only in the creation, maintenance, and retelling of the narratives, but also in finding, sorting, interpreting, and assessing them. Librarians, as well as parents and teachers provide such assistance, but through the Internet more and more strangers are involved as well, be they list-serve editors, bloggers, reviewers, or other readers. In this rich mix of potential stories and interpretations the need for strong hermeneutic skills and "crap detectors" has grown in importance. Thus children, as well as those who help them sort through the morass of potential stories, can take an active role to determine which stories are most edifying as well as entertaining. We need excellent guides from an early age, but we also need to learn to "tune" in the truth when we are young. Becoming authentic is a collaborative effort.

I Am More Than a Story

In Louisville, at the corner of Fourth and Walnut, in the center of the shopping district, I was suddenly overwhelmed with the realization that I loved all those people, that they were mine and I theirs, that we could not be alien to one another even though we were total strangers. It was like waking from a dream of separateness, of spurious self-isolation in a special world, the world of renunciation and supposed holiness... This sense of liberation from an illusory difference was such a relief and such a joy to me that I almost laughed out loud... I have the immense joy of being man, a member of a race in which God Himself became incarnate. As if the sorrows and stupidities of the human condition could overwhelm me, now I realize what we all are. And if only everybody could realize this! But it cannot be explained. There is no way of telling people that they are all walking around shining like the sun.—Thomas Merton, describing his mystical experience that occurred in 1958.

I would be remiss to ignore a most serious challenge to our new theory of authenticity if I failed to consider a perspective found in most religious traditions. These traditions claim, while at the developmental level of the ego there is no real self, at the deeper or transcendent level we *are* pure awareness. This "witness" is our true self. Mystics from every culture have sought to leave behind the ego and identify with awareness itself, which is to achieve the state of mystic union with all that is. However this state is described or understood, the claim is that pure awareness is the one unchanging thing about us and thus is most fundamentally who we are. When people achieve this state they claim to feel whole and totally at home.[22] They are truly authentic because they have identified with their true, inner core essence.

One response we might give to this powerful challenge is that very few people achieve this vaunted level of spiritual development, and therefore while it might well be the ultimate authenticity, most people will never attain it. The theory of authenticity we have been developing will have to suffice for most of us. If Ken Wilber is right, however, we need not accept this spiritual essentialism that looks like the process of peeling the onion until getting to its golden inner core. Especially in his most recent book, *Integral Spirituality*, Wilber contends that even those who accomplish the highest experience of spiritual insight carry with them major aspects of identity from the stages of development in which they have grown. Wilber also distinguishes between *stages* of spiritual development through which seekers must pass (which are parallel or similar to stages of moral, cognitive, and emotional development) and *states* of religious experience. Someone can be at the lowest stage of development and have a mystical experience. The difference between them and someone at a higher stage will not be the quality or legitimacy of the experience, but rather the interpretation or understanding of the experience.

---

22 Lex Hixon's *Coming Home*, e.g., is about various holy people who have achieved this mystical union.

Advanced spiritual heroes like Jesus transcend the limitations of lower levels of development, but Jesus remained his mother's son on the cross, he struggled with temptation until the end, he had great difficulty living out his advanced spiritual insights in the face of immense political, social, and physical challenges, he was supported by a community of followers, and so on. Thomas Merton, on the other hand, had his famous religious experience on a street corner in Louisville, Kentucky, when he was at a relatively early stage of spiritual development. Nevertheless this profound experience of oneness with everyone and everything informed the rest of his life and spiritual development. Merton would have been inauthentic if he had not built his life around the experience on that street corner, but it would be inaccurate to say he was only, or even most, authentic in that moment. His ego disappeared, he experienced oneness and bliss, but whether or not he had been or was to be authentic was based on how he wove his experiences into a coherent story.

Wilber's perspective helps us comprehend Merton, Jesus or any one of us by highlighting a crucial aspect of being authentic—*integrity*. At each stage of development, we naturally attempt to integrate the various aspects of our lives—our emotions, social relations, values, metaphysics, factual knowledge, and so on—into a coherent narrative. To fail such integration is to be open to the kinds of anxiety and emptiness that we have associated with inauthenticity. This challenge to become integrated exists for the most advanced as well as the least developed spiritual beings among us. In fact, advanced spiritual people have a greater challenge because they not only need to integrate the dimensions of the world with their advanced spiritual experience, but they must also integrate all of the material from their lower levels of development as well. What they have going for them, of course, is deep understanding and the flexibility of mind that comes with having gone through many previous transformations to higher levels of development. As we discussed earlier, the Dalai Lama is open to changing even his most precious beliefs if science tells him something important he had not known, whereas many religious people at a lower stage are unable to accept scientific truths because they are inflexibly attached to interpretations of dogma (to narratives at a certain level) and feel terribly threatened at the prospect of moving to a more sophisticated level of understanding.

Integrity is achieved when one comes to a coherent narrative. However, not just any coherent narrative will do. For a narrative to bring integration that is authentic it must fit who I am with the world I experience. Everyone, including advanced spiritual people, uses language, ideas, and tropes they learn from their culture, and therefore success in this enterprise of building an integral narrative happens better in some cultures, and with the use of certain images or linguistic usages, than in others. And once again, people who have grown through several stages of development tend to have greater capacities for narrative formation because they are more familiar with a richer variety of stories and have more nimble and rich hermeneutic abilities. They tend to have greater strengths and flexibility of mind and creativity just as they tend to be more capable of letting go of stories, habits, beliefs, and values that keep them tied to a developmental stage instead of embracing transformation.

You might still wonder if the "witness," our pure and simple awareness, isn't the deep, core essence we have been missing in our search for the real me. If what you seek is some unchanging aspect of your self, awareness itself is it. By definition the content of consciousness is always changing, and this includes aspects of our identity—our desires, beliefs, values, memories, roles, and so on—but that which is aware of this content, or awareness itself, seems fixed. Mystics who have attained this remarkable state, however, report some interesting features. First, to become this witness is to leave behind ordinary concerns and experience, including one's identity and ego. Second, when in this state there is no action, no ordinary doing possible. You must be in a trance-like state of meditation. Third, the purest expression of what this state is like comes from the Vedic tradition in Hinduism which claims that all is one (or there is only one, not many.) Finally, in this state of deep meditation there is no thinking, imagining, or narrating going on. In that sense this highest or deepest or most authentic spiritual experience is beyond depiction. It is ineffable.

Often times, when mystics return from their blissful forays they put together coherent stories to communicate what they can to the rest of us. Or, as many an apprentice has experienced, these masters poke and prod their followers to grow, to move beyond their current level of development by achieving a more sophisticated or satisfactory integrity. I am not denying the wonder of the blissful union the great mystics achieve, nor am I discouraging anyone from working toward that experience. I do want to emphasize that reaching that state is a social/cultural journey and accomplishment and is a matter of passing through a series of stages that are both built into our DNA and culturally defined. Our natural pilgrimage is between these two. Also, it is important to note that professional basketball players, e.g., can be authentic players or athletes at each stage of their development and their highest accomplishments as professionals make them paragons but not necessarily any more authentic than they were when their talents were less developed. The same is true for people on their spiritual journeys. You may not achieve Nirvana until your final stage, but you may have been a genuine seeker throughout your pilgrimage.

What marks whether or not someone is authentic, then, are two things: if they have (or live) a coherent story, and if that story fits with the realities within and without the person. A story with integrity. Much of what I have been attempting to do in this book is to call your attention to false starts and dark alleys that distract us from knowing ourselves and our worlds and from living with integrity. The good news that Wilber brings us is that there are remarkable cross-cultural and trans-historical patterns that can help us in our attempts to understand our lives and create integral narratives. We can stand on the shoulders of giants. Nevertheless, we each must find our way.

Pilgrimage - Wandering on the Way

> Pilgrimage requires stories that try to glean meaning from the chaotic incidents along the way. –Phil Cousineau

I love the phrase, "wandering on the way," as does Victor Mair, who chose it as the title to his collection of the tales and parables of Zhuangzi,[23] the greatest of the classical Daoists. When we think of pilgrimage we often have the image of a carefully planned trip to a specific place for a specific purpose, and certainly many pilgrimages have such trappings. But the inner workings of pilgrimage usually are much more like wandering than careful planning.

In 2000 I taught for a semester at Bradford University in Yorkshire, England. We were fortunate that our entire family could experience what to us was an exotic place and way of life, and we were doubly fortunate that we had time to travel across the British Isles, from London to Edinburgh to Tintagel to Wales to the remote corners of Ireland. I thought that my main focus would be teaching a new subject (sociology) in a new context (A-level exam preparation), but while that was my official assignment, in retrospect it was the mechanism to launch a

---

23 Victor H. Mair, ed. and trans., *Wandering on the Way: Early Taoist Tales and Parables of Chuang Tzu.*

far more significant venture. As we drove to the far reaches of Britain and hiked over hill and moor, we began to notice that our attention was increasingly drawn to ancient holy sites—standing stones, holy wells, hallowed battlefields, legendary glens and graveyards, churches and cathedrals, and monasteries. Many of these places, like the great Edwardian castles built to protect the empire against Welsh insurrectionists, were natural tourist sites, but we began finding ourselves at small holy sites many tourists never discover. The itineraries for our weekend and holiday travels were roughly planned—we decided to go to northern Scotland or to St. Kevin's monastery in eastern Ireland—but we made a point to saunter, to wander. The most significant experiences we had came from our openness to the unexpected. What Lori and I realized late in our six-month sojourn to England was that we were on pilgrimage.

Pilgrimage usually happens best when people follow the classic formula for any religious or spiritual experience: lengthy preparation, an intense experience, and a lengthy period of "debriefing," of reflecting on the experience. Our preparation had been for a five-month trip to Britain, for teaching, for our boys being in an English school, for living in a village, for driving on the other side of the road, and so on. Not for spiritual experience. Yet as the trappings of our everyday lives changed, and as we shed our identities, we became open to whatever, to the unbidden. In the process we were changed at a deep and subtle level. Neither of us had an "ah-ha" moment, a blinding flash, a profound shaking of our being, and neither of us had a sense that we were ready for personal transformation. Yet we were, and if we had read our own signals, as an outsider might, we would have realized our readiness. After all, we had opted to pack up, exchange lives with our English counterparts who were living in our house and driving our car and doing my job while we were doing the same in their stead. Surely we were ready for change at a pretty deep level.

For me the quest turned out to be the perennial question of authenticity: how do I want to spend my life? Back in Iowa I was spread very thin with too many commitments at work and in my personal life. Our sojourn in Britain helped me realize that if I wanted to be effective in working for the causes that meant the most to me, I would have to choose, to narrow my focus. But how? Our pilgrimage helped me choose. What I found myself drawn to were holy sites that were natural places where the Celts of old practiced their worship in and through nature. It finally dawned on me that more than almost anything, I cared for nature, and after that it was easier to sort out my priorities so that I could spend my life in a way that fit who I was.

My "awakening" came through many excursions that reinforced the ideas animating the chapter of this book on nature. I was most alert and most quiet when sitting on a hillside or near a holy spring, walking near the ocean, exploring ancient stone passage graves, and hiking over dales. I noticed a cumulative effect wherein I simultaneously became increasingly self aware *and* open to the world around me. I became especially aware of how the layers of tasks and responsibilities that had come to occupy my psyche had seriously narrowed my vision and my abilities to respond to what was around me. In my 45 years of college teaching this was the closest I had to a sabbatical, but it was more of a pilgrimage than a typical sabbatical wherein most academics narrow their focus and hunker down to a serious professional study.

Pilgrimage: Into the "Wilderness"

As a single footstep will not make a path on the earth, so a single thought will not make a pathway in the mind. To make a deep physical path, we walk again and again. To make a deep mental path, we must think over and over the kind of thoughts we wish to dominate our lives.—Thoreau, Walden

I am not surprised to find a growing number of studies that show the importance of time in nature for human flourishing. To mention a few: even a few minutes of exercise outdoors are better for people, mentally and psychologically as well as physically, than similar activities indoors, and people's brains function differently when hooked up to electronic communications than when they're doing outdoor activities, and this is especially true with regard to concentrated, in-depth thinking. Furthermore, a few moments spent in outdoor activities can lessen stress, that most insidious component of many maladies people suffer today. People who keep the Sabbath (i.e., who take a serious day away from everyday routines and responsibilities), especially those who include outdoor time, are better able to focus with equanimity on those responsibilities during the week. These and other positive effects of connecting to and in nature have strong implications for our educational practices, environmental policies, personal habits, technology uses, and spiritual practices. But how are they connected to wandering and authenticity?

I once viewed a documentary wherein a Hindu holy man made the simple but crucial point that while some people seem to be born with a genius for spiritual practice, as with most talents, most of us need props and much assistance to learn well the spiritual art. Thus holy music, liturgy, incense, spiritual directors, and time in nature can be much needed aids on our paths. In like manner, very few people follow a straight path to enlightenment while most of us wander—we are more or less focused on our spiritual practices at any given time and we often flit from one strategy to another, depending on a wide variety of factors. One of the great gifts of traditions like Daoism is the recognition and valorization of this common pattern of human life. Countless people have commented on how much people tend to miss who turn their image of how to live or how to achieve something into a rigid or habitual pattern that results in their overlooking much of what is delightful and interesting. Perhaps this is especially true of spiritual activity. One function of calling the holy "mysterious" is to remind us that there is no playbook, no formula, no one right way to approach this dimension of life.

At the same time, it is instructive that Daoism, like every other wisdom tradition, but also like a growing chorus of modern brain scientists and therapists, counsels regular sojourns into what nature has to offer—silence, diminishment of the distractions of our frenzied lives, time to reflect, and full embodiment. If Hegel is correct that what we truly desire gets lost in our everyday din, then time in nature holds the best likelihood for peeling away the false desires that keep us from this critical self discovery. It is less that there is a deep self hidden by the trappings of civilization than that there are aspects of our selves that must see the light of day if we are to integrate the inner and outer into a coherent self that has gravity of character. In like manner, it is less that openness to the mysteries of reality will put us in touch with the absolute or with absolute truth than that we will live in an enchanted world where every encounter can be a call. Bugbee calls this living in "reality as a wilderness":

> Reality as a wilderness...is the theme which unifies my own
> life. It enfolds and simplifies, comprehends and completes.
> Whenever I awaken, I awaken into it. It carries with it the

gift of life. And it lives in the authenticity of every authentic gift, every true blessing confirms it deeper; it is always with me when I come to myself. Through it I find my vocation, for the wilderness is reality experienced as call and explained in responding to it absolutely.[24]

Being Real...In Between

We are constantly invited to be who we are.—Thoreau

Many observers have commented on the power of naming—to name something or someone is to establish a special kind of relationship with almost God-like powers and Satanic temptations. Naming usually involves some kind of knowing, which can be a source of power. Used with wisdom naming opens up worlds; without wisdom it can destroy them. No wonder the ancient Hebrews believed that what it means to be made in the likeness of God is to be able to name the creatures. A common feature of many psychological therapies is to help people acquire a richer vocabulary of emotions so that they, for example, can differentiate being enraged from being angry or piqued or aggravated. Richer emotional vocabularies bring richer and more nuanced emotional and social life, and can result in the difference between a too-heavy and harmful reaction to an insult and an appropriate quip that reconciles the disputants. A rich vocabulary, like a rich array of edifying narratives, can make great differences in the quality of people's lives. The power to name improves our abilities to understand and shape our selves as well as the world around us.

Philosophical ideas function in similar ways. Like it or not, we live our (often unspoken or inchoate) metaphysics. What we consider to

---

24 *Inward Morning*, 128.

be real or valuable, and what we believe are the limits of our abilities to comprehend, have a great deal to do with the qualities of our experiences. This book has been an attempt, on the one hand, to show how important the concept of authenticity is for people today, and on the other to work toward a better version of authenticity than we have inherited from modern culture. I hope I have shown that to operate with the belief that the authentic self is an essence that exists in us from birth (or conception) is to condemn ourselves to a life of fruitless introspection and to ignore realities about how embedded in our worlds we really are. If you add to that misconception the common view that to be an individual is to be stuck making our worlds by ourselves, the very quest for authenticity becomes a major source of the emptiness, loneliness, and alienation that our quest is meant to combat. I have also tried to show that to reject both essentialism and individualism by concluding that the self is an illusion and that we are simply socially constructed is to endure a hopeless cynicism that only adds to our ennui. If you add to this post-modern perspective the view that we should eschew any talk about our subjective experiences, you will have discarded fundamental building blocks of authentic personhood.

I have proposed a theory of authenticity that is a *both/and* rather than an *either/or*, or *neither/nor*. The self emerges in the complex interactions between our interiority and what is exterior to us, and an authentic self takes shape when we act with an integration of our deepest desires and our external commitments and responsibilities. Because we are hyper-social and storied beings, this emergence takes place under the auspices of edifying stories learned from our communities and cultures. At the same time, because we desire to be individuals we need to shed the distractions that keep us from developing our unique voices. Because everyone of us is different, we cannot define what any person's authentic self will turn out to be. The person of gravity we become makes us more, rather than less, predictable. We will become unique but predictable. Our natural tendency to become authentic, like our innate impulse to become an adult, brings with it responsibilities we often shy away from, but if we don't lose our abilities to hear and respond to those calls, we may eventually find ourselves on a pilgrimage to a more authentic self. May this one day be true for you.

Bibliography

Abram, David, *Becoming Animal: An Earthly Cosmology* (New York: Pantheon, 2010).

———, *The Spell of the Sensuous* (New York: Vintage Books, 1996).

Adorno, Theodor, *The Jargon of Authenticity* (trans. K. Tarnowski and F. Will. London: Routledge & Kegan Paul, 1973).

Appiah, Anthony, "Identity, Authenticity, Survival: Multicultural Societies and Social Reproduction" in Amy Gutman, ed, *Multiculturalism: Examining the Politics of Recognition* (Princeton, NJ: Princeton University Press, 1994).

———, *Ethics of Identity* (Princeton, NJ: Princeton University Press, 2004).

Aslan, Reza, *Beyond Fundamentalism: Confronting Religious Extremism in the Age of Globalization* (New York: Random House, 2010).

Bender, Rudiger, "The Aesthetics of Ethical Reflection and the Ethical Significance of Aesthetic Experience: A Critique of Alasdair MacIntyre and Martha Nussbaum" (EESE 1/1998, 1-15).

Bercovitch, Sacvan, *The Puritan Origins of the American Self* (New Haven, CT: Yale University Press, 1975).

Bergmann, Frithjof, *On Being Free* (South Bend, In: University of Notre Dame Press, 1977).

Bernstein, J.M., "The Very Angry Tea Party" (*The New York Times*, June 14, 2010).

Blechman, Andrew, *Leisureville: Adventures in America's Retirement Utopias* (New York: Atlantic Monthly Press, 2008).

Borgmann, Albert, *Technology and the Character of Contemporary Life* (Chicago, IL: University of Chicago Press, 1987).

———, *Crossing the Postmodern Divide* (Chicago, 1993).

Brittan, Gordon G., Jr., "Autonomy and Authenticity." Edward F. Mooney, ed, *Wilderness and the Heart: Henry Bugbee's Philosophy of Place, Presence, and Memory* (Athens, GA: University of Georgia Press, 1999), 129-49.

Brooks, David, *Bobos in Paradise: The New Upper Class and How They Got There* (New York: Simon & Schuster, 2001).

———, *The Social Animal: The Hidden Sources of Love, Character, and Achievement* (New York: Random House, 2011).

Bryant Smith, Olav, *Myths of the Self: Narrative Identity and Postmodern Metaphysics* (Lanham, MD: Lexington Books, 2004).

Bugbee, Henry, *The Inward Morning* (Athens, GA: University of Georgia Press, 1955).

Camus, Albert, *Resistance, Rebellion and Death* (New York: Knopf, 1961).

———, *The Myth of Sisyphus* (London: Hamish Hamilton, 1955; originally published by Libraire Gallimard, 1942).

———, *The Plague* (New York: Knopf, 1948; originally published by Libraire Gallimard, 1947).

———, *The Rebel* (New York: Penguin, 1974, 36-47. Originally *L-Homme Revolte*, Random House, 1954).

———, *The Stranger* (New York: Knopf, 1946; originally published by Libraire Gallimard, 1942).

Campbell, Joseph, *Myths to Live By* (New York: Viking, 1972).

Caputo, John, *Against Ethics: Contributions to a Poetics of Obligation With Constant Reference to Deconstruction* (Indiana University Press, 1993).

Casey, Edward S., *The Fate of Place: A Philosophical History* (Berkeley: University of California Press, 1997).

Cousineau, Phil, *Once and Future Myths: The Power of Ancient Stories in Our Lives* (Newburyport, MA: Conari Press, 2003).

———, *The Art of Pilgrimage: The Seeker's Guide to Making Travel Sacred* (Newburyport, MA: Conari Press, 2000).

Crawford, Matthew, *Shop Class as Soulcraft: An Inquiry into the Value of Work* (New York: Penguin, 2009).

Creswell, Tim, *Place: A Short Introduction* (New York: Blackwell, 2004).

Csikszentmihalyi, Mihalyi, *Flow: The Psychology of Optimal Experience* (New York: Harper & Row, 1990).

DeZengotita, Thomas, *Mediated: How the Media Shapes Your World and the Way You Live in it* (New York: Bloomsbury Publishing, 2005).

Dominguez, Joe and Vicki Robin, *Your Money or Your Life: Transforming Your Relationship With Money and Achieving Financial Independence* (New York: Penguin Books, 1993).

Dostoevsky, Fyodor, *Notes from Underground* (Originally published in Russian in 1864; first English translation published by Everyman's Library in 1913).

Ellul, Jacques, *The Technological Society* (New York: Vintage, 1967).

Erickson, Lori and Robert Sessions, "A Case for Sabbaticals," in John DeGraaf, ed., *Take Back Your Time: Fighting Overwork and Time Poverty in America* (San Francisco: Berrett-Koehler, 2003), 167-71.

Ewen, Stewart, *All-Consuming Images: The Politics of Style in Contemporary Culture* (Harper-Collins, 1988).

Fallows, James, "Be Nice to the Countries that Lend You Money." *The Atlantic*, Dec., 2008, 62-65.

Frank, Thomas, *The Conquest of Cool: Business Culture, Counterculture, and the Rise of Hip Consumerism* (Chicago, IL: University of Chicago Press, 1998).

———, *One Market Under God: Extreme Capitalist Market Populism and the End of Economic Democracy* (New York: Anchor, 2001).

———, *What's the Matter with Kansas?: How Conservatives Won the Heart of America* (New York: Holt, 2005).

Frankfurt, Harry G., *The Importance of What We Care About: Philosophical Essays* (Cambridge University Press, 1988).

Friedman, Jonathan, *Cultural Identity and Global Process* (London: Sage Publications, 1996).

Froese, Katrin, *Nietzsche, Heidegger and Daoist Thought* (Albany, NY: SUNY Press, 2006).

Gardner, Howard, *The Unschooled Mind: How Children Think and How Schools Should Teach* (New York: Basic Books, 1993).

Golomb, Jacob, *In Search of Authenticity: From Kierkegaard to Camus* (New York: Routledge, 1995).

Gruchow, Paul, *Grass Roots: The Universe of Home* (Minneapolis, MN: Milkweed Press, 1995).

Guignon, Charles, *On Being Authentic* (New York: Routledge, 2004).

Guthrie, Stewart, *Faces in the Clouds: A New Theory of Religion* (London: Oxford University Press, 1993).

Haidt, Jonathan, *The Happiness Hypothesis: Finding Modern Truth in Ancient Wisdom* (New York: Basic Books, 2006).

Heath, Joseph and Andrew Potter, *Nation of Rebels: Why Counterculture Became Consumer Culture* (New York: Harper paperback, 2004).

Heidegger, Martin, *The Question Concerning Technology* (trans. W. Lovitt; New York: Harper & Row, 1977).

Herbert, *Culture, Inc.: The Corporate Take-Over of Public Expression* (New York: Oxford, 1991).

Hoge, Dean R. and Larry G Keetor, "Determinants of College Teachers' Religious Beliefs and Participation" (*Journal for the Scientific Study of Religion*, 1976 15 (3): 221-35).

Holstein, James A. and Jaber F. Gubrium, *The Self We Live By: Narrative Identity in a Postmodern World* (New York: Oxford University Press, 1999).

Hurley, S.L., *Justice, Luck and Knowledge* (Cambridge, MA: Harvard, 2005).

Hymowitz, Kay S., *Manning Up: How the Rise of Women Has turned Men Into Boys* (New York: Basic Books, 2011).

Jeffers, Robinson, *Not Man Apart* (New York: Sierra Club/Ballantine, 1969).

Kierkegaard, Søren, *Either/Or* (Howard and Edna Hong, trans. Princeton, NJ: Princeton University Press, 1988. First published in 1846).

Kimbrell, Andrew, *The Masculine Mystique: The Politics of Masculinity* (New York: Ballantine Books, 1995).

Kimmel, Michael, *Guyland: The Perilous World Where Boys Become Men* (New York: Harper Collins, 2008).

———, *Manhood in America* (New York: Oxford University Press, 2005).

Kunstler, James Howard, *The Geography of Nowhere* (New York: Free Press, 1994).

Laslett, Peter, *The World We Have Lost* (New York: Charles Scribner's Sons, 1965).

Layard, Richard, *Happiness: Lessons from a New Science* (New York: Penguin, 2006).

Lee, Dorothy, *Freedom and Culture* (Upper Saddle River, NJ: Prentice Hall, 1959).

Lee, *Valuing the Self* (Long Grove, IL: Waveland Press, 1986).

Leonard, Annie, "Story of Stuff" (www.storyofstuff.com).

Leventhal, Allan, and Christophe Martell, *The Myth of Depression as Disease: Limitations and Alternatives to Drug Treatment* (Santa Barbara, CA: Praeger, 2005).

Light, Andrew, *Philosophies of Place* (Lanham, MD: Rowman & Littlefield, 1999).

Lindholm, Charles, *Culture and Authenticity* (Hoboken, NJ: Blackwell, 2008).

Lopez, Barry, *Rediscovery of North America* (New York: Vintage, 1992).

Louv, Richard, *Last Child in the Woods: Saving Our Children from Nature-Deficit Disorder* (Chapel Hill, NC: Algonquin Books, 2005).

Lynbomirsky, Sonja, *The How of Happiness: A Scientific Approach to Getting the Life You Want* (New York: Penguin, 2007).

MacIntyre, Alastair, *After Virtue: A Study in Moral Theory* (South Bend, IN: University of Notre Dame Press, 1981).

Mails, Thomas E., *The Mystic Warriors of the Plains* (New York: Barnes & Noble, 1972).

Mair, Victor H. trans., *Wandering on the Way: Early Taoist Tales and Parables of Chuang Tzu* (Honolulu: University of Hawaii Press, 1998).

Margolis, Diane Rothbard, *The Fabric of Self: A Theory of Ethics and Emotions* (New Haven, CT: Yale University Press, 1998).

Martin, Mike W., ed., *Self-Deception and Self-Understanding* (Lawrence, KS: University of Kansas Press, 1985).

Mauro, Claudio, ed., *In Praise of Fertile Land: An Anthology of Poetry, Parable, and Story* (Seattle: Whit Press, 2003).

May, Gerald G., *The Wisdom of Wilderness: Experiencing the Healing Power of Nature* (San Francisco: Harper, 2006).

McAdams, Dan P., *The Redemptive Self: Stories Americans Live By* (New York: Oxford, 2005).

McCloskey, Deirdre, *The Bourgeois Virtues: Ethics for an Age of Commerce* (Chicago: University of Chicago Press, 2007).

McKibben, Bill, *Deep Economy: The Wealth of Communities and the Durable Future* (New York: Times Books, 2007).

———, *The Age of Missing Information* (New York: Random House, 1982).

Merleau-Ponty, Maurice, "Cezanne's Doubt," in *Sense and Nonsense* (Evanston, IL: Northwestern University Press, 1964). Originally published in France as *Sens et non-sens* (Les Editions Nagel, 1948).

Miller, Mark Crispin, *Boxed In: The Culture of TV* (Evanston, IL: Northwestern University Press, 1988).

Mooney, Edward F., ed, *Wilderness and the Heart: Henry Bugbee's Philosophy of Place, Presence, and Memory* (Athens: University of Georgia Press, 1999).

Moore, Kathleen Dean, et al., eds, *How It Is: The Native American Philosophy of V.F. Cordova* (Tucson: The University of Arizona Press, 2009).

Morris, Errol, "The Anosognosic's Dilemma: Something is Wrong But You'll Never Know What It Is (Part 1)" (*The New York Times*, June 20, 2010).

Nagel, Thomas, *The Possibility of Altruism* (Princeton, NJ: Princeton University Press, 1979).

Needleman, Jacob, *Money and the Meaning of Life* (New York: Doubleday, 1991).

Neiman, Susan, *Evil in Modern Thought: An Alternative History of Modern Philosophy* (Princeton, NJ: Princeton, 2002).

Nelson, Richard, *Make Prayers to the Raven: A Koyukon View of the Northern Forest* (Chicago: University of Chicago Press, 1983).

New York Times writers, *Class Matters* (New York: Henry Holt & Company, 2005).

Norris, Kathleen, *Dakota: A Spiritual Geography* (Boston: Ticknor & Fields, 1993).

————, *Acedia and Me: A Marriage, Monks, and a Writer's Life*, (New York: Penquin, 2008)

Nussbaum, Martha, "Finely Aware and Richly Responsible: Moral Attention and the Moral Task of Literature" (*The Journal of Philosophy*, 1985, 515-29).

————, *The Therapy of Desire: Theory and Practice in Hellenistic Ethics* (Prineton, NJ: Princeton University Press, 1994).

————, *The Fragility of Goodness: Luck and Ethics in Greek Tragedy and Philosophy* (New York: Cambridge University Press, 1986).

————, *Upheavals of Thought: The Intelligence of Emotions* (New York: Cambridge University Press, 2003).

O'Donohue, John, *Anam Cara: A Book of Celtic Wisdom* (New York: Harper-Collins, 1998).

Olds, Jacqueline and Richard S. Schwartz, *The Lonely American: Drifting Apart in the 21st Century* (Boston, MA: Beacon Press, 2009).

Orr, David W., "The Ecology of Giving and Consuming." In Roger Rosenblatt, ed., *Consuming Desires: Consumption, Culture, and the Pursuit of Happiness* (Washington, D.C.: Island Press, 1999), 137-54.

Palmer, Parker, "The Woodcarver" in *The Active Life: Wisdom for Work, Creativity and Caring* (New York: Harper, 1991).

————, *A Hidden Wholeness: The Journey Toward An Undivided Life, Welcoming the Soul and Weaving Community in a Wounded World* (Hoboken, NJ: Jossey-Bass, 2004).

Pecqueur, Jean-Paul, *The Case Against Happiness* (Farmington, ME: Alice James Books, 2006).

Piercy, Marge, *Circles on the Water* (New York: Knopf: 1982).

Polanyi, Carl, *The Great Transformation: The Political and Economic Origins of Our Time* (Boston, MA: Beacon Press, 1944).

Pope, Stephen J., *The Evolution of Altruism and the Ordering of Love* (Washington, D.C.: Georgetown University Press, 1995).

Postman, Neil, *Amusing Ourselves to Death: Public Discourse in the Age of Show Business* (New York: Penguin, 1985).

Potter, Andrew, *The Authenticity Hoax: How We Get Lost Finding Ourselves* (New York: Harper, 2010).

Prochnik, George, *In Pursuit of Silence: Listening for Meaning in a World of Noise* (New York: Doubleday, 2010)

Putnam, Robert, *Bowling Alone: The Collapse and Revival of American Community* (New York: Simon & Schuster, 2000).

Rawls, John, *A Theory of Justice* (Cambridge, MA: Harvard, 1972).

Reding, Nick, *Methland: The Death and Life of an American Small Town* (New York: Bloomsbury USA, 2009).

Ricard, Matthieu, *Happiness: A Guide to Developing Life's Most Important Skill* (New York: Little, Brown & Co., 2003).

Robinson, Joe, *Don't Miss Your Life: Find More Joy and Fulfillment Now* (Hoboken, NJ: Wiley, 2010).

Ruben, Gretchen, *The Happiness Project* (New York: Harper, 2009).

Sapir, Edward, "Culture, Genuine and Spurious," reprinted in *Katarxis*, No. 3, 1-7 (http://www.katarxis3.com/Sapir.htm).

Sartre, Jean Paul, *Being and Nothingness* (most recent English translation by Hazel Barnes, New York: Citadel, 2001).

———, "No Exit" (first published in 1946 by Stuart Gilbert; republished most recently in English as *No Exit and Three Other Plays*, Vintage, 1989).

———, *Existentialism and Human Emotions* (New York: Kensington Publisher, 1957).

———, *Nausea* (1964 edition by New Directions Publishing Corporation. *Nausea* was first published in French in 1938 and first translated into English in 1959.).

———, *The Imaginary: A Phenomenology of the Imagination* (first published by Editions Gallimard, Paris, in 1940; Routledge republished *The Imaginary* in 2010).

Scanlon, Thomas M., *What We Owe Each Other* (Cambridge, MA: Harvard, 2000).

Seligman, Martin, *Authentic Happiness: Using the New Positive Psychology to Realize Your Potential for Lasting Fulfillment* (New York: Free Press, 2002). His website is http://www.authentichappiness.sas.upenn.edu/Default.aspx

Sessions, Robert and Jack Wortman, *Working in America: A Humanities Reader* (South Bend, IN: Notre Dame University Press, 1991).

———, *Working in America: Supplemental Readings* (Acton, MA: Copley Custom Publishing Group, 2002).

Shank, Joshua Wolf, "What Makes Us Happy" (New York: Atlantic, June, 2009).

Singer, Peter *How Are We to Live* (New York: Harper, 2001).

———, *Practical Ethics* (New York: Cambridge, 1999).

———, *Writings on an Ethical Life* (New York, Harper, 2001).

Sober, Elliott, *Unto Others: The Evolution and Psychology of Unselfish Behavior* (Cambrdige, MA: Harvard, 1999).

Stivers, Richard, *Technology as Magic: The Triumph of the Irrational* (New York: Continuum, 2001).

Strong, David, *Crazy Mountain: Learning from Wilderness to Weigh Technology* (Albany, NY: SUNY Press, 1995).

Tallis, Raymond, *Enemies of Hope: A Critique of* Contemporary *Pessimism* (Houndsmills, U.K.: Palgrave Macmillan, 1997).

Tayac, Gabrielle, "Keeping the Original Instructions," in Gerald McMaster and Clifford "E. Trafzer, eds., *Native Universe: Voices of Indian America* (Washington, D.C.: National Geographic Society, 2004), 73-84.

Taylor, Charles, *A Secular Age* (Cambridge, MA: Belknap Press, 2007).

———, *Ethics of Authenticity* (Cambridge, MA: Harvard, 1992).

———, *Sources of the Self* (Cambridge, MA: Harvard, 1992).

Todd, Richard, *The Thing Itself* (New York: Riverhead Hardcover, 2008).

Turkle, Sherry, *Alone Together: Why We've Started Expecting More from Technology and Less from Each Other* (New York: Basic Books, 2011).

Twenge, Jean M. and W. Keith Campbell, *The Narcissism Epidemic: Living in the Age of Entitlement* (New York: Free Press, 2009).

Twitchell, James, *Branded Nation: The Marketing of Mega Church, College Inc, and Museumworld* (New York: Simon & Schuster, 2004).

Unger, Peter, *Living High and Letting Die* (New York: Oxford, 1996).

Vannini, Philip and J. Patrick Williams, *Authenticity in Culture, Self and Society* (Farnham, U.K.: Ashgate, 2009).

Vitek, William, and Wes Jackson, eds., *Rooted in the Land: Essays on Community and Place* (New Haven, CT: Yale University Press, 1996).

Weisman, Alan, *The World Without Us* (New York: Thomas Dunne Books, 2007).

Wilber, Ken, *A Brief History of Everything* (Boston: Shambala, 2001).

———, *A Theory of Everything: An Integral Vision for Business, Politics, Science and Spirituality* (Boston: Shambala, 2003).

———, *Integral Psychology: Consciousness, Spirit, Psychology, Therapy* (Shambala, 2000).

Williams, Bernard, *Truth and Truthfulness: An Essay in Genealogy* (Princeton & Oxford: Princeton University Press, 2002).

———, *Moral Luck* (New York: Cambridge University Press, 1982).

Williams, Rosalind, *Retooling: A Historian Confronts Technological Change* (Cambridge, MA: MIT Press, 2002).

Wilson, Colin, *The Outsider* (New York: Tarcher, 1987).

———, *Beyond the Outsider* (New York: Carroll & Graf Pub, 1991).

———, *The Outsider and Beyond* (Rockville, MD: Borgo Press, 2007).

Wilson, Eric G., *Against Happiness: In Praise of Melancholy* (New York: Farrar, Straus and Giroux, 2009).

Zielenziger, Michael, *Shutting Out The Sun: How Japan Created Its Own Lost Generation* (New York: Vintage, 2007).

A native of South Dakota, Robert Sessions earned a BA from Drake University and a PhD in philosophy from the University of Michigan. He has taught philosophy and humanities at four colleges, including twenty-six years at Kirkwood Community College in Iowa City. He is the co-author of *Working in America: A Humanities Reader* and has published articles on environmental philosophy, the philosophy of work, and the philosophy of technology. Bob is the proud father of five children and grandfather of three. He lives in Iowa City with his wife, Lori Erickson.

A native of South Dakota, Robert Sessions earned a BA from Drake University and a PhD in philosophy from the University of Michigan. He has taught philosophy and humanities at four colleges, including twenty-six years at Kirkwood Community College in Iowa City. He is the co-author of *Working in America: A Humanities Reader* and has published articles on environmental philosophy, the philosophy of work, and the philosophy of technology. Bob is the proud father of five children and grandfather of three. He lives in Iowa City with his wife, Lori Erickson.

The Ice Cube Press began publishing in 1993 to focus on how to live with the natural world and to better understand how people can best live together in the communities they share and inhabit. Using the literary arts to explore life and experience in the heartland of the United States we have been recognized by a number of well-known writers including: Gary Snyder, Gene Logsdon, Wes Jackson, Patricia Hampl, Greg Brown, Jim Harrison, Annie Dillard, Ken Burns, Kathleen Norris, Janisse Ray, Alison Deming, Richard Rhodes, Michael Pollan, and Barry Lopez. We've published a number of well-known authors including: Mary Swander, Jim Heynen, Mary Pipher, Bill Holm, Connie Mutel, John T. Price, Carol Bly, Marvin Bell, Debra Marquart, Ted Kooser, Stephanie Mills, Bill McKibben, and Paul Gruchow. We have won several publishing awards over the last nineteen years. Check out our books at our web site, join our facebook group, visit booksellers, museum shops, or any place you can find good books and discover why we strive to "hear the other side."

Ice Cube Press, LLC (est. 1993)
205 N. Front Street
North Liberty, Iowa 52317-9302
steve@icecubepress.com
www.icecubepress.com

to my authentic
forms of ultimate reality
Fenna Marie & Laura Lee

New Work School
New Work Culture

COMPARE
BERGMANN TO
ANDRÉ GORZ
PAUL GOODMAN
ROBERT REICH ?

CPSIA information can be obtained at www.ICGtesting.com
Printed in the USA
LVOW042201211111

256000LV00001B/5/P